The Periodic Table of Ideas

History Changing Ideas and Why They Matter to You

By Benjamin Cheung, Ph.D.

Copyright © 2021 by Benjamin Cheung

Copyright registration TX 8-932-187

All rights reserved. No part of this book may be reproduced or transmitted in any form or by any means, electronic or mechanical, including photocopying, recording, or by any information storage and retrieval system, without permission in writing from the copyright owner.

ISBN: 9798578887949

ASIN: B08RSZ1514

Table of Contents

Preface ix
PART I – INTRODUCTION 1
   Chapter 1 – PERIODIC IDEAS INTRODUCTION 2
PART II – PHILOSOPHY IDEAS 6
   Chapter 2 – PHILOSOPHY IDEAS 7
   Chapter 3 – DIALECTIC METHOD 10
   Chapter 4 – EMPIRICISM 13
   Chapter 5 – PROBLEM SOLVING 16
   Chapter 6 – INTUITION 20
   Chapter 7 – HISTORICAL PHILOSOPHY 23
   Chapter 8 – PRAGMATISM 26
   Chapter 9 – ANALYTICAL PHILOSOPHY 29
   Chapter 10 – EXISTENTIALISM 33
   Chapter 11 – HERMENEUTICS 36
   Chapter 12 – PUBLIC SPHERE 39
   Chapter 13 – PHILOSOPHY PERSONAL RELEVANCE 42
PART III – SCIENCE IDEAS 44
   Chapter 14 – SCIENCE IDEAS 45
   Chapter 15 – STANDARDS 48
   Chapter 16 – MEASUREMENT 52
   Chapter 17 – ELEMENTS 56
   Chapter 18 – FEEDBACK 60
   Chapter 19 – MODEL 63

Chapter 20 – EXPERIMENTATION 67

Chapter 21 – SCIENTIFIC METHOD 71

Chapter 22 – ANALYSIS 74

Chapter 23 – SYSTEM 77

Chapter 24 – CLASSIFICATION 81

Chapter 25 – SCIENCE PERSONAL RELEVANCE 84

PART IV – TECHNOLOGY IDEAS 86

Chapter 26 – TECHNOLOGY IDEAS 87

Chapter 27 – TRANSPORTATION TECHNOLOGY 90

Chapter 28 – PROTOTYPING 93

Chapter 29 – COMPUTATION 96

Chapter 30 – COMMUNICATIONS 99

Chapter 31 – ROBOTICS 102

Chapter 32 – ARTIFICIAL INTELLIGENCE 105

Chapter 33 – NETWORKING 108

Chapter 34 – VIRTUAL REALITY 111

Chapter 35 – SOCIAL MEDIA 114

Chapter 36 – PERSONALIZATION 117

Chapter 37 – TECHNOLOGY PERSONAL RELEVANCE 120

PART V – ECONOMIC IDEAS 122

Chapter 38 – ECONOMIC IDEAS 123

Chapter 39 – MARKETS 126

Chapter 40 – CURRENCY 129

Chapter 41 – CREDIT 132

Chapter 42 – DIMINISHING RETURNS 135

Chapter 43 – TRADE 138

- Chapter 44 – ECONOMIC CYCLE 141
- Chapter 45 – MARGINAL UTILITY 144
- Chapter 46 – INCENTIVES..147
- Chapter 47 – SOCIAL CAPITAL 150
- Chapter 48 – CREATIVE DESTRUCTION 153
- Chapter 49 – ECONOMIC PERSONAL RELEVANCE.....................................156

PART VI – BUSINESS IDEAS 159
- Chapter 50 – BUSINESS IDEAS..160
- Chapter 51 – COMPANY 163
- Chapter 52 – DIVISION OF LABOR 166
- Chapter 53 – MULTI-DIVISIONS...169
- Chapter 54 – MANAGERIAL CAPITALISM 172
- Chapter 55 – INTELLECTUAL CAPITAL 176
- Chapter 56 – BUSINESS PERSONAL RELEVANCE 180

PART VII – PSYCHOLOGY IDEAS...182
- Chapter 57 – PSYCHOLOGY IDEAS..183
- Chapter 58 – PERSONALITY TRAITS 186
- Chapter 59 – PROPINQUITY EFFECT 190
- Chapter 60 – FIELD THEORY 194
- Chapter 61 – SOCIAL PSYCHOLOGY 198
- Chapter 62 – COGNITIVE PSYCHOLOGY 204
- Chapter 63 – PSYCHOLOGY PERSONAL RELEVANCE 208

Part VIII – CONCLUSION 210
- Chapter 64 – CROSS FERTILIZATION & CREATIVITY....................................211
- Chapter 65 – CONCLUSION 216

Part IX – Appendices 220

Appendix-1 – THE PERIODIC TABLE OF IDEAS 221

Appendix-2 – PHILOSOPHY PERIODIC IDEAS 222

Appendix-3 – SCIENCE PERIODIC IDEAS 226

Appendix-4 – TECHNOLOGY PERIODIC IDEAS 230

Appendix-5 – ECONOMIC PERIODIC IDEAS 234

Appendix-6 – BUSINESS PERIODIC IDEAS 238

Appendix-7 – PSYCHOLOGY PERIODIC IDEAS 241

Appendix-8 – CANDIDATE PERIODIC IDEAS 245

Part X – References 249

Appendix-8 – References 250

Tables

Table 1 — Periodic Philosophy Ideas 9
Table 2 — Steps in Socratic Method 11
Table 3 — Problem Solving steps 17
Table 4 — Steps in Induction 30
Table 5 — Steps in deduction 31
Table 6 — Periodic Philosophy Ideas Personal Relevance 43
Table 7 — Periodic Science Ideas 47
Table 8 — Types of Standards 49
Table 9 — Steps in the Scientific Method 72
Table 10 — Periodic Science Ideas Personal Relevance 85
Table 11 — Periodic Technology Ideas 89
Table 12 — Periodic Technology Ideas Personal Relevance 121
Table 13 — Periodic Economic Ideas 125
Table 14 — Periodic Economic Ideas Personal Relevance 158
Table 15 — Periodic Business Ideas 162
Table 16 — Periodic Business Ideas Personal Relevance 181
Table 17 — Periodic Psychology Ideas 185
Table 18 — Periodic Psychology Ideas 209
Table 19 — Functional Grouping of Periodic Ideas 213
Table 20 — Periodic Philosophy Ideas (Appendix) 223
Table 21 — Periodic Philosophy Ideas Personal Relevance (Appendix) 225
Table 22 — Periodic Science Ideas (Appendix) 227
Table 23 — Periodic Science Ideas Personal Relevance (Appendix) 229
Table 24 — Periodic Technology Ideas (Appendix) 231
Table 25 — Periodic Technology Ideas Personal Relevance (Appendix) 233
Table 26 — Periodic Economic Ideas (Appendix) 235
Table 27 — Periodic Economic Ideas Personal Relevance (Appendix) 237
Table 28 — Periodic Business Ideas (Appendix) 239
Table 29 — Periodic Business Ideas Personal Relevance (Appendix) 240
Table 30 — Periodic Psychology Ideas (Appendix) 242
Table 31 — Periodic Psychology Ideas Personal Relevance (Appendix) 244

Figures

Figure 1 – Periodic Table of Ideas 5
Figure 2 – The Periodic Table of Elements 57
Figure 3 – Purpose of Money 129
Figure 4 – The Economic Cycle 142
Figure 5 – Big Five Personality Trait Model with Facets 188
Figure 6 – The Solomon Asch Line Test Conformity Experiment 201
Figure 7 – Periodic Ideas Grouped by Function 212
Figure 8 – The Periodic Table of Ideas (Appendix) 221

Preface

This is a book of ideas. Ideas that were and continue to be important in world history. They are fundamental ideas in their disciplines. They span the areas of business, economics, philosophy, psychology, science and technology. Each of the ideas in this book is told as a story of how made its mark in history, and how it can matter to you. The inspiration for this book stemmed from my first book, the 32 innovation factors whose theme was that certain concepts are recurrent in engineering.

I was born in Syosset, New York and grew up in South Bend, Indiana in the USA. I graduated with my bachelor's degree and Master of Electrical Engineering degree at Purdue University in West Lafayette, Indiana. I did my Ph.D. in Operations Research at Walden with a dissertation on Manifold Wireless networks. I am fluent in mandarin Chinese, American Sign Language (ASL) and English. I have taught ASL at work and helped to teach ASL at Fairleigh-Dickinson University.

I have travelled to 30 countries on 6 continents and have been to many advanced and developing countries. I was the 2008 Heroclix World Champion (a chess-like game). I have designed three games the Tech Deck (2020), Peer to Peer (2020) and Star Trek Expeditions Expansion (2012).

In 1991, I joined General Electric (GE) Medical systems as a software engineer. I worked on Computed Tomography (CT) and Magnetic Resonance Imaging (MRI). I became the lead software developer for the calculations package on GE Ultrasound products. I joined Lucent Technologies in November 1996 as a software engineer to develop 2G (TDMA) wireless base stations. Later, Lucent became Alcatel-Lucent in 2007 and then merged with Nokia in 2016. I have been a system architecture working on 3G (UMTS), 4G (LTE), and 5G wireless systems.

I transitioned from architecture to join Bell Laboratories within Nokia. I am currently (2021) working in the wireless standards group within Bell Labs.

I have three USA granted patents #8,755,805 (USA Patent No. 8,755,805 B2, 2014), #7,443,804 (USA Patent No. 7,443,804 B2, 2008), and #9,918,232 (United States of America Patent No. 9,918,232, 2018) and numerous patents pending. They are all in wireless industry. I have been published in the Bell Laboratories Technical Journal with an article on statistical algorithms in fault detection and prediction (Cheung, Kumar, & Rao, Statistical algorithms in fault detection and prediction: Toward a healthier network, 2005).

I have published five books before this one: 32 Innovation Factors (Cheung, 32 Innovation Factors, 2003), 3G Cellular Systems in 90 minutes (Cheung, 3G Cellular Systems in 90 Minutes, 2003), Robotics in 90 minutes (Cheung, Robotics in 90 minutes, 2005), Renewable systems in 90 minutes (Cheung, Renewable Systems in 90 Minutes, 2005). In 2019 I published The Four Elements of Thinking (Cheung, The Four Elements of Thinking, 2019) which associates the four key aspects of thinking reasoning, creativity, evaluation and synthesis with earth, air, fire and water respectively.

To find out more about my bio, you can visit my personal website at http://cheung.interzone.com

DEDICATION

This book is dedicated to Sherman D. Cheung, Franklin Cheung and my friends Ed Arnold-Berkovits, David Fu, Doc McLaury, Richard Kopacz, Scott W. Din, and Steve O. Chew.

The Periodic Table of Ideas

PART I – INTRODUCTION

Chapter 1 – PERIODIC IDEAS INTRODUCTION

The Periodic Table of ideas celebrates human creativity. It is a collection of brilliant concepts. These products of human creativity have endured the test of time and occur repeatedly throughout history. The periodic ideas have been faithful companions in pivotal human affairs. They have been created by some of the most gifted minds in history. You can inherit these intellectual treasures by learning to apply the ideas in this book. All the periodic ideas have made a significant impact in their disciplines. These are among the best ideas of Mankind, developed by the brightest minds in history. Each of the periodic ideas are recurring, significant, and potentially relevant to you.

To make the table tractable, 50 ideas were selected from a myriad of ideas. These concepts have steered civilizations through the turbulent rivers of time. The periodic table of ideas was distilled from 1,190 candidate ideas through the filters of periodicity, historical impact, and personal significance. The candidate ideas are in Appendix 8.

As you set off for new horizons and start new projects, you can look to the periodic ideas for inspiration and guidance. If you want to make a difference in the world, build from the ideas of the most brilliant minds in history. These ideas span business, economics, philosophy, psychology, science, and technology.

The philosophy periodic ideas guide your reasoning. Philosophy prompts you to ask probing questions. The philosophy notions foster critical thinking and provide insights on how to think about the world. Philosophy asks profound questions as the basis of comprehension. The scientific concepts empower your thinking. Science provides you with methods to analyze problems. The science periodic ideas add tools to your mental toolbox. The technology notions provide practical tools to propel your projects to success. Technology offers solutions you can apply to your projects. The products of technology have revolutionized society and improved every aspect of our lives. The economic ideas give your projects a social and financial footing. Economics indicate where your ideas will thrive and where your efforts will pay off. The business conceptions show you how enterprises can transform lives. The psychology periodic ideas give you insights into yourself and those around you. Psychology explains the workings of your attention systems, creativity, memory, perception, and personality.

The inspiration for the periodic table of ideas came from Mendeleev's periodic table of elements (Mendeleev D. I., 1901). The periodic table of atomic elements were arranged such that elements that share a chemical property, such as the halogens or alkali metals, are grouped together. Likewise, the periodic table of ideas group concepts together by discipline. For example, there is a column devoted to philosophy and another to technology. The left columns of the table are more conceptual; and the right columns are more pragmatic. Philosophy is the left-most column in the periodic table of ideas and serves as an intellectual basis. Next, the sciences explore the workings of natural phenomena. The next column are the technology ideas because technology often builds upon the discoveries of science. Finally, the economic, business and psychology ideas are on the right-side of the periodic table of ideas. In the table of elements, properties recur at periodic intervals of atomic numbers. In the periodic table of ideas, concepts recur throughout history.

For an idea to have been included in the table, it must be potentially relevant to you. For example, the atomic sciences and nuclear technologies have been periodic and significant in history. However, they are unlikely to be directly relevant to you and were culled. The final periodic ideas were selected from the candidate ideas because they could be personally relevant to you and make a difference in your life. According to the 2019 World Intellectual Property Indicators report, innovators filed 3.3 million patents in 2018 alone (World Intellectual Property Organization, 2019). However, in a modern society, most of these innovative ideas have specialized applications that will not be relevant to a typical person.

Each of the periodic ideas are color coded. The philosophy periodic ideas are color-coded with blue. The science ideas are colored in red. Technology concepts are shaded with orange. The economic ideas are colored in green. The psychology ideas are brown colored. The business ideas are tinted in yellow. The color scheme is based on the Academic Costume Code and Academic Ceremony Guide (Sullivan, 2001). The color coding makes it easier for you to associate a periodic idea to a discipline. This will be important in considering alternate ways to group the Periodic ideas and to cross-fertilization them in Chapter 64.

Unfortunately, many disciplines were not represented. Examples include architecture, mathematics, medicine, law, political science, and sociology. However, due to the interdisciplinary nature of the periodic ideas, concepts from these other areas have influenced their development. For example, mathematics and statistics play a vital role in the analysis science periodic idea.

The chapters of this book follow the logic of the table layout. Each of the book sections are a collection of periodic ideas within a discipline. Those sections are interchangeable when reading this book. Thus, if you have an interest in technology, you can start reading from those chapters first. The chapters in philosophy and science are more theoretical than those of technology. The ideas in technology, business and psychology tend to be practical. Each chapter has a description of the periodic idea, an inventor, a notable work, an illustrative story, and describes how it might be relevant to you. Each periodic table entry has the name of the idea, the year it debuted, and a symbolic image representing the concept. A header at the top or bottom of each of the columns shows that ideas in that column fall into the same domain. The psychology and business ideas were combined into the same column. Within each column the periodic ideas are arranged by the year it debuted.

The following diagram shows the periodic table of ideas:

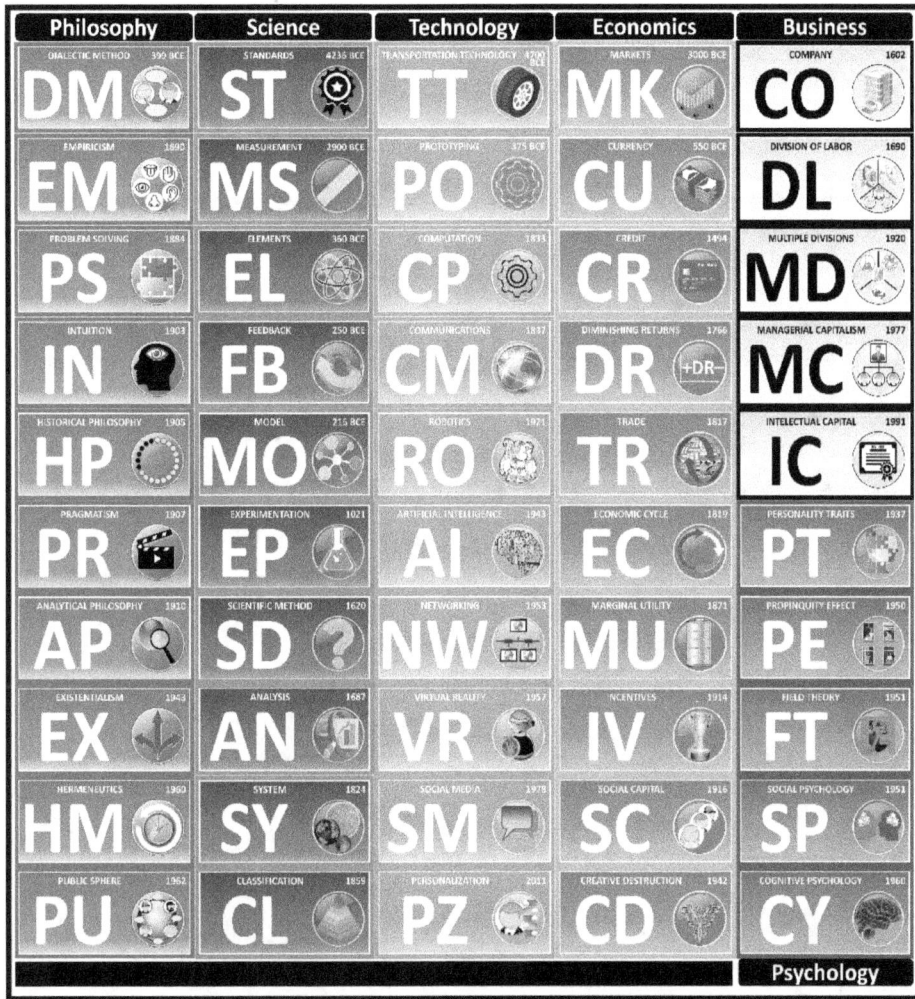

Figure 1 – Periodic Table of Ideas

PART II – PHILOSOPHY IDEAS

Chapter 2 – PHILOSOPHY IDEAS

People are naturally curious. Philosophers have pondered and then attempted to explain the world around them for thousands of years. The word philosophy is derived from the Greek word *philosophia* which means a love of wisdom. Philosophy is the study of questions about existence, knowledge, values, reason, mind and language. Philosophers seek to answer universal questions (Russell B., A History of Western Philosophy, 1967). What is the nature of things? How do we know something to be true? What is art? What is justice? What is our moral responsibility? Why are we here? Philosophers question and probe at the limits of our current knowledge (Durant, 1926).

The first scientists were called natural philosophers. They asked, "what is the best way to study the natural world?" This quest resulted in the scientific method (Gower, 1996). Natural philosophy encompassed astronomy, medicine, and physics which eventually became distinct disciplines of study. Likewise, psychology, sociology, linguistics and economics that were once a part of philosophy are now separate academic disciplines (Durant, 1926). Because philosophy explores the boundary of our knowledge, it has had a broad a scope over the centuries. Today, philosophy encompasses many sub-fields including metaphysics, epistemology, ethics, aesthetics, political philosophy, logic and the philosophy of science (Durant, 1926). Philosophers try to decipher the mysteries of life and the enigmas that claw at our minds. Armed with nothing more than their wits, early philosophers plumbed the depths of knowledge and nature with observation, critical thinking, debate, and rhetoric.

Of the disciplines in the periodic table of ideas, philosophy, over the millennia, has commanded the broadest range of exploration. The following chapters will explore ten key ideas in philosophy. We will take a journey with some of the most brilliant philosophical thinkers in history. By its nature, the questions posed by philosophy and the topics explored are relevant to everyone. You will find the topics of problem solving and pragmatism practical and useful. Existentialism and intuition encourage you to engage in self-introspection. The periodic philosophical ideas of analytical philosophy and the dialectic method foster critical thinking.

The following table summarizes the periodic philosophy ideas. They are sorted by date of introduction. This table can also be found in the Appendix 2 of this book for quick reference. The candidate philosophy ideas can be found in Appendix 8.

PHILOSOPHY IDEA	ID	DESCRIPTION
DIALECTIC METHOD 399 BCE	DM	Socrates. The dialectic method is an exploratory process using dialogue to ask and answer questions, encourage critical thinking, coax out assumptions, and find contradictions to improve a hypothesis.
EMPIRICISM 1690	EM	John Locke. Empiricism states that knowledge primarily comes from our senses. Evidence discovered through experiments, sensory experience, observation, and experiment form the basis of our knowledge.
PROBLEM SOLVING 1884	PS	John Dewey. Problem solving is practical thinking with the aim of resolving a problem. The seven basic steps of problem solving are formulation, root causes, knowledge, ideation, selection, reasoning, and evaluation.
INTUITION 1903	IN	Henri-Louis Bergson. Intuition is the ability to acquire knowledge without conscious reasoning. It includes the ability to access unconscious knowledge. Intuition includes insight, instinctive understanding, and unconscious cognition.
HISTORICAL PHILOSOPHY 1905	HP	George Santayana. Historical philosophy is a metaphysical naturalism stating that knowledge arises not just from pure reasoning but from the interaction of the mind and its environment. Progress builds upon the accomplishments of the past.
PRAGMATISM 1907	PR	William James. Pragmatism asserts that ideas have merit based on the practical consequences they have in everyday human experience. Knowledge is obtained through practical application of theory.

PHILOSOPHY IDEA	ID	DESCRIPTION
ANALYTICAL PHILOSOPHY 1910	AP	Bertrand Russell. Analytical philosophy encompasses formal logic, conceptual analysis, deduction and induction. The four steps of induction are pattern, hypothesis, experiment and theory. The four steps of deduction are theory, hypothesis, evidence and confirmation.
EXISTENTIALISM 1943	EX	Jean-Paul Sartre. Existentialism is the study of the human individual. Everyone can freely live life passionately and authentically by defining what will be significant and meaningful in their lives.
HERMENEUTICS 1960	HM	Hans-Georg Gadamer. Hermeneutics is the study of how humans interpret the world. We understand the world through interpretation. However, this interpretation is anchored to a historical era which creates biases and prejudices.
PUBLIC SPHERE 1962	PU	Jürgen Habermas. The public sphere is a place where people can congregate and freely discuss and identify societal problems. Through public debate in the public sphere, people inspire political action.

Table 1 – Periodic Philosophy Ideas

Chapter 3 – DIALECTIC METHOD

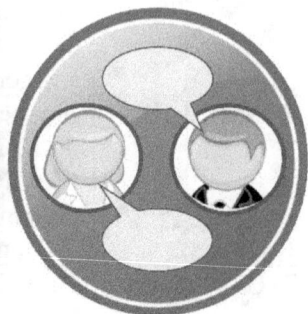

DESCRIPTION: Socrates developed the dialectic method, or the Socratic method. It is a cooperative exploratory process using conversational dialogue to ask and answer questions (Adler, 2010). It is a discourse between people holding different points of view with the aim of establishing the truth through reasoned argumentation. The goal is to encourage critical thinking, coax out assumptions, and identify contradictions in order to improve a hypothesis. The dialogue is intended to eliminate or refine a hypothesis which has contradictory elements. The method involves three stages. First, a thesis is proposed which states an idea. Second, the antithesis is a reaction that contradicts or negates the thesis. Last, the synthesis resolves the differences between the first two points.

The method is captured in the writings of Plato in the Euthyphro (Plato, Euthyphro, 2012), Apology (Plato, The Apology of Socrates, 2012), Crito (Plato, Crito, 2012), Phaedo (Plato, Phaedo, 1998), and Symposium (Plato, Symposium, 1980). Dialectics was taught in medieval universities along with logic, rhetoric and grammar (Adler, 2010). In the 19th century, Georg W. F. Hegel developed dialectics into a logical method which proceeds from a thesis through antithesis resulting in a synthesis. The following table shows the steps in the Dialectic method:

STEPS IN SOCRATIC METHOD	
STEP	DESCRIPTION
HYPOTHESIS	First, ask a challenging open-ended question as a basis to explore a subject. Then, develop a possible explanation or solution for the question or problem.
THINK & INVESTIGATE	Think critically and develop ideas that might contribute towards a solution. Phrase insights in the form of questions. Employ questions to explore a subject and establish a foundation of what is known.
IDENTIFY WEAKNESSES	Identify weaknesses or contradictions in an explanation or hypothesis. Look for things that are illogical.
POSE QUESTIONS	A moderator asks questions to interrogate the proposal and find weaknesses in a hypothesis.
ITERATE	The hypothesis is revised, and the process iterates.

Table 2 – Steps in Socratic Method

NOTABLE WORK: Apology (Plato, The Apology of Socrates, 2012)
PERSON: Socrates
SYMBOL: DM. The image of two people having a dialogue is representative of the dialectic method.
DATE: 399 BCE
STORY: Socrates wrote no book. He founded no school. Yet, he is one of the most influential thinkers in philosophy. He has been world famous even thousands of years after his death. A founder of western philosophy, he was influential in the development of ethics and epistemology which is the theory of knowledge. He developed the *elenchus*, or Socratic method of exploring a subject through questions and answers. Socrates is famous for saying *"the unexamined life is not worth living"* (Plato, The Apology of Socrates, 2012). We learn of his teachings through one of his students, Plato. The dialectic method survives in the form of his dialogues. Euthyphro (Plato, Euthyphro, 2012) is a dialogue about piety and justice. The Crito (Plato, Crito, 2012) a dialogue exploring justice and injustice. The Phaedo (Plato, Phaedo, 1998) is a dialogue on the soul. The Symposium (Plato, Symposium, 1980) is about a banquet with speeches on love (Eros). The dialectic method employs questions to explore a subject by establishing a foundation of what is known and to expose contradictions in other positions and explanations. Opposing arguments clash with the objective of improving understanding and refining a hypothesis. The resultant opinion is a synthesis of conflicting ideas which is more robust and logical than the original assertion.

Each dialectic discovers flaws in an accepted model or competing hypotheses. Thus, the debate gradually approaches the truth.

RELEVANCE TO YOU: The heart of philosophical activity is to attempt to understand the world around us. Thus, asking profound questions is at the epicenter of philosophy. You can practice the dialectic method to study a subject, or to proceed from a hypothesis. Use questions to explore and understand. Philosophy has come a long way from Socrates' time. However, asking questions and seeking answers to achieve comprehension is timeless.

Follow the steps of the Dialectic Method to get at the truth. Setup a debate. Find a friend or a group of people to discuss a problem or topic. Start with a provocative question to answer. You can also start with a hypothesis as a possible explanation for something. Think critically and creatively. Establish a foundation of what is known about the subject. Ask questions to encourage discussion and debate. See if you can find contradictions or opposing viewpoints. Then revise the original hypothesis to account for the discrepancies. The Socratic method seeks to find contradictions in differing hypotheses to make headway on the journey towards the truth.

The saloons of the Victorian era were the equivalent of modern social media. A forum where people ask and discuss a wide range of topics. A child asks innocent questions. A philosopher asks profound questions. An investigator asks exploratory questions. A researcher asks hypothetical questions. A writer asks fantastical questions. A reporter asks journalistic questions: Who? What? Where? When, and why? Questions are at the core of intellectual exploration, and comprehension. Questions can illuminate your path towards enlightenment.

Chapter 4 – EMPIRICISM

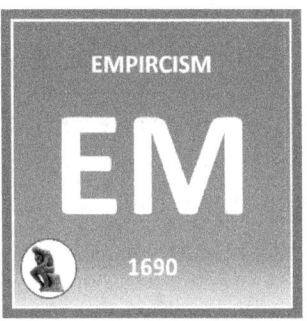 

DESCRIPTION: Empiricism asserts that knowledge primarily comes from our senses. Evidence discovered through experiments, sensory experience, and observation form the basis of our knowledge. The modern scientific method proceeds from a hypothesis and theory that is tested against observations and then subject to continuous revision based on the collected evidence. Empirical research and experiments validated through observation and measurements is at the core of the scientific method. Epistemology is the theory of knowledge. Its three main branches are empiricism, rationalism and skepticism.

Empiricism originated from the Vaisheshika school of Hindu philosophy and the Empiric school of ancient Greece. Galileo Galilei was a famous empiricist from the renaissance. In the 17th century, Francis Bacon and Thomas Hobbes laid the foundation for modern science (Bacon, 1620). In the 18th century enlightenment, John Locke, George Berkeley, and David Hume further developed Empiricism. Then, logical empiricism, also known as logical positivism, synthesized empiricism with mathematical logic. It was developed by Gottlob Frege and Ludwig Wittgenstein. In the 1870s, Charles Sanders Pierce championed the use of inductive, deductive and abductive reasoning as the basis for an empirically based scientific method still in use today.

The Prussian philosopher Immanuel Kant (1724-1804) once wrote that all that we can know of the world is from our five senses of taste, touch, vision, smell, and hearing (Kant, Critique of Pure Reason, 2008). He was the last major philosopher of the Enlightenment; and one of history's most influential thinkers. He said, ultimately, any information that we get about the world around us is from our senses (raw stimulus). To comprehend our reality, the mind organizes stimulus from our senses into perceptions. We try to make sense of the world from our perceptions. For example, my touch senses something round, smooth and light. My sense of smell detects the aroma of a fruit. My vision indicates something red with a stem on top. There is an audible crunching sound when eaten. My sense of taste indicates sweetness. Our minds organize this raw stimulus into the perception of an Apple. Kant asserts that organized perceptions lead to concepts and organized concepts become knowledge (Kant, Critique of Pure Reason, 2008). Our perceptions are the basic building blocks of our individual knowledge and understanding (Kant, Critique of Practical Reason, 2004).

NOTABLE WORK: Essay Concerning Human Understanding (Locke, 1690)
PERSON: John Locke
SYMBOL: EM. The image of the five human senses symbolizes the Empiricism concept that knowledge arises from sensory experience.
DATE: 1690
STORY: I learned sign language 20 years ago, and I became conversationally proficient after 3 years of courses and study. Eventually, I taught sign language courses at work and helped teach courses at Farleigh-Dickinson University. I forged many friendships within the deaf community. My interactions with that community made me appreciate that body language and facial expressions convey significant meaning. Communicating with your hands tickles a different part of your brain than talking. I could hold a long conversation in a loud setting, such as a bar, without losing my voice. I learned how the deaf creatively utilize light-based or vibration-based solutions for devices that would normally require hearing, such as a telephone, doorbell, fire alarm, and alarm clock.

In another example, a restaurant chain called the Blind café (The Blind Cafe, 2015) has as its mission to positively engage people socially in 100% darkness with live music, meaningful discussion and the act of breaking bread communally. They describe the experience as a dinner with discussion and intimate music as a force for positive social change. It is held in 100% darkness with no blindfolds. The Blind café was started by Rosh, an American singer-songwriter inspired by his visit to a dark café in Reykjavik, Iceland in 2007 (The Blind Cafe, 2015). Imagine eating a dinner with friends and family in total darkness. Your senses of taste, touch, hearing and smell would roar to life.

RELEVANCE TO YOU: To put empiricism to work for you, hone your skills of observation. Savor tastes as you eat. Smell the roses. Look at the visual details. Listen attentively to sounds around you. Feel textures as you touch things. In the Victorian era, people were encouraged to explore museum works using all their senses (Purnell, 2017). Museum visitors could lick and feel museum works! Michael Gelb's book *"How to think like Leonardo da Vinci"*, encourages you to take the time to cultivate each of your five senses (Gelb, 2000). Pick one of your senses each week and engage in activities that let you cultivate and sharpen the chosen sense. Observations made from your senses are first-hand evidence. Use your sense of sight, sound, taste, touch, and smell to explore the world.

For example, Matt Hercek has received a mystery gift with a card for the holidays. It has no return sender information. For fun, he wants to figure out what it is and from whom before he opens it and the card. He considers everyone who might send him a gift and eliminates everyone who has already sent him a gift. He uses all his senses to make observations. He observes the dimensions, gift wrapping, packaging, shape, size, smell, texture, weight, and weight distribution. He listens for sounds when he shakes it. He observes the postmark and origin of shipping. You can try this exercise yourself. Have someone place an object in a box and then try to solve the mystery.

Observe the world around you. Do not just see with your eyes but register details in your mind. Learn to see minute details such as colors, imperfections, labels, mechanisms, printing, and ornamentation. Listen to the sounds that surround you. Identify the sources of those sounds. Pay attention and be mindful of others and your environment. Empiricism encourages you to engage your senses whenever possible. When you come across an object, perceive as a detective might. Consider the color, condition, form, function, labels, make, manufacturer, model, product name, shape, size, and weight. When you engage a person, observe their clothing, distinguishing features, facial features, gait, idiosyncrasies, ornamentation, mannerisms, speech patterns, and weight.

Chapter 5 – PROBLEM SOLVING

DESCRIPTION: Pragmatism posits that ideas have merit based on the practical affect they have in everyday human experience. The origin of pragmatism is attributed to Charles Sanders Pierce with his 1878 essay, *"How to make our ideas clear"* (Pierce, 1878). Pierce defines a *clear idea* as one that can be apprehended and recognized wherever encountered. He then proceeds to write about doubt, belief, and habits of thought. Pierce claims our apprehension of a concept is rooted in its practicality. Today, pragmatism is characterized by action and problem solving.

Pragmatists are concerned with how to act effectively in the world. They distill the symptoms down to actual problems to address. They also account for consequences and implications. As we go about our lives, how should we engage the problems that we encounter to realize our aspirations? In *Kant and the Philosophic Method,* John Dewey asserts that people only think when confronted with problems (Dewey, Kant and the Philosophic Method, 1884). We should seek to understand the world and gain control of our environment. Dewey encourages the development of effective responses to practical problems in life.

John Dewey wrote in his book, Logic the theory of Inquiry, *"It is a familiar and significant saying that a problem well put is half-solved* (Dewey, Logic - The

Theory of Inquiry, 1938)". He suggests that a well-formulated problem focuses the problem-solving activity and helps to reveal a solution. Thus, his aphorism suggests that a problem well stated propels you towards a solution.

The seven basic steps of problem solving are:

STEP	DESCRIPTION
Problem Formulation	You define the problem or issue to be solved or investigated. Describe the problematic situation and the objectives.
Root Causes	The root causes of the problem are identified. What are the sources of the problem? The 5 Whys techniques can be used. Start by asking, "*Why does this happen?*" When you have an initial explanation, keep asking "Why?" to reveal deeper levels of causes. In the *Fishbone* method a problem is written at the head of the fish, and possible causes are listed on a branching skeleton. During the investigation the bone tree coaxes you to consider each of the causes on the fish bones.
Knowledge	Gather evidence that is relevant to the problem. Investigate articles and books to gather facts.
Solution Ideation	Idea generation techniques, such as *brainstorming*, can be used to craft candidate solutions.
Selection	The candidate solutions are evaluated and selected through decision-making methods.
Reasoning	Logical reasoning should be applied throughout the problem-solving journey. Reason can refine the formulation, isolate root causes, separate facts from opinions, and help evaluate solutions.
Evaluation	Proposed solutions are evaluated. Selected options can be documented and implemented. Results are evaluated for efficacy.

Table 3 – Problem Solving steps

NOTABLE WORK: Kant and the Philosophic Method (Dewey, Kant and the Philosophic Method, 1884)
PERSON: John Dewey
SYMBOL: PS. The interlocking puzzle pieces iconifies to steps of problem solving as they come together to form a solution.
DATE: 1884

STORY: One of the most famous problem solvers was Albert A. Einstein. He was the father of modern physics and one of the most influential physicists in throughout history (Einstein, Einstein's Miraculous Year: Five Papers That Changed the Face of Physics, March 2005). His mass-energy equation, $E=mc^2$, is synonymous with physics. In 1921, he received the Nobel Prize in Physics. Einstein left us with some insightful advice on problem solving. Einstein once said, ""*Our situation is not comparable to anything in the past. It is impossible, therefore, to apply methods and measures which at an earlier age might have been sufficient. We must revolutionize our thinking, revolutionize our actions, and must have the courage to revolutionize relations among nations of the world. Clichés of yesterday will no longer do today, and will, no doubt, be hopelessly out of date tomorrow* (Einstein, A Message to Intellectuals, 1948)." This has been transformed into the contemporary aphorism, *"We can't solve problems by using the same kind of thinking we used when we created them."* Sometimes we need to open new avenues of thinking in order to make progress. We may need to look at a situation differently to imagine a solution. We may need to try a different approach to arrive at an effective solution. Einstein said, *"It's not that I'm so smart, it's just that I stay with problems longer* (Einstein, Bite-Size Einstein: Quotations on Just About Everything from the Greatest Mind of the Twentieth Century, 2015)". Problem solving requires patience and persistence. Don't quit. Allow your mind to ponder upon a problem. Creativity requires an incubation time to allow ideas to hatch. Einstein also stated, *"if I had only one hour to save the world, I would spend 55 minutes defining the problem, and only 5 minutes finding the solution"*. Solving problems requires careful study of the situation and circumstances of the problem. Problem solving needs to work from a solid foundation of knowledge. Take time to gather and understand the relevant facts. When you spend time to understand and define a problem, effective solutions are produced.

RELEVANCE TO YOU: The problem-solving periodic idea is one that is relevant and useful to everyone. As we make our way through life, everyone encounters problems large and small on daily basis. People get lost, have interpersonal conflicts, encounter obstacles, deal with unexpected events, experience failures, and encounter work issues. Following Einstein's advice, to solve problems, first define your problem. *Problem formulation* defines an issue to solve or a situation that needs improvement. It defines the destination for the thinking journey. Next, try to identify *root causes* of the problem. How did this problem come about? Why is this an issue? You can employ the *5 Whys* method by initially asking "*Why does this happen?*". Determine an answer. Then, continue to ask "*Why?*" five more times to home in on root cause. The *Fishbone* technique encourages you to consider each of the potential causes as you seek a root cause. Understanding causes allows you to address the effects (McInerny, 2005). Aristotle defined efficient cause, material cause, formal cause, and final causes (Aristotle, 2012). An *efficient cause* directly creates an effect. A *material cause* is the creator of a cause. A *formal cause* identifies the nature of something. A *final cause* is the purpose of an activity.

Next, you need to collect evidence and facts relevant to the problem. Exploration, experimentation and inquiry produces a body of *knowledge* to work from. Then, *solution ideation* involves identifying your options and thinking of solutions. *Brainstorming* creates potential solutions (Offner, Kramer, & Winter, 1996). In 1939, Alex Osborn coined the term and wrote *Applied Imagination* (Osborn, 1953). The ground rules for brainstorming are to create a quantity of ideas, focus on originality, encourage collaboration and to suspend judgment. Creativity generates original solutions. Leigh Thompson advocated electronic brainstorming with computers to exchange ideas (Thompson L. , 2003).

Proposed solutions are then *selected*. Decision making techniques help you pick a proposal by considering constraints, criteria, and consequences (Lehrer, 2010). Finally, solutions are *evaluated* for effectiveness. You can refine proposals after they are scrutinized. Experience can highlight potential pitfalls and guide the way towards an effective solution. This technique of problem solving is practical for everyday use. My prior book, *the Four Elements of Thinking* provides more detail on this seven step method of problem solving (Cheung, The Four Elements of Thinking, 2019).

Chapter 6 – INTUITION

 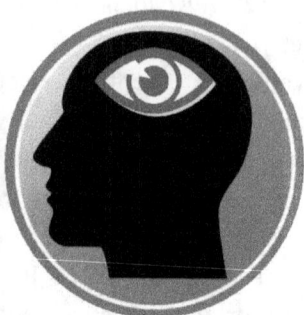

DESCRIPTION: Intuition is defined as the ability to acquire knowledge without conscious reasoning. The word intuition derives from the Latin verb *intueri* which means "to consider". Intuition has different meanings including the ability to access unconscious knowledge, unconscious cognition, insight, and instinctive understanding. Rene Descartes defined intuition as preexisting knowledge gained through rational reasoning or discovering truth through contemplation (Descartes R. , Meditations on First Philosophy, 1993).

In his book, *An Introduction to Metaphysics*, Henri-Louis Bergson wrote that an object can be known absolutely and relatively (Bergson, 1903). Relative knowledge is obtained through analysis and reasoning. Absolute knowledge comes from an intuitive grasp of the truth. Bergson writes that intuition is an intellectual sympathy whereby you can place yourself within an object and know its absolute nature. For Bergson, the flow of time and "*mobile reality*" are integral to intuition. We understand objects via a direct connection to its *élan vital*, or life-force, by our experiences through time. For example, science analyzes static images of a city to develop a relative knowledge of it. A person wanders through the city and gets a direct connection to it over time. This connection to the city affords insights into its operation.

NOTABLE WORK: An Introduction to Metaphysics (Bergson, 1903)
PERSON: Henri-Louis Bergson
SYMBOL: IN. The mind's eye symbolizes intuition.
DATE: 1911
STORY: In 1997, four researchers at the University of Iowa had people gamble using a card game (Bechara, Damasio, Tranel, & Damasio, 1997). Each participant in the study was given $2,000 to start with. They had to choose cards from any of four decks. Most cards yielded varying monetary rewards, but some cards incurred a penalty. The researchers rigged the decks. Two of the decks had only modest penalties while the other two decks carried significant monetary penalties. The pattern was unpredictable. The researchers noted that players reported liking some decks better than others. They observed that bodies tensed, and careful measures of sweat were indicators of anticipation of penalties. Players developed an intuition for which decks were favorable. Today, researchers now refer to this experiment as the *Iowa Gambling Task*. This experiment was an attempt to understand intuition.

Later in 2009, five researchers at King's College in London performed brain scans of people engaged in the Iowa Gambling Task (Lawrence, Jollant, O'Daly, Zelaya, & Phillips, 2009). They found that the orbitofrontal cortex, involved in decision making, and the insula, responsible for cohesive feeling is involved in intuitive hunches. Gut feelings about threats or opportunities are not always correct. However, the human system which evolved for survival is apparently quite sensitive in some individuals. Instincts and intuitive insight can help you navigate a variety of situations.

RELEVANCE TO YOU: Your intuition clues you into other people's motives, stock market picks and when to fold in poker. How do we cultivate and practice using our intuition? For Bergson, intuition entails understanding the world through our sense of time. As we interact with our environment, we make a connection to it. That connection can offer insights into how the things work. You should pay attention to your intuition. You should listen when your inner voice and gut feeling speaks. However, Intuition is an insufficient criterion of truth. Try to balance your hunches against rational thought. You will need to follow up on hunches to ascertain their veracity.

Intuition is lost in the turbulence of mental noise and the chaos of daily life. Quiet time will foster intuition. Learning to quiet the mind requires solitude.

Meditation and mindfulness encourage intuition. Erika Carlson defined mindfulness as paying attention to your current experience and observing it in a non-judgmental way (Carlson, 2013). Mindfulness can help you control mental chatter, assess situations objectively and let you tune into your intuition.

Dreams and intuition both emerge from the unconscious mind. Analyzing your dreams can clue you into your subconscious thoughts. Gaining knowledge and experience will boost your intuition because it lets you connect the dots subconsciously. You should note when coincidences, surprising insights and intuitive leaps happen to you. When you see your intuition kick in, you become more attuned to it. You incubate solutions when your intuition mulls over a problem. Graham Wallas stated the importance of incubation in creativity (Wallas, 1926). Henri Poincare described how the unconscious mind incubates ideas (Poincare, 1929). Emma Policastro claimed intuition is important to creativity (Policastro, 1995).

Take time to develop and nurture your creativity. Intuitive people are often creative. Taking time to connect with people will also develop your intuition. Socializing offers an opportunity to communicate your thoughts. When you express your thoughts, you give substance to your intuitive insights. Progress often comes from the crossbreeding of your hunches with those of others. When you have a gut feeling, pay attention. Take note of the instinctive reaction and consider its merits. It often warrants further investigation. Your subconscious mind can make intuitive leaps of insight that bypasses analytical reasoning.

Chapter 7 – HISTORICAL PHILOSOPHY

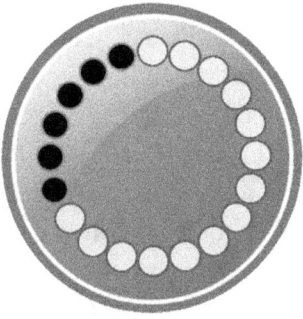

DESCRIPTION: Historical philosophy is a metaphysical naturalism concept that asserts that knowledge arises from the interaction of the mind and its environment. Progress builds upon the accomplishments of the past. The essence of the concept is captured in the aphorism "Those who cannot remember the past are condemned to repeat it". This adage appears in the book *Reason in Common Sense* which is the first volume in *The Life of Reason* by George Santayana (Santayana, 1905). Santayana was a metaphysical naturalist, who believed that culture and society develop to harmonize with their environment. Naturalism espouses that knowledge arises not just from pure reasoning but from the interaction of the mind with its environment. The Life of Reason is a work about pragmatism. Santayana claimed that progress builds on previous developments. The developments of civilization are cumulative. He writes that retentiveness is the condition of progress (Santayana, 1905). He ponders on change and constancy. Inheritance is a social mechanism of persistence. Habit, heredity and memory are a form of persistence for the individual. We remember our own personal past and we develop habits from our experiences. Since he penned this famous aphorism, it has been used to apply to many things aside from progress including the avoidance of atrocities.

NOTABLE WORK: The Life of Reason (Santayana, 1905)

PERSON: George Santayana
SYMBOL: HP. This is symbolized by the progress circle working its way towards completion.
DATE: 1905
STORY: Schools and universities are the way a society preserves information and passes on Mankind's knowledge to future generations. Through the ages, schools have developed in all countries to teach their children. Schools and universities transfer knowledge so that it may persist generation after generation. The first universities emerged in Europe during medieval times in the 11th century specializing in the arts, law, theology and medicine (Ruegg, 1992). Education has undergone major epochs. During the Renaissance, in the 15th century, education systems became more international because people traveled and spread knowledge and culture (Campbell, 2019). The development of modern scientific techniques helped to standardize scientific and technological educational content. In the 1800s, during the Colonial Era, international trade and suzerain relations promoted education. Colonies adopted the governing suzerain country's culture and educational system. During the world wars (1914-1918 and 1937-1945) mass migrations by refugees spread their knowledge and educational techniques to host countries. Mobility cross-fertilized knowledge. After the Cold War ended in the 1990s, commerce, education, scientific endeavors, and commercial products became more global.

RELEVANCE TO YOU: *Those who cannot remember the past are condemned to repeat it* (Santayana, 1905). While George Santayana wrote this aphorism in the context of progress, it has other applications. At a personal level, it urges you to remember your mistakes in order to avoid repeating them in the future. For example, in the process of learning any skill, hobby, or vocation, you will make mistakes along the way. When you encounter failures, learn from them. Mistakes make for an effective teacher. Experience guides you when you encounter the same tricky situations again.

An expert knows the pitfalls commonly encountered in their craft. His experience encompasses the knowledge needed for a plan to succeed. He can employ solutions that have been effective with similar problems. He accepts that making mistakes is part of the learning process. An expert has put Santayana's wisdom to use by remembering his past mistakes and letting those experiences guide him in the future. He tries something and assesses where it went wrong. His experience allows him to navigate and course correct around hazards.

Experience allows you to scrutinize a proposal by identifying where a solution is likely to run into problems. Humanity has built up a body of experience from the success and mistakes of others. Science is founded on the principle of sharing observations and experimental results with other researchers in the attempt to prove a hypothesis. Subsequent researchers then build upon those experiences resulting in scientific progress. In any discipline, such as math and chemistry, a lineage of thinkers and scientists have built up a rich legacy of knowledge. You can watch a video or read about the experience of others who have attempted to do what you want to learn. Learn to see far by standing on the shoulders of giants.

Wisdom is the soundness of an action or decision using experience, knowledge, and good judgment. Wisdom is marked by learning from your past experiences and the ability to identify situations where you can apply your learning. Wisdom is also obtained by learning from other's mistakes and avoiding those mistakes yourself. *Schadenfreude* is the fascination with the suffering of others due to their mistakes or misfortune. Why do we find the mistakes of other people so interesting? We are curious because we can gain wisdom by learning from their mistakes. Mistakes are learning opportunities. Santayana's aphorism advises us to learn from experience and dodge similar mistakes. You can learn from your own experiences and those of others. Through the trials of human folly arises wisdom.

Chapter 8 – PRAGMATISM

DESCRIPTION: Pragmatism asserts that ideas have merit based on the practical consequences they have in everyday human experience. The origin of pragmatism is attributed to Charles Sanders Pierce with his 1878 essay *How to make our ideas clear* (Pierce, 1878). He defined *clear ideas* as those that are easily recognized. Pierce defined his pragmatic maxim as, *"consider what effects, that might conceivably have practical bearings, we conceive the object of our conception to have. Then, our conception of these effects is the whole of our conception of the object* (Pierce, 1878)." Subsequently, William James developed and popularized pragmatism (James, Pragmatism A New Name for Some Old Ways of Thinking, 1907). Progress is made through the practical application of theory. Theory is useful when applied in practice. An important product of philosophical thought is how to live life intelligently. What better way to live than to live practically by using what works? Putting an idea into practice materializes it into reality. If one idea is more effective than another, then it should be adopted. The idea of pulling cargo is replaced with the more pragmatic idea of a cart with wheels. The concept of steam ships, starting with the Turbinia, replaced sailing ships (Osler, 1981). The practicality of printed text from printing presses overtook oral traditions (Hook, 2009). The heliocentric (sun-centered) model of the solar system by Copernicus was had more explanatory value than an earth-centered model (Copernicus, 1543). Pragmatist philosophers assert that reality and truth arise from their practical utility. Applying pragmatism is discovering what works and applying it.

NOTABLE WORK: Pragmatism – A New Name for Some Old Ways of Thinking (James, Pragmatism A New Name for Some Old Ways of Thinking, 1907)

PERSON: William James

SYMBOL: PR. Pragmatism is symbolized by the clapper board used in making movies to initiate action.

DATE: 1907

STORY: Thomas A. Edison is remembered for being a prolific inventor, holding 1,093 patents (Josephson, 1992). Edison changed the world and the course of human history with his practical ideas. Edison embodied pragmatism and a pragmatic approach to engineering. He invented the electric power generator, functional electrical light bulb, fluoroscope, motion picture camera (kinetoscope), phonograph, sound recorder, and rechargeable battery (accumulator). He created inventions in a practical and methodical manner. He is famous for developing a practical electric light bulb in 1879 (US patent #223,898). He exhaustively tried over 6,000 elements in search of a feasible light bulb filament. After 1,200 experiments, he succeeded. In 1879, he identified a carbon filament that lasted for 13.5 hours (Simmons, 2016). Edison eventually discovered that a carbonized bamboo filament could last more than 1,200 hours. Edison sought practical approaches and based his designs on empirical evidence and experimentation. He created one of the first industrial research laboratories located in Menlo Park, New Jersey (USA). Its charter was to develop practical, commercially viable inventions (Stross, 2007). This concept has proliferated to most large companies around the world.

RELEVANCE TO YOU: Action and problem solving are the hallmarks of pragmatism. Ideas underpin decisions. Decisions become actions, transforming our ideas into reality. When you embark on a new project, make the necessary preparations, then act. From our actions we learn and improve. Actions create our experiences. Those experiences allow us to perform intelligently and wisely when we next encounter a similar situation. When you are confronted with an obstacle, let experimentation help you find an answer. Take a hands-on approach and see if it works. Learn from your successes and mistakes. Make the most of what works and see what you can improve based on your mistakes. You will eventually find a practical approach that works. John Dewey advocated hands-on learning rather than rote memorization encouraging the discovery of knowledge firsthand (Dewey, 1899).

Four kinds of difficult choices exist. The first are dilemmas. The definition of a dilemma is a situation with two unappealing choices. Dilemmas all have consequences through inaction. If you are trapped or lost when catastrophe strikes, inaction may be disastrous. Moral and ethical dilemmas challenge you with difficult courses of action. The second kind is one where you wrestle with too many appealing choices to choose from. You become paralyzed by analysis. The third type is a quandary trap where it appears to only have a single solution with no choices. However, through action we generate new possibilities. The fourth kind of difficult choice is a Sophie's choice where selecting any option has catastrophic consequences (Styron, 1979).

Most of the choices you make are simple with few long-term consequences. For example, what you choose to eat for breakfast today. Some choices will have lasting effects that shape your destiny. For instance, choosing a career. Some situations you only get one shot and you need to make your decision count. Landing on the moon is an illustrative example. Experience or analysis can guide you towards a solution. For the big decisions in life, give yourself some time to think, research and plan before you act.

You need to consider trade-offs. You only have 24 hours in a day and finite resources. What you choose to invest in comes at an opportunity cost. Kevin Maney claimed that a common trade-off is between fidelity (quality) and convenience (Maney, 2010). Trade-offs you make in your career, finances, personal matters, and projects influence how well you navigate through life.

In the second century BCE, the playwright Terence wrote *"fortis fortuna adiuvat"* which means *"fortune favors the bold"*. In 1854, the chemist and pioneer of the germ theory of disease, Louis Pasteur said *"Dans les champs de l'observation le hasard ne favorise que les esprits prepares"* from French this translates into "in the fields of observation chance favors the prepared mind." This has also been translated more simply to "chance favors the prepared mind (Pasteur, 1854)." Success emerges from preparation and action.

Chapter 9 – ANALYTICAL PHILOSOPHY

DESCRIPTION: Analytical philosophy encompasses formal logic, conceptual analysis, deduction and induction. The writings of Bertrand Russell (Russell, Principia Mathematica, 1910), Ludwig Wittgenstein (Wittgenstein, 1922), G. E. Moore, Gottlob Frege (Frege, 1879), have all contributed to the development of analytical philosophy. Logical positivism emphasizes the logical structure of philosophical propositions. Analytical philosophy employs the logical form of propositions. Formal mathematical and logical systems are used to analyze elementary propositions. Logical operations such as addition, association, disjunction, negation, permutation, and summation are used to manipulate logical statements. Statements are created about a subject using variables. Then, logical operators can deduce conclusions from a premise. As a simple example, consider the statement: all healthy dogs have a good sense of smell. A logician might represent D as the set of healthy dogs, and S to represent the set of things with a good sense of smell. A logical statement is all D are in the set S. Rover is a healthy dog and a member of D. Logic concludes that Rover has a good sense of smell.

The basic steps of induction are pattern, hypothesis, experiment, and theory (Copi, Cohen, & Flage, 2007). Information is gathered and patterns identified. A hypothesis is proposed which explains and accounts for the observable evidence. Occam's Razor asserts that among competing hypotheses, the one with the fewest assumptions should be selected (Sober, 2015). If two theories explain the data, the simpler theory will be more amenable to verification. Its empirical content is greater (Sober, 2015). Experiments are performed to test the hypothesis. Finally, a general theory, rule or conclusion is developed based on the data and hypothesis. The following table describes the steps of induction:

STEPS IN INDUCTION	
STEP	DESCRIPTION
PATTERN	Relationships are identified among the data. Patterns are found within the body of evidence.
HYPOTHESIS	A hypothesis is a plausible explanation for a phenomenon based on limited evidence as a starting point for investigation. A hypothesis is proposed as a basis for reasoning without any presumptions as to its truthfulness. A hypothesis should account for assumptions. Occam's Razor suggests using the hypothesis with the fewest assumptions.
EXPERIMENT	Experiments are undertaken to make a discovery, test a hypothesis, or demonstrate a known fact. Experiments are performed to gather evidence supporting or denying the hypothesis.
THEORY	A theory is a system of ideas intended to explain something usually based on general principles (for example Darwin's theory of natural evolution). The evidence is analyzed to determine whether conclusions can be drawn. The objective in inductive reasoning is to ascertain if the hypothesis can be supported or denied. It may also suggest that further investigation is necessary. Critical reasoning, and formal logic can be applied to assist in determining whether a hypothesis is true or false.

Table 4 – Steps in Induction

Deduction is often used in logical arguments. Deductive arguments assert that the conclusion necessarily follows from the truth of the premises. Deduction follows four main steps: theory, hypothesis, evidence, and confirmation (Terrell, 1967). A theory is a system of ideas that is intended to explain something, often based on general principles. From these general principles, a hypothesis is proposed as a given explanation for something. Then, evidence is gathered relevant to the hypothesis. Lastly, confirmation for or against the hypothesis can be determined by analyzing the evidence.

STEPS IN DEDUCTION	
STEP	**DESCRIPTION**
THEORY	A theory is a system of ideas intended to explain something, usually based on general principles. For example, Einstein's theory of general relativity.
HYPOTHESIS	A hypothesis is a proposed explanation based on limited evidence as a starting point for further investigation. A hypothesis is proposed as a basis for reasoning without any presumptions as to its truthfulness. A hypothesis should account for *assumptions*.
EVIDENCE	Observations and facts are gathered related to the hypothesis.
CONFIRMATION	The evidence is analyzed to determine whether conclusions can be drawn. Typically, the objective is to ascertain if the hypothesis can be supported or denied. It may also suggest if further investigation is necessary. An argument, syllogism, critical reasoning, and formal logic can be applied to assist in determining whether a hypothesis is true or false.

Table 5 – Steps in deduction

NOTABLE WORK: Principia Mathematica (Russell, Principia Mathematica, 1910)
PERSON: Bertrand Russell
SYMBOL: AP. A magnifying glass examining the world symbolizes this idea.
DATE: 1910
STORY: Who was the world's greatest detective? Many fictional characters come to mind. Some examples are Batman, Sherlock Holmes, Hercule Poirot, or Edgar Alan Poe's Le Chevalier Auguste Dupin. But have you heard of William J. Burns, Ellis Parker, or Raymond Schindler who were hailed as master detectives in their day? William Burns was the director of the Bureau of Investigation (BOI) which eventually became the Federal Bureau of Investigations (FBI). Raymond C. Schindler was the protégé of William J. Burns (Hughes R. , 2014). In 1910, Ray established the Schindler Bureau of Investigation. He was famous in America as an astute private investigator. By his death in 1959, he was widely renown as America's leading private detective. He pioneered scientific detective work long

before modern forensic science. He had exclusive use of the dictograph, a remote sound recording machine. He investigated 10,000 cases during his illustrious career (Hughes R. , 2014). Ray outsmarted a wide variety of criminals on his way to becoming a modern Sherlock Holmes. He caught blackmailers, cheats, confidence men, murderers, political grafters, racketeers, saboteurs, swindlers, and thieves. On January 20, 1952 on NBC, the Goodyear Television Playhouse aired *Raymond Schindler, Case One*. Frank Maxwell portrayed Detective Schindler (Hughes R. , 2014). A detective gathers evidence, does his research and observes the crime scene. He uses deduction and induction to draw conclusions based on the evidence. **RELEVANCE TO YOU:** You can learn to apply deductive and inductive thinking to your problems. Think as a detective would when you tackle a conundrum. To follow the steps of induction, first craft a plausible explanation for your problem at hand. Inductive reasoning produces general principles from specific observations. Then, develop a hypothesis, gather evidence, and confirm the theory. Inductive thinking works from the specifics to the general. Deduction proceeds from the general to the specifics. The deductive reasoning steps are theory, hypothesis, evidence and confirmation. You should try to propose a theory, generate a hypothesis, gather evidence and confirm the hypothesis.

Suppose you want to explain a mystery at work. First, you need to identify the facts. Gather relevant evidence to the problem. Who is involved? What details can you observe? Why is the problem important to you? What significant facts can you gather? Where did the events take a place? What was the timeline of events? Next, produce a theory that might provide an explanation. Develop a hypothesis that fits the facts. Then, you can develop an experiment and gather evidence that might support or deny the hypothesis. Then, finally draw reasonable conclusions based on the evidence that you have.

Imagine you are a private detective. You are called in to investigate to murder of Harry Oakes. Harry was an investor, developer and entrepreneur in the Bahamas. Mr. Oakes became wealthy from a gold mine in Ontario, Canada. He was murdered after midnight with an ice pick and then burned. How would you investigate this case? What kind of information would you seek out? Whom would you talk to? Where would you go to investigate? What sort of hypothesis might you create? What questions come to mind? This was an actual case that Ray Schindler investigated that has been the focus of numerous books and four films (Bocca, 1959).

Chapter 10 – EXISTENTIALISM

DESCRIPTION: The human individual is the central subject of interest in existentialism. What makes a human unique and different from animals? In a universe without purpose, why are humans here? Is it even meaningful to ask that question?

Ancient Greek philosophers pondered these timeless, philosophical questions. Socrates and Plato deliberated on "what is a good life" (Shields, 2013). The Greek term *Eudaimonia* translates to a flourishing life. They reflected how someone could deliberately lead a meaningful life.

Søren Kierkegaard, Fyodor Dostoevsky, Jean-Paul Sartre, and Friedrich Nietzsche pioneered existential philosophy. Søren Kierkegaard in his work, Either / Or considers how choice affects our lives as we search for a meaningful existence (Kierkegaard, 1992). A meaningless world creates a sense of dread, which has been called *existential angst*.

Jean-Paul Sartre asserted that a central tenet of existentialism is that existence precedes essence (Sartre, 1943). Individuals *exist* as conscious, independent, and responsible beings with values. They should determine meaning in their lives. This existence eclipses *"essence"*, those labels, roles, and stereotypes that are assigned to them. Sartre stated that humans have no intrinsic purpose (Sartre, 1943). Thus, a person is free to define what is meaningful for their lives. Every individual is responsible for living life passionately and authentically. They accomplish this by defining what is significant and meaningful in their lives. The actual life of an individual is their "true essence".

NOTABLE WORK: Being and Nothingness (Sartre, 1943)
PERSON: Jean-Paul Sartre
SYMBOL: EX. The three arrows symbolize that people choose a direction for their lives. They define what is meaningful to them.
DATE: 1943
STORY: In August 1931, Karl Jansky at Bell Laboratories detected radio waves from our Milky Way galaxy (Jansky, 1933). In 1937, Grote Reber built a radio telescope and performed the first systematic survey of astronomical radio waves (Verschuur, 2015). These humble beginnings kicked off the field of radio astronomy. Astronomy is the science which studies celestial objects and phenomena. These phenomena include supernovas, quasars, and the cosmic microwave background radiation (Zeilik, 2002).

The search for extraterrestrial intelligence (SETI) is the scientific search for intelligent life on other planets. SETI monitors electromagnetic radiation for signs of intelligent transmissions from civilizations on other planets. In 1960, astronomer Frank Drake at the National Radio Astronomy Observatory (NRAO) conducted the first modern SETI experiment, dubbed "Project Ozma" (SETI Institute, 2020). Drake used a radio telescope 85 feet (26 meters) in diameter at Green Bank, West Virginia, USA to examine the stars Tau Ceti and Epsilon Eridani. In 2015, Stephen Hawking and Yuri Milner started a SETI project called *Breakthrough Listen* based at the Berkeley SETI Research Center (Rees, et al., 2017).

SETI tries to answer the question, *"are we alone in the universe?"* By contrast, existentialism poses the questions, *"In the vast meaningless cosmos, does anything we do truly matter? Do our lives have any purpose?"* Profound philosophical questions give you pause for reflection.

RELEVANCE TO YOU: Existentialism coaxes you to consider what is important in your life. What do you value? What do you find meaningful? What makes your life worth living? If you have nothing to aim for, you will wander aimlessly. In the vast emptiness of the universe, people give space and time meaningfulness through their actions as they contribute to the collected works of Mankind.

Would you want to live your life over again? What are good decisions you have made in your life? Are there decisions you wish you had made differently? How can you learn from your mistakes? Friedrich Nietzsche wrote "*My formula for greatness in a human being is amor fati* (love fate): *that one wants nothing to be different, not in the future, not in the past, not for all eternity.* (Nietzsche, 1992)" Nietzsche suggests an attitude where you should accept the things that happen in you. You should accept that the journey of life has both good and bad moments. If you live life with purpose you will not have any regrets.

The fundamental human desires are to live, to learn, to love, and to leave a legacy. The desire to live encompasses core values such as achievement, success, and wealth. The desire to learn has growth values such as curiosity, exploration, knowledge and reasoning. The desire to love entails social values such as community, cooperation, devotion, empathy, family, justice, and teamwork. The desire to leave a legacy employs transcendent values including fame, accomplishment, discovery and innovation.

Think back on your peak experiences. What moments made you feel alive? What must you have in your life to experience fulfillment? The questions that help you discover your values and what you find meaningful are the most important you will consider throughout your life. They will shape your destiny and allow you to live a productive and fulfilling life.

Chapter 11 – HERMENEUTICS

DESCRIPTION: Hermeneutics is derived from the Greek word *hermeneuo* which means to *interpret*. It is the study of how people interpret the world. History does not belong to us, but we belong to it. Hermeneutics is the art of understanding and making oneself understood. It includes both verbal, non-verbal communication, semiotics and presuppositions. *Semiotics* is any kind of communication that involves signs and symbols. Semiotics is employed in history texts, philosophy, law, and theology. Hans-Georg Gadamer asserted that the purpose of philosophy is to interpret our existence. We understand the world through interpretation. However, any interpretation is anchored to a historical era which gives rise to biases and prejudices (Gadamer, 1960). The historical context, scientific understanding, and culture of the time shapes the investigations that people conduct. It steers the questions that people ask. For example, medieval astronomers believed that the stars were nestled in an aethereal transparent element like jewels set in glass orbs (Grant E. , 2009). Thus, investigations they launched would have been framed in that historical context.

NOTABLE WORK: Truth and Method (Gadamer, 1960)
PERSON: Hans-Georg Gadamer

SYMBOL: HM. Hermeneutics is symbolized by a clock face with a rewinding time arrow to indicate the historic past.

DATE: 1960

STORY: When I visited the Lalbagh Botanical Garden in Bangalore, India, my taxi driver asked me if he could drink water from my water bottle. I declined, trying to explain to him what germs and bacteria were to no avail. Instead, I bought him a bottle of water. The discovery of bacteria by Antonie van Leeuwenhoek in 1675 changed our view of the world. In 1849, a London outbreak of Cholera killed 15,000 people. The conventional *miasmic theory* of Cholera held that it was carried by polluted air. Thus, the investigation was performed in this historical context. An industrialized, over-crowded London polluted the River Thames. Epidemiology is the science devoted to studying the causes and effects of health and disease. Its development changed our interpretation of the world. It is the basis for public health policy and preventative healthcare. Epidemiologists analyze data to understand the propagation of diseases. The term Epidemiology comes from the Greek language meaning *"the study of what is upon the people"*.

In 1854, John Snow investigated the cause of cholera in Soho, London, England. He is considered the father of modern Epidemiology (Johnson, 2007). John Snow hypothesized that Cholera was carried in the water. The pathogenic hypothesis for the mechanism of Cholera transmission changed the course of history. William Farr gathered evidence and confirmed Snow's conjecture. Farr statistically correlated where deaths occurred relative to where people obtained their drinking water from (Johnson, 2007).

In modern times, scientists are no strangers to bacteria, germs and viruses. In 2020, the SARS-CoV-2, or COVID-19, pandemic raged across the world. However, thanks to John Snow and advancements in epidemiology, our approach to manage and investigate COVID-19 are better. For example, Scientists employ metagenomic nanopore sequencing for the identification of viral pathogens (Lewandowski, et al., 2020). Hermeneutics suggests that we are a product of our times. Our approach to managing a viral pandemic is grounded in our current scientific knowledge.

RELEVANCE TO YOU: Hermeneutics is about interpretation and historical context. Armed with this knowledge, you can make hermeneutics work for you. You constantly interpret the world around you. Everything you are exposed to from articles, conversations, and news are nestled in the popular culture, political, scientific and technological references of your time. The journalists, politicians, and scientists research topics and ask questions relevant to their historical time. People quote cultural and political references for their time. Your perception of the world goes through a filter based on the knowledge of society at the time. The time that you live in provides a historical context which defines your reality filter. How you perceive news and information goes through this filter. When you process information for a project, consider how history, culture and historical context have affected your perception. Historical eras come and go. The rise of the internet, the personal computer revolution, the smart phone era, the social media era. The beginning or end of an era shapes your approach to the world.

Hans-Georg Gadamer claimed when we read historical texts, we come to understand their traditions, prejudices and cultural norms (Gadamer, 1960). In a sense, we have a "conversation with history". The result of which is a better understanding of our personal biases. Hans-Georg called this a "fusion of horizons". For example, the more you expose yourself to works from the renaissance, enlightenment and industrial revolution the better you come to understand your own time.

Chapter 12 – PUBLIC SPHERE

DESCRIPTION: The public sphere is a place where people can congregate and freely discuss and identify societal problems and through that public debate inspire political action. In the 18th century, during the enlightenment, coffee houses and salons were places where people would gather and freely discuss social problems. These places were public spheres that straddled the private sphere and the state. Jürgen Habermas asserted that society depends on its citizens to scrutinize and reason collectively about existing traditions (Habermas, 1962). The public sphere encourages people to identify social problems through public discourse and as a result initiate political action. Today, public discussion occurs in conventions, mass media, meetings, publications, and social media. Discourse in the public sphere is amplified by the media creating public opinion. Social media sites such as Facebook, WhatsApp, YouTube, and Twitter allow people to publicly discuss and debate social traditions. In modern society, the public sphere includes public institutions such as galleries, museums, schools, theaters, town halls, and universities.

In modern times, societies need to adapt to keep pace with a dynamic world. Habermas suggests that individuals can transform society by reasoning together in the public sphere. The public sphere allows people to build consensus to bring about change that results in a better society. Participation in a democracy entails exercising the freedom for collective expression. History is replete with social movements such as the Arab spring, civil rights movement, green movement, human rights movement, and woman's suffrage movement. Most movements for social change have used the public sphere. Dictators and totalitarianism squelch the public sphere to get a stranglehold on the citizenry. People are naturally gregarious and social. The public sphere serves as a place where people can congregate and discuss ideas for improving society.

NOTABLE WORK: The Structural Transformation of the Public Sphere (Habermas, 1962)
PERSON: Jürgen Habermas
SYMBOL: PU. The public sphere is symbolized by a group of people having a discussion.
DATE: 1962
STORY: On February 2, 2011 the Adbusters website proposed a protest initiated by Kalle Lasn and Micah White titled, "*A Million Man March on Wall Street*" (Lasn & White, 2011). The movement proposed a peaceful occupation of the financial district to protest corporate influence on democracy, lack of legal consequences, and increasing disparity in wealth. On June 9, 2011, Lasn registered OccupyWallStreet.org as a web address. The occupy Wall Street movement utilized numerous public spheres including an online forum and organized meetings. The movement garnered international media attention and sparked similar movements across the world. The protest began with about 150 people assembling at Zuccotti Park in New York City on September 17, 2011. Their movement's slogan, "*We are the 99%*" referred to the income and wealth inequality in the United States between the wealthiest 1% and the rest of the population. When people gathered in the public sphere, they used a "stack" system to give speakers turns to talk. The movement produced numerous media pamphlets and a free newspaper to disseminate information. It gained attention from President Barack Obama, the Daily Show broadcast, labor unions, political commentators, and celebrities. The occupy wall street movement illustrates how discussion in the public sphere can raise awareness of social issues and motivate change.

RELEVANCE TO YOU: Partaking in the public sphere allows you to observe or join the conversation even if you are not a political activist. Where the spotlight of the media shines, so turns the gaze of the public. If you have a social media presence or hold discussions in any public forum, you have connected with the public sphere. Your conversations beyond your dining room table are likely in the public sphere. Jürgen Habermas suggests the public sphere improves society through public discourse with the aim of questioning social tradition. Social improvement begins with just one person with an idea for change. It starts with one conversation about improving society. Social media can amplify that idea and spark a movement. People going about their business will see where change needs to happen. Institutions far away are removed from the problems at hand. Change in society is created incrementally with the people closest to the problems tackling the ills of society and improving the world one issue at a time.

The public sphere allows people to congregate, share their experiences, and discuss problems together. It magnifies the voice of one person allowing it to resonate throughout groups and then to society at large. Authors inspire us to dream of a better future. Read a book. Journalists who write about current affairs raise our awareness of the world. Explore the news. Artists create social commentary through their art. Visit a museum. Talk show hosts explore pressing social issues. Tune into a debate. These are all examples of the public sphere in action.

Chapter 13 – PHILOSOPHY PERSONAL RELEVANCE

This chapter collects and summarizes the personal relevance of each of the philosophy periodic ideas. Problem solving and pragmatism encourage critical thinking. Philosophers pose thoughtful and meaningful questions. Their journeys and discoveries are often personally relevant to everyone. The philosophy periodic ideas provide insights into how you observe and think about the world. They can spur you towards a fulfilling and satisfying life.

The following table is a digest of the personal relevance for the philosophy periodic ideas. The periodic ideas table and their personal relevance tables are also collected in the appendix of this book for quick reference.

PHILOSOPHY IDEA	ID	PERSONAL RELEVANCE
DIALECTIC METHOD 399 BCE	DM	The dialectic method drives you to think critically, coax out assumptions, and find contradictions in a hypothesis. It inspires you to ask challenging open-ended questions as a basis to explore a subject.
EMPIRICISM 1690	EM	Empiricism encourages you to utilize your senses. It urges you to make first-hand observations and explore the world through sensory experiences. It gets you to hone your powers of observation.
PROBLEM SOLVING 1884	PS	Problem solving helps you methodically work through your problems in a seven-step approach. Practical problem solving allows you to intelligently conquer issues at work, home, community, and recreation.

PHILOSOPHY IDEA	ID	PERSONAL RELEVANCE
INTUITION 1903	IN	Intuition allows you to acquire knowledge without conscious reasoning. Intuition causes you to make leaps of insight and arrive at an instinctive understanding that bypasses analytical reasoning. Intuition urges you to balance your hunches against rational thought.
HISTORICAL PHILOSOPHY 1905	HP	Historical philosophy spurs you to remember your mistakes and to avoid repeating them in the future. When you make mistakes and encounter failures, Historical philosophy encourages you to learn from them. Mistakes can be an effective teacher for you.
PRAGMATISM 1907	PR	Pragmatism advises you to consider how practical something is. It encourages you to live a practical life by using what works. Pragmatism urges you to take a hands-on approach to life's challenges.
ANALYTICAL PHILOSOPHY 1910	AP	Analytical philosophy helps you engage and develop your critical thinking. Its methods allow you to solve challenging problems.
EXISTENTIALISM 1943	EX	Existentialism inspires you to live life to its fullest by defining what is significant and meaningful to you.
HERMENEUTICS 1960	HM	Hermeneutics gets you to consider how history, culture and historical context affect your reality filter. When you read historical texts, Hermeneutics helps you understand from the perspective of their traditions, prejudices and cultural norms. This helps you uncover your own biases, what Hans-Georg called a *"fusion of horizons"*.
PUBLIC SPHERE 1962	PU	The public sphere gets you to engage in public debate that aims to identify societal problems. Through public debate in the public sphere, you can inspire and influence social transformation. Social improvement begins with your ideas for social change.

Table 6 – Periodic Philosophy Ideas Personal Relevance

PART III – SCIENCE IDEAS

Chapter 14 – SCIENCE IDEAS

Science builds and organizes knowledge through testable explanations and predictions about nature and the universe. Modern science is divided into three major branches consisting of the natural sciences, social sciences, and formal sciences. The natural sciences include astronomy, biology, chemistry, geology, and physics to investigate nature and natural phenomena (Barr, 2014). The social sciences are comprised of anthropology, economics, psychology, and sociology which study individuals and societies (Michie, 2014). The formal sciences consist of logic (Smith P. , 2003), mathematics (Pickover, 2009), and theoretical computer sciences (Dasgupta, 2016) which focus on abstract concepts. The synergy of science and mathematics underpins technology.

Much of what a typical person knows is directly or indirectly a product of science. Our conception of living things, the mechanisms of the world around us, how things work, and the composition of matter are described by astronomy, biology, chemistry, geology, and physics. From biology, we scry the genetic makeup of living organisms. Chemistry imparts an understanding of plant chemistry through botany, the formation of igneous rocks via geology (Rothery, 2016), how ozone forms through ecology, and how medications work by pharmacology (Myers, 2003). From physics, we divine the motion of a projectile, the thermodynamics of systems (Wark, 1983), the nature of the atom, and the composition of stars (Ling, Sanny, & Moebs, 2017). Engineers create inventions based on scientific understanding. For example, the science of motion, fluids, and gases resulted in the study of aerodynamics which, in turn, allowed us to design airplanes (Brandt, 2015).

Science is a cumulative endeavor. When scientists first observe an unfamiliar phenomenon, they develop a hypothesis to try to explain it. For example, the

Ancient Greeks tried to explain lightning bolts with Zeus hurling them (Hamilton, 2011). Thor threw lightning in Norse mythology (Crossley-Holland & Love, 2017). Ukko explained lightning in the Finnish culture (Salo, 2006). As scientists uncover new evidence, they revise their theories. Between 1600 to 1800, William Gilbert, Otto von Guericke and Benjamin Franklin pioneered research into the study of electricity (Stewart J. V., 2001). Today, science describes lightning as an electrostatic discharge where two electrically charged regions between the atmosphere or ground equalize producing electromagnetic radiation (Rakov & Uman, 2007).

The following table summarizes the science periodic ideas. They are sorted by date of introduction. This table can also be found in the Appendix 3 of this book for quick reference. The candidate science ideas can be found in Appendix 8.

SCIENCE IDEA	ID	DESCRIPTION
STANDARDS **4236 BCE**	ST	(Ancient Egyptians). Standards are a set of rules or guidelines established by an authority as a model, criterion, or measure. You can apply them as standards of assessment, conduct, criterion, instruction, or practices.
MEASUREMENT **2900 BCE**	MS	Khnum Khufu (Pharaoh). Measurement is the assignment of a number to a characteristic of an object or event. Researchers can then compare and analyze measurements. Metrology establishes a uniform system of weights and measures with fundamental units to link human activities.
ELEMENTS **360 BCE**	EL	Plato. Elements are the simplest chemical substances and are irreducible through chemical reactions. Elements can only be changed into other elements using nuclear methods. A *combination* merges two or more individual component elements. A *permutation* is a varied order or arrangement of a set of things.
FEEDBACK **250 BCE**	FB	Ktesibios of Alexandria. Feedback is defined as the return of a portion of the output of a process or system back to the input. Feedback is typically used to maintain performance or to control a system or process. Closed loop systems measure the output of a system and compare it to a desired target.

SCIENCE IDEA	ID	DESCRIPTION
MODEL 216 BCE	MO	Aristarchus of Samos. Models in math and science make the world easier to understand through components based on existing knowledge. Models represent objects, phenomena, and processes in a simplified and objective way. Models simulate an observed phenomenon to facilitate understanding.
EXPERIMENT 1021	EP	Ibn al-Haytham. Experiments are a scientific procedure undertaken to make a discovery, test a hypothesis, demonstrate a known fact, or determine the efficacy of an idea. It is a procedure under controlled conditions to verify, refute, or establish a hypothesis when trying to explain phenomenon.
SCIENTIFIC METHOD 1620	SD	Francis Bacon. The scientific method is a procedure consisting of systematic observation, measurement, and experiment. The five steps of the scientific method are question formulation, hypothesis development, prediction, testing, and analysis. These steps refine a hypothesis to explain natural phenomenon.
ANALYSIS 1687	AN	Isaac Newton. Analysis is the processing of collected evidence and data to make sense of the information. Modern scientific evaluation is often accomplished through statistical analysis of data such as an Analysis of Variance (ANOVA) test.
SYSTEM 1824	SY	Nicholas Carnot. A system is defined as a group of interacting, interrelated, or interdependent elements forming a complex whole. A system is also characterized by its structure, purpose and function.
CLASSIFICATION 1859	CL	Charles Darwin. In biology, classification is done with taxonomy which is the science of naming and classifying groups of organisms based on shared characteristics. Other systems of classification include phylogenetics, cladistics, systematics, economic taxonomy, and Bloom's taxonomy.

Table 7 – Periodic Science Ideas

Chapter 15 – STANDARDS

DESCRIPTION: Standards are a set of rules or guidelines established by an authority as a model, criterion or measure. Standards are employed in science, technology, education, industry and governments. They allow people to coordinate by following a standard procedure. Procedures create repeatability and ensures quality. Standards result from scientific analysis to allow people to follow a procedure. For example, the scientific study of radiation resulted in people wearing radiation suits when working with radioactive materials. Industrial standards create precision uniformity in production and manufacturing. For example, an assembly line is a way to use standardization in the manufacture of a product (Nye, 2015). Aside from measurements, standards are used for processes. Testing standards ensure the quality of a product. For example, Underwriters Laboratories (UL) develops safety standards related to the certification, inspection, and testing of electrical devices for manufacturers (Underwriters Laboratories, n.d.). Standardized tests and procedures deliver repeatable outcomes.

Standards are used in instruction, assessment, conduct, criterion and practice. Standardized instruction defines guidelines for an educational system. Standards of practice allow practitioners to capitalize on the best techniques developed in their profession. Standards of conduct propose a set of rules governing behavior. Standardize criterion of truth gauge what a thing should be. Criterion applies to anything used as a test of quality. The following table summarizes the five different types of standards:

TYPE	DESCRIPTION
Standards of Assessment	Standards-based assessment evaluates something based on expected outcomes. For example, a set of criteria demonstrates mastery of a concept by a student.
Standards of Conduct	A code of conduct is a set of rules outlining the norms and proper practices for an individual. For example, companies create a code of conduct for employees.
Standardized Criterion of Truth	A standard of judging the truth. An established rule or test, by which facts, or principles are gauged against. For example, criterion to judge the validity of a science experiment.
Standards of Instruction	An academic system of instruction, assessment and reporting define guidelines for the goals of an educational system. Students are expected to demonstrate an understanding of knowledge as a result.
Standards of Practice	Guidelines set down for a set of procedures. These are developed so all practitioners use the best techniques available. For example, there are standards of practice expected to be used by every physician.

Table 8 – Types of Standards

Science is a collaborative effort. Confirmation of scientific experimental outcomes are independently verified. Dependable replication of an experiment lends credibility to the results. If multiple independent sources arrive at the same conclusion, a consensus is established. This can eventually lead to social standards and standardized procedures. For example, epidemiology leads to standardized behaviors of hygiene and the development of standardized medical practices and procedures.

William Trochim defined *validity* as the best approximation to the truth of a given conclusion. He defined the four standardized criteria of truth as *conclusion validity, internal validity, construct validity, and external validity* (Trochim, 2001). There are also false or inadequate criteria of truth (Sahakian & Sahakian, 1993). The erroneous criteria are custom, emotions, instinct, intuition, majority rule, revelation, time, and tradition. People use these unconsciously as a standardized criterion of truth. However, they are inadequate as true measures of determining the truth. Be wary of them.

Within any scientific discipline, a body of peer-reviewed articles defines its theoretical boundaries. As the body of scientific knowledge grows, standardized criteria of truth are used to assess new theories and ideas. Standardized procedures are used to ensure safety and responsibility during scientific studies.

Scientific organizations exist to ensure consistency between scientific endeavors and activities. These organizations include statistical institutes, medical associations, mathematical societies, and science academies. Reference works serve as a baseline that other scientists can build from. They also disseminate standardized knowledge. This serves as a touchstone to gauge new scientific ideas.

NOTABLE WORK: 365 Day Calendar based on the rising of Sirius (the "Dog Star") every 365 days.
PERSON: Egyptians
SYMBOL: ST. The standard idea is symbolized by a medal.
DATE: 4236 BCE
STORY: At 10:48 AM on Sunday, February 7, 1904 an ominous fire alarm blared in the John E. Hurst & Company Building in Baltimore, Maryland, USA. A fire consumed the building then leapt from building to building until it engulfed an 80-block area of the city (Petersen, 2004). It was the third worst conflagration in American history. Fire fighters from New York, Philadelphia, Virginia, and Washington, DC responded, but to no avail. Their fire hoses could not connect to Baltimore fire hydrants because they did not fit their hydrants. They watched helplessly as the flames rampaged through central Baltimore. The fire destroyed 1,500 buildings, covered 140 acres, and raged for more than 30 hours (Petersen, 2004). It was the impetus for the development of a national standard to prevent a similar occurrence in the future. Until then, each municipality had its own unique fire-fighting equipment. Research was conducted on the 600 fire hose couplings in use around the country. One year later, a national standard was created to ensure uniform fire safety equipment. Baltimore also enhanced their building code to emphasize the use of fireproof materials. This story illustrates how standardization facilitates coordination of groups.
RELEVANCE TO YOU: Standards of assessment, criterion, conduct, instruction, and practice all have practical uses. Standards of assessment can help you track your learning progress. Standardized criterion can assess the safety of retail products. Standards of conduct are used to create social cohesion. Standardized

procedures assist newcomers to acclimate to an organization. Standards of instruction are used in schools to help students learn optimally. Standardized practices let professionals share the best ideas in their discipline. Standards produce consistency of outcomes.

An example of a standard of assessment is a test that assesses the learning progress of a student. Bacterial checks against ricin or Escherichia coli in food illustrates standardized criterion. An example of a code of conduct are ethical standards that are used by organizations to define proper behavior. A classroom textbook, or virtual instruction from an expert exemplifies standards of instruction. An example of a standards of practice is a doctor taking your blood pressure during a hospital visit. In science, the peer-review process solicits the examination of fellow scientists to increase the quality of the scientific effort.

You can consider where standards apply in your life. Standards are used ubiquitously in society. Try to observe where they are used. Standards of assessment allow you to test your learning progress. Language teaching software programs use tests to drill home new knowledge. Standardized criteria are used to gauge the truth of something. Standards of conduct synchronize behaviors. Society uses ceremonies to standardize behavior. For instance, graduation and wedding ceremonies mark rites of passage. Standardized instruction creates efficient teaching practices to optimize learning. For example, when you try to learn something, you may watch an instructional video. Standards of practice are a way to share best procedures used by the foremost experts in the field. Brushing your teeth to maintain oral hygiene exemplifies a standard of practice.

Chapter 16 – MEASUREMENT

DESCRIPTION: A measurement is the assignment of a number to a characteristic of an object or event, which can be compared with other objects or events (Pedhazur & Pedhazur Schmelkin, 1991). Metrology is the science of measurement. Measurement has become an integral part of modern society.

Early civilizations needed systems of weights and measures for agriculture, construction, government, and trade. In 2900 BCE, the first permanent standard was created to build the Khufu Pyramid. The royal Egyptian *cubit* defined a fixed standard of length and was carved from black granite (Dodson A., 2000).

Measures were regional with different locales developing their own standards for lengths, areas, volumes and masses. Often such systems were tied to agriculture, food and land management. For example, units of length started with the Egyptian cubit which evolved to the inch, foot and yard (Measurement Science Conference, 2020). The Romans introduced the mile (Beard, 2016). Ancient Mediterranean traders used grains of wheat and barley for units of mass. The stone, quarter, hundredweight, and ton were units of mass developed in Britain. The Sumerians and Babylonians, with a sexagesimal system of numbers, divided a day into hours, minutes, and seconds which is still the basis of modern timekeeping (Dohrn-van Rossum, 1996).

In 1585, Simon Stevin advocated the use of decimal numbers in measurements (Stevin, 1585). This led to the creation of the metric system in 1668. It was officially adopted by France in 1799 (Isakov, 2014). The industrial revolution from 1764 to 1840 fostered international trade which made standardized weights and measures critical (Stearns, 2012). Consequently, a modernized and uniform systems of weights and measures with precise fundamental units was developed (Pedhazur & Pedhazur Schmelkin, 1991). The use of electricity also motivated international standardized units. To drive international conformity, the International Bureau of Weights and Measures was established in 1875 (Quinn, 1991). Located in Saint-Cloud, France, it is often referred to as BIPM, the initials of its French name, *Bureau International des Poids et Mesures*.

Modern science breaks down the world into discrete values. We have divided our world into perfectly uniform units to better study it (Isakov, 2014). This effort is rooted in the European Renaissance of the 14th century. The quantification of the world led to precision instrumentation and engineering marvels (Winchester, 2019). We measure acceleration (meters/second^2), area (square meters), brightness (candle), distance (meters), energy (kilowatt), force (Newtons), geography (latitude, longitude), mass (kilogram), pressure (Pascal), sound (decibel), temperature (degree), time (second, minutes) (Wonning, 2018), velocity (kilometers per hour), and volume (teaspoon) (Fenna, 2002). Accordingly, we have devices that give precise quantized readings including the clock, GPS, measuring cup, ruler, speedometer, and thermometer. Precise measurements facilitate consistency, interchangeability, and manufacturability. The four types of data and measurements scales are: nominal (labels), ordinal (ordered choices), interval (numeric value) and ratio (intervals).

NOTABLE WORK: Monarchs of the Nile (Dodson A. , 2000)
PERSON: Khnum Khufu (Pharaoh)
SYMBOL: MS. A ruler represents the measurements periodic idea.
DATE: 2900 BCE
STORY: The First Transcontinental Railroad in the United States of America (U.S.) was constructed between 1863 and 1869 (Bain, 1999) and spans 1,912 miles (3,077 kilometers). It was originally called the Pacific Railroad and later the Overland Route. It connected the existing eastern U.S. rail network at Council Bluffs, Iowa with San Francisco Bay on the Pacific coast. The Western Pacific Railroad Company started building from the western terminus at Alameda, California. Then, the Central Pacific Railroad Company of California (CPRR)

continued to build eastward 690 mi (1,110 km) from Sacramento. Simultaneously, the Union Pacific Railroad (UPRR) built westward 1,085 mi (1,746 km) from the eastern terminus at Council Bluffs, Iowa. On May 10, 1869 the CPRR president, Leland Stanford, hammered in the last "Golden Spike" at Promontory Summit, Utah Territory to inaugurate service. Measurement allowed the two lines being built simultaneously to meet precisely at a single point (Bain, 1999).

A further complication was that there were two standards for track gauge which is the distance between the two rails. The British standard gauge of 4 ft 8½ inches (1,435 mm) was used in the north. The other was 5 feet (1,524 mm) gauge used in the south (Bain, 1999). The incompatibility was reconciled by adopting the standard gauge (Daspit, 2020). Also, timekeeping was not standardized with time zones across the United States until November 18, 1883. To solve this measurement problem, in 1865, each railroad set its own time to help coordinate schedules. Telegraphy allowed railroads to coordinate timetables. The 15 tunnels of the project each required precision measurements to build and stay true to course. Measurement plays a vital role in all large-scale projects of engineering.

RELEVANCE TO YOU: The concept of measurements is woven into our lives. The things that use measurements are ubiquitous. Try to consciously observe where measurements are used. You will find we are surrounded by products that use the measurement concept. Have you looked at a clock today? Measurement in timekeeping governs our day. The measurement of time allows people to schedule a meeting. Have you used a geolocation application to find your way? The measurement of latitude, longitude and altitude allows us to navigate to any destination. Map applications measure distance in miles or kilometers to give us a sense of span. Do you drive a vehicle? Velocity measurements (miles or kilometers per hour) are displayed to the driver. Have you used a computer? The quantization of information into bits allows a computer to process data. Digital video pixelates images by representing color with discrete values. Are you trying to lose weight? The scale weighs your mass in pounds or kilograms. Have you ever had a fever? A thermometer measures temperature in degrees Fahrenheit or Celsius. Cooking recipes use measurements for volume such as teaspoons and cups. The electricity meter in your home measures energy usage in kilowatt hours. Nearly all the manufactured things you use rely on measurements to produce or operate.

What if we thought about measurements creatively? What if we considered them as a resource? For example, consider the measurement of time in managing your day. Could you manage your schedule in fixed "chunks" of time? When you plan your day, think of time as a measured resource. Consider time in hourly units and plan accordingly. Try to plan one day an hour at a time. Then, try it for a week. As another example, what if we thought about volume differently? Your possessions take up volume. Can you rearrange them in different ways? Can you group things by dimension or by function? When you need to pack for a trip, measurement, space and volume become all important. I have travelled all around the world with just a backpack. That can only happen with a good sense of measurement and volume. Try to think creatively with the use of time, space, or volume measurements.

Measurement can also be meaningful in the abstract. The measure of man is a symbolic assessment of his character. Protagoras said that *"man is the measure of all things"* (Plato, Dialogues (Theaetetus), 2007), implying that knowledge is subjective, being derived from human observation. Martin Luther King, Jr. stated "The ultimate measure of a man is not where he stands in moments of comfort and convenience, but where he stands in times of challenge and controversy. (King M. L., 1968)" Abstract qualia such as creativity, intelligence, or wisdom are hard to measure quantitatively; yet, we have a sense when someone has a good measure of those characteristics.

Chapter 17 – ELEMENTS

DESCRIPTION: Since time immemorial, Mankind has wondered what things are fundamentally made of. The concept of an element as an undividable substance has three major historical phases: classical definitions, chemical definitions and atomic definitions. In the classical definition, Empedocles (490-430 BCE) of ancient Greece proposed that everything was made of four elements: earth, air, fire and water (Simplicius, 2011). He called them the four "roots". Plato was the first to use the term *element* in reference to earth, air, fire and water (Plato, Timeus, 360 BC). This view lasted through the middle ages into the Renaissance (1300-1600). Medieval alchemy was developed by Jabir ibn Hayyan. It consisted of the classical elements with the addition of sulphur and mercury (Norris, 2013). Alchemists considered this set of elements as the irreducible components of the universe.

1661 marked the era of chemical definitions. Elements are chemically the simplest substances and are irreducible by chemical reactions. Elements can only be changed into other elements using nuclear methods. Robert Boyle proposed a corpuscular theory of nature. He proposed that matter was composed of irreducible units of matter called *atoms* (Boyle, 1661). The atoms of an element must all have the same number of protons. Though, they can have different numbers of neutrons and hence different masses. Atoms of the same element with different numbers of neutrons are called isotopes. The first modern list of chemical elements was produced by Antoine Lavoisier in his 1789 book, *Elements of Chemistry* (Lavoisier, 1789). He identified thirty-three elements. In 1869, Dmitri Mendeleev proposed his periodic table of elements which had sixty-six elements arranging them by atomic weight (Mendeleev D. I., 1901). He predicted the properties of germanium, gallium and scandium before their discovery based on his table.

The following is a diagram of the modern periodic table of elements:

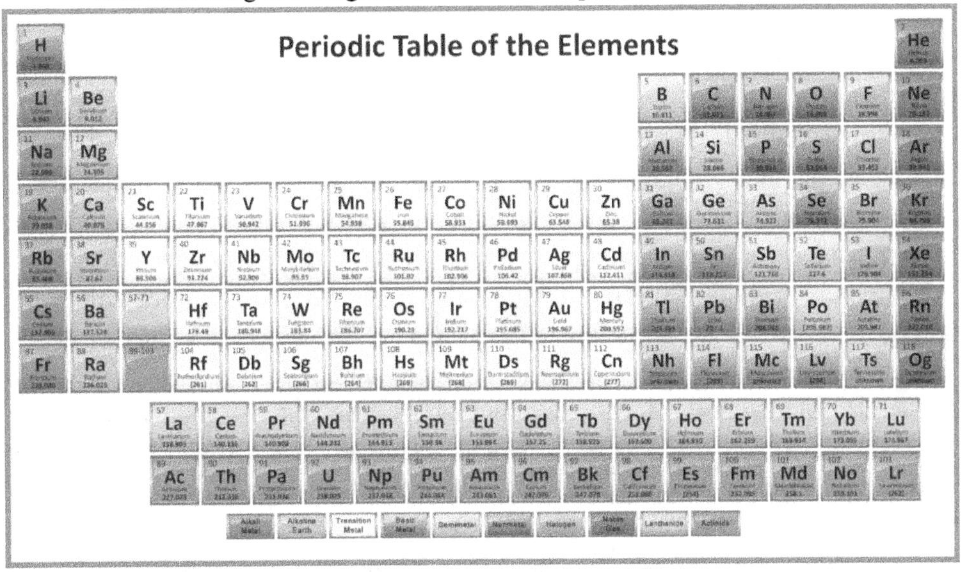

Figure 2 – The Periodic Table of Elements

The physicist Henry Moseley inaugurated the atomic definitions era. In 1913, he discovered a mathematical relationship between atomic numbers and X-ray wavelengths using X-Ray spectroscopy and Bragg's diffraction law (Moseley, 1913). Thus, the nuclear charge became the basis for the atomic number of an atom. An understanding of neutrons and protons led to the modern definition of an element based on atomic number (Scerri, 2013). The use of atomic number had greater predictive value than using the atomic weight. By 1914, seventy-two naturally occurring elements were identified (Aldersey-Williams, 2011). Today, the International Union of Pure and Applied Chemistry (IUPAC) is the world authority in developing standards for the naming of the chemical elements and compounds (International Union of Pure and Applied Chemistry, 2020). Most recently, scientists synthesized element number 117, Tennessine (Glanz, 2010) and element 118, Oganesson (Soby, 2016). Scientists estimate anywhere from 1×10^{18} to

1×10^{200} possible different stable chemical compounds could be created from the 118 known elements (Science Forums, 2013). The Chemical Abstract Services has a chemical registry containing over 30,000,000 chemicals in it (American Chemical Society, 2020).
NOTABLE WORK: Timeus (Plato, Timeus, 360 BC)
PERSON: Plato
SYMBOL: EL. An icon of an element represents this periodic idea.
DATE: 360 BCE
STORY: Combinatorics started in ancient India with Sushruta and ancient Greece with Chrysippus and Hipparchus (Wilson & Watkins, 2013). A *combination* is a merging of individually distinct component elements. A *permutation* is one of several possible variations, where a set of things are ordered or arranged. Together permutations and combinations produce variety and diversity. There are many examples of combinations and permutations. Case in point, there are only five basic tastes (salty, sweet, sour, bitter, and umami). However, when combined, they give rise to a myriad combination of tastes. Computers use only ones and zeros to represent data using a binary counting system. A stream of ones and zeros are used to represent numbers, codes, and letters. The resulting binary stream can represent video, voice, and data. As another example, there are but seven primary colors (red, orange, yellow, green, blue, indigo, and violet) and yet they produce a medley of colors when blended. The possible number of patterns that the 100 billion neurons of your brain can make is more than the number of atoms in the observable universe (Hawkings & Blakeslee, 2005). As another example, the combination of DNA and genes produces diversity in living organisms (Urry, et al., 2016). Set theory, algebraic group theory, and sorting algorithms are mathematical areas that use combinations and permutations (Jech, 2006).

      The combination of elements produces a variety of molecules. Just the elements of carbon and hydrogen can combine to produce a plethora of forms. Hydrocarbons come in the form of alkanes, alkenes, cycloalkanes, and arenes. They can be gases (methane and propane), liquids (hexane and benzene), waxes (paraffin wax and naphthalene), or polymers (polyethylene, polypropylene, and polystyrene) (Tro, 2016).
RELEVANCE TO YOU: The atomic elements are relevant to you in the sense of building blocks. The basic concept of an elemental building block has far reaching and wide-ranging applications from the fashion industry to nutrition. This book uses the elements principle to outline key ideas in history that have become

fundamental building blocks for many disciplines. Basic elements combine in many different combinations and permutations to create compounds and materials. Likewise, elemental building block ideas combine to produce an endless variety of outcomes. Basic scientific ideas combine to empower and enrich society.

Identify the basic concepts and elements in your project. Key ideas often produce new avenues of thinking. Consider a knowledgeable chef plying his craft. He can combine basic ingredients and spices to produce a variety of culinary creations. Cultural cuisine is characterized by a set of basic spices used in many dishes. The basic colors are combined by a maestro in endless ways to create masterpieces. The stroke of a paintbrush with elemental paints converge on the canvas to produce a magnum opus. The words in a language are combined to spin a story and produce wonderous captivating tales. In his book, *20 Master Plots*, Ron Tobias describes elemental plot components that are combined to produce interesting stories (Tobias, 2012). The musical notes of instruments combine in an orchestra to produce a symphony. The basic components of life – muscle, organs, bone and tissue combine in a variety of ways to produce diversity in animals. Basic dance steps are manipulated and combined by a choreographer to create dance pieces. Basic elemental ideas in architecture create distinctiveness in buildings. Elemental ideas in Photography create visual masterpieces on film. A movie director animates a story script by manipulating the elements of theater including the props, lighting, performers, set, and stage.

The concept of combinations and permutations find a wide variety of everyday applications. For example, a tailor sees different combinations and permutations as he mixes and matches elemental pieces of clothing and accessories. A chef will see culinary possibilities by combining different spices and sauces with different ingredients. You can use combination and permutation to dress or prepare a meal. You can test two ideas together and see if there is a meaningful combination. You can alter the arrangement of things in your project and see if it produces something useful. Combinations and permutations can stimulate creativity. You can try to bond two concepts together to see if the union is meaningful. Handshaking elements coaxes you to think fundamentally about those concepts. You can test to see if a combination produces a new creative application (Barabasi, 2014).

Chapter 18 – FEEDBACK

DESCRIPTION: Feedback is defined as the return of a portion of the output of a process or system back into the input, especially when used to maintain performance or to control a system or process. Feedback mechanisms are present in biological systems. For example, humans are endotherms that maintain a body temperature of 37° C (98.6° F). So, when you are hot, you sweat and vasodilate using blood convective cooling. This example of biological feedback is called homeostasis, where the body uses a self-regulating process to maintain an equilibrium. Feedback is used in many engineering systems. For example, a cruise control system uses feedback to keep a constant velocity for a vehicle. There are many feedback mechanisms in the climate. For example, a warm atmosphere holds more water vapor which leads to more cloud formation. Increased clouds lead to increased albedo which limits cloud formation. Albedo is the amount of light reflected by a surface. This is an example of a negative feedback loop (Zeigler & Praehofer, 2000). The concept of feedback is used in cybernetics, control systems, audio feedback, feed forward, optical feedback, recursion, and resonance.

There are two kinds of feedback loops, positive and negative feedback. A positive feedback mechanism increases the effect of something, while a negative feedback loop works to dampen the effect. An example of a positive feedback loop is ice albedo feedback (Lian & Cess, 1977). Albedo is the ratio of the light reflected by a planet to that received by it. Snow and ice reflect sunlight. By reflecting incoming solar radiation back into space, the temperature of the Earth drops. If the Earth becomes colder, more ice grows, covering more area. Thus, reflecting even more incoming sunlight, which in turn cools the Earth further. Scientists study feedback loops in nature and biology to understand those systems better.

There are two basic types of control systems: open-loop and closed-loop. Open-loop systems do not use feedback, while closed-loop systems rely on feedback (Nise, 2019). Both types of systems have a control mechanism that can adjust the behavior of the output. Closed loop systems measure the output and compare it to a desired target. For example, in a heating and cooling system, the output of the system is the temperature in the home. The controller, the thermostat in this case adjusts the temperature based on a comparison of present level to the desired set point temperature. Open loop control systems do not correct its output. For example, a time-based traffic light that uses a fixed period of time for its green, yellow and red lights.

NOTABLE WORK: Ktesibios's clepsydra water clock used water to regulate a timekeeping mechanism (Cowan, 2012).

PERSON: Ktesibios of Alexandria, Egypt

SYMBOL: FB. Feedback is symbolized by a cycle of arrows.

DATE: 250 BCE

STORY: Insulin and glucagon made by the pancreas use feedback loops to cause your liver to maintain constant blood glucose levels in homeostasis (Bliss, 2007). Glucose is used in cell respiration to produce ATP for energy. The body uses two hormones to regulate blood glucose. The pancreas regulates blood glucose through its alpha and beta cells. When you eat a sugary dessert, your blood glucose rises and the pancreas releases insulin. The insulin causes your cells to absorb glucose. It also causes the liver to store glucose in the form of glycogen. This feedback loop reduces your blood glucose level. If you have not eaten in a while, your blood glucose level drops. Consequently, the alpha cells in the pancreas release glucagon which causes the liver to break down glycogen and release glucose into the blood increasing your glucose level. Thereby, maintaining a relatively constant level of blood glucose in your body throughout the day (Bliss, 2007).

In 1921, Frederick Banting and Charles Best discovered the hormone insulin in pancreatic extracts from dogs. They injected the hormone into a diabetic dog and discovered that it lowered its glucose levels. With the help of chemist James Collip and John J.R. Macleod, they successfully purified insulin. In 1922, they treated a boy suffering from severe diabetes (Banting & Best, 1922). In 1923, Banting and Macleod received the Nobel Prize in Medicine for their discovery.

RELEVANCE TO YOU: Feedback has many applications in science and engineering. However, it also has a similar usage in a social sense. When someone gives you feedback, they are commenting on your behavior or performance so that you can improve yourself. This is akin to the feedback loop of a closed system. The output, your behavior, is observed by someone. They describe your behavior based on a target behavior, and you take their feedback as input to alter your future behavior. Feedback allows you to course correct and change your behavior.

Feedback is one mechanism by which we learn. Through trial and error, we try something, observe the outcome and adjust actions to improve performance. We learn from our mistakes. Our triumphs are a positive feedback loop where we analyze our successes and nurture what worked well. Engaging in an activity which leads to the accumulation of knowledge is what we call experience. The feedback cycle of experimentation and results creates experiences that we benefit from.

You should learn how to identify your biological feedback mechanisms and take appropriate action. Listen to your body. If you are exhausted, you should rest. If you lack vitamins or certain nutrients, your body will show signs of the deficiency. For example, a prolonged lack of vitamin C (ascorbic acid) causes scurvy with symptoms of swollen gums, bulging eyes, scaly dry skin and very dry hair. Eat more vitamin C rich foods such as oranges, brussels sprouts, and broccoli. Pain is a feedback mechanism in your body that signifies a physical problem. Nurse the injury. Learn to identify feedback cycles and see if you can modify the inputs to achieve favorable outcomes.

Chapter 19 – MODEL

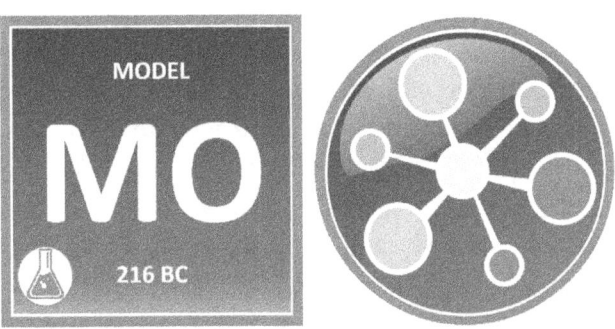

DESCRIPTION: Models in mathematics and science try to make a part of the world easier to understand through components based on existing knowledge. Models represent objects, phenomena and processes in a simplified, objective and logical way. Simulations of the real world require selecting relevant aspects of a subject to model (Bailer-Jones, 2013). Models simulate an observed phenomenon to facilitate mathematical or scientific understanding. Modeling is an essential activity in many engineering, mathematics, and scientific endeavors. While models simulate the real world, they must simplify reality to make the model tractable. Despite being an approximation, they are invaluable. A complete representation of reality is impossible, but scientists try to build a model which has predictive utility (Bailer-Jones, 2013). Models help researchers visualize phenomena.

    There are three basic kinds of models: conceptual, operational, and mathematical. Each model has different objectives and focuses on different information. *Conceptual models* try to understand a subject better. The conceptual model allows scientists to gain insights into nature through an abstraction of reality. *Operational models* seek to understand processes. For example, the operational model may help an engineer optimize industrial performance. Finally, *Mathematical models* quantify and visualize information (Page, 2018).

If the model helps the researcher understand the world better, it has achieved its objective. Models are deployed in many areas including biological studies, catastrophe management, economics, epidemiology, future studies, geologic studies, software development, statistics, and systems dynamics. For example, a climate model is crafted to forecast weather systems. Catastrophe modeling estimates damage caused by devastating events such as hurricanes or earthquakes. Economic models are used to understand resource flows and commercial markets. As another example, ecology models are created to better understand natural processes and the ramifications of human interaction with an ecosystem. Modeling are used when it is impractical to create direct experiments and measure outcomes. For example, stellar models of the solar system or milky way galaxy. A computer simulation is an efficient way to implement a model. Models are invaluable because they have analytical potential and can predict consequences. Animal studies are performed by pharmaceutical companies because animal models help scientists understand the side effects of new medications. The world is a complex place. Complex interactions take place in any natural ecosystem (Hurlbut, 1976). A model can zoom in on one part of a complex system to make it mentally digestible. For example, Aerospace engineers study just the wing of a model airplane in a wind tunnel.

To develop a model, first delineate a system to be studied. A system is a set of interacting and interdependent entities that form an integrated whole. For more information, see the systems periodic idea chapter. Next, identify the abstractions simplifying the real world. The assumptions are listed. Then, the structure of a model is defined which details the patterns and relationships of elements in the model. The developed model is employed and tested. Afterwards, the model is analyzed and evaluated for its predictive capability. Models that generate reproduceable results and are consistent with observations gain credibility. For example, in vivo and in vitro models are used in vaccine development (Youngdahl, Hammond, Sipics, Hicks, & Cicchini, 2013). This analysis refines the model. Finally, the model is deployed for practical applications or used to make real-world decisions. Many software applications are available to help you create and use a model including Adobe dimension, Wolfram Mathematica, and MATLAB.

NOTABLE WORK: The Sand Reckoner wherein he proposed a heliocentric model of the solar system (Archimedes, 216 BC)
PERSON: Aristarchus of Samos

The Periodic Table of Ideas

SYMBOL: MO. The model idea is represented by a ball and stem molecular model kit.

DATE: 216 BCE

STORY: Wind tunnels have been used to study model airplanes, golf balls, automobiles, Olympic cyclists, racing helmets, spacecraft, tennis balls, and wings. The science of aerodynamics emerged with the development of airplanes. Wind tunnels are large tubes with air blowing through them and are used to study aerodynamics. They allow researchers to study the aerodynamic efficiency of test scale models. The motion of the air can be studied by smoke, dyes, and colored threads. In 1746, the British military engineer Benjamin Robins invented a whirling arm apparatus to carry out some of the first experiments in aviation theory (Robins, 1761). In 1883, Osborne Reynolds showed that a scale model airflow pattern matches that of a full-sized vehicle if the ratio of the inertial forces to the viscous forces can be preserved (Reynolds, 1883). This fluid-flow parameter is now known as the Reynolds number. Scale test models try to preserve the geometric proportions, Mach number and Reynolds numbers of the actual object. The Wright brothers used a simple wind tunnel in 1901 to study the effects of airflow during the development of the first successful heavier-than-air flying machine, the *Wright Flyer* (Dodson, 2005).

RELEVANCE TO YOU: A model is a way to look at the world in a simplified manner making it easier to understand. For example, consider a model railroad set. The miniature train set in a diorama is a microcosm of the world, a scaled down representation of the real world. Models are useful when you can't perform experiments or get real-world data. For instance, virtual reality simulations let you explore natural phenomenon on other planets and star systems.

For your project, see if you can create a model, storyboard or flowchart. Abstract the key elements of your project to reduce a complex problem down into a manageable simulation. Identifying key abstractions focuses you on the relevant parts of a complicated problem. It allows you to gain a deeper understanding of your subject matter. Models can help you visualize a process. For example, a flow chart can help you understand how the parts of a production process integrate. Models help you gain insight into a problem and tame it. Simplifying a system makes it easier to see the pivotal aspects of it. You can visualize the key parts of a system with a model. You can create a model to identify bottlenecks in a process. It lets you discover constraints and obstacles. Mental meandering frustrates problem solving. Models examine a problem in miniature to guide your exploration towards a solution.

You can start with a simple model. To create a model, first define your problem and the relevant system. A system is a set of interdependent entities in an integrated whole. For example, "Doc", a teacher, wants to see how educational videos will affect his student's retention of knowledge. In this case, the classroom system is composed of the teacher, students, training material, and learning environment. Next, identify the key parts of a process, or system. For example, in a classroom, the key elements are the activities, class environment, students, teacher, and training material. In a process, you want to find the key decision points. So, the next step to develop a model is to identify the patterns and relationships. In our example, a learning model might relate training videos to a quantifiable change in learning progress and test scores. The analysis refines the model. Finally, the finished model is put into operation and evaluated. Deploy the model for a practical application or use it to make real-world decisions. The teacher in this example, may integrate educational videos as part of his regular curriculum.

Chapter 20 – EXPERIMENTATION

DESCRIPTION: Experiments are a scientific procedure undertaken to explore, gather evidence, test a hypothesis, demonstrate a fact, or determine the efficacy of an idea. Science is quintessentially associated with experimentation. An experiment is a procedure under controlled conditions to verify, refute, or establish a hypothesis when trying to explain phenomenon. Experiments also investigate the performance, qualities, or suitability of something. It is a crucible of truth, a test designed to verify an assertion. Experiments establish scientific theories from consistent results by repeatable tests and observation. Experiments can come in many forms, from simple to elaborate. Tests take into consideration available evidence, environment, known variables, subjects, and time constraints.

Trochim described three kinds of studies: descriptive, relational and causal (Trochim, 2001). *Descriptive tests* are used to describe a situation or a thing. *Relational tests* establish a connection between two or more variables. *Causal experiments* identify cause and effect patterns between variables. Test designers consider data reliability, data sampling, interviews, measurement, problem formulation, scaling, and variables to create experiments.

The design of an experiment requires choices and considerations. A causal experiment tries to establish a relationship between two variables. A simple method is a two-group experiment where one group is a control group and the other is the treatment group. Participants are randomly assigned to the groups. Pre-tests and post-tests assess the efficacy of an experiment. Another type of experiment is a factorial design which uses factors as independent variables. Each of the factors may have a level, or a subdivision. For example, a factorial design may have temperature and pressure as factors in the experiment. Statistical analysis is used to evaluate the outcomes of an experiment, such as an *analysis of variance* (ANOVA), or a *t-test* (Aczel & Sounderpandian, 2005).

Experiments encourage a trial-and-error approach to investigation. This approach reaches a solution iteratively. Each successive trial reduces errors. These series of tests eventually converge to a satisfactory result or provide plausible theories. Exploration through a series of tests points the investigation in the right direction.

Experimentation begins with asking insightful questions and formulating a possible answer. That candidate answer is called a hypothesis. Then, you can try to verify the validity of the hypothesis through an experiment. Experimentation encourages investigation. Examination produces observations to help craft an experiment. Inquiry and knowledge are essential to the creation of experiments.

A *Gedanken experiment* is a thought experiment to consider a theory and think through its consequences. Lindsay Yeates described the seven types of Gedanken experiments as pre-factual, counter-factual, semi-factual, prediction, hind-casting, retro-diction, and back-casting (Yeates, 2004). *Pre-factual* thought experiments speculate on a possible future outcome given the occurrence of a specific event. *Counter-factual* experiments theorize on the possible outcomes of a different past. It considers what might have happened if event A had happened instead of B. *Semi-factual* thought experiments consider the likelihood of the present given a different past. Even though event A happened instead of B, would event C still have occurred? *Predictive* experiments anticipate a future outcome from a set of circumstances. *Hind-casting* tests the validity of a simulation after an event has already occurred. *Retro-diction* establishes the cause of an event by moving backwards in time. Reverse engineering and forensics are examples of retro-diction. *Back-casting* takes a future outcome and moves backwards in time step-by-step until the present is reached. Back-casting determines the mechanisms by which the future could be attained from the present.

NOTABLE WORK: Book of Optics (al-Haytham, 1989)
PERSON: Ibn al-Haytham

The Periodic Table of Ideas 69

SYMBOL: EP. A chemistry beaker represents experimentation.
DATE: 1021
STORY: Some experiments were landmark scientific achievements. Cosmology is a branch of astronomy that pertains to the origin, structure, and space-time relationships of the universe (Webster's New World Dictionary, 1984). It is built upon the knowledge of the fundamental particles, their interactions and the physics of space-time and gravitation. The "big-bang" model proposes a rapid expansion scenario for the origin of the universe. One of its predictions was experimentally verified when Arno A. Penzias and Robert W. Wilson discovered the cosmic microwave background radiation in 1960 (Penzias & Wilson, 1965). They shared the Nobel Prize in the Physics in 1978. This radiation is an afterglow of the violent, fiery processes in the early stages of the big bang. It is called the cosmic background radiation because it is nearly uniform when observed from different directions. The universe cooled for 13.8 billion years to reach its present equilibrium temperature of 3.5 degrees kelvin. They performed their landmark experiments at the Holmdel Horn Antenna of Bell Labs at Crawford Hill, New Jersey, USA (Penzias & Wilson, 1965).
RELEVANCE TO YOU: We think experiments are only performed by lab scientists in white coats in a remote research laboratory. However, anyone can conduct an experiment. Just bear in mind that experimentation is simply used to test a claim. You can perform an experiment with a simple conversation with someone. It does not necessarily have to involve white lab coats and chemistry beakers. The objective of scientific experimentation is to find out if a hypothesis is true. Use experimentation to gain insight and knowledge.

For example, suppose you have a hypothesis that you will enjoy sky diving. Without jumping out of a plane, how could you first test that hypothesis? You could try an experiment with a life-size simulator. You might conduct an experiment with a virtual reality computer program jumping out of a virtual airplane. You might have a friend who is an experienced sky diver. They could record their sky diving experience with a helmet camera. Thus, you could experience their adventure vicariously. You could perform experiments watching sky diving videos on social media sites, such as YouTube.

Experimentation comes in many different forms. They are often used outside of scientific endeavors. You can use simple down to earth experiments. Experiments are just tools for mental exploration and discovery. Experiments are a good way to explore a subject. If you want to design formal experiments there are many established types of standard experiments to use (Singleton & Straits, 2005). Resources are available to help you design experiments should you need to call upon them. Statistical tests ascertain whether to accept or reject a hypothesis within a certain probability of confidence.

Experimentation only requires the willingness to try new things, explore new ways of thinking, and hop onto new trains of thought. For example, a child frequently performs experiments to understand the world. Vera and Crossan looked at how an experimental culture can stimulate creativity in improvisation performers (Vera & Crossan, 2005). Experimentation is a willingness to explore the mysterious.

Exploration is the investigation the unfamiliar. Great explorers such as Magellan charged into the unknown to circumnavigate the world. Christopher Columbus had a thirst for exploration which led him to discover the "new world". He was willing to risk life and limb to further Mankind's knowledge of the world. Columbus and his crew thought they might be sailing over the edge of the earth into an abyss. His crew conquered their fear of the unknown and ventured forth in the face of adversity (Morison, 1991).

Chapter 21 – SCIENTIFIC METHOD

DESCRIPTION: The scientific method involves systematic observation, measurement, and experimentation. The procedure involves the formulation, testing, and modification of a hypothesis to explain natural phenomenon. It has been the basis of our understanding of the universe around us (Cowles, 2020). The scientific method is a procedure that has characterized science since the 17th century. The five steps of the scientific method are question formulation, hypothesis development, prediction, testing, and analysis. A scientific quest starts with a hypothesis. A hypothesis proposes an idea to explain a phenomenon (Gower, 1996). The proposals are tested through observation and experimentation. The experimentation affirms or denies the hypothesis. The research explores those ideas that are promising and shelves those that are not. Scientists follow the evidence wherever it leads them. They establish scientific theories by careful observation and consistent results from repeatable experiments (Goldstein & Goldstein, 1981). Researchers investigate promising leads to gain further insight and refine a hypothesis. Eventually, mathematical models or equations are developed resulting in the ability to predict natural phenomena.

The scientific method consists of five parts: question formulation, hypothesis development, prediction, testing, and analysis (Gower, 1996). The start of a thinking journey should begin with a good question. The hypothesis formulates a conjecture to explain the observations and evidence. Scientific formulations define a null hypothesis which is a conjecture that the hypothesis is false while an alternative hypothesis posits that the hypothesis is true. A prediction determines the logical consequences of a hypothesis. If the hypothesis aligns with observations, and explains a phenomenon, it has predictive value. Scientific experiments are designed to test and verify a hypothesis. After experiments are performed and data is gathered, analysis is used to ascertain the validity of the hypothesis. Statistical analysis is typically used. For example, an ANOVA, t-test, or chi-squared test are used to mathematically estimate a confidence level that the hypothesis is true (Aczel & Sounderpandian, 2005). Science is a collaborative endeavor, results are published, and other experimenters strive to repeat and verify the findings.

STEPS IN SCIENTIFIC METHOD	
STEP	DESCRIPTION
FORMULATION OF QUESTION	Developing a question will serve as the basis for a scientific study. Questions will guide the thinking journey and serve as the basis for exploring the unknown.
DEVELOPMENT OF HYPOTHESIS	A hypothesis is a proposed explanation made based on limited evidence as a starting point for further investigation. A hypothesis is proposed as a basis for reasoning without any presumptions as to its truthfulness. A hypothesis should account for assumptions. Scientific formulations define a null hypothesis which is the conjecture that the statistical hypothesis is false while an alternative hypothesis postulates that the hypothesis is true.
PREDICTION	A prediction determines the logical consequences of a hypothesis. If the hypothesis aligns observations and available evidence to explain a phenomenon, it may have predictive value which is the ability to predict outcomes from inputs.
TESTING	Scientific experiments are designed to test and verify a hypothesis. *Descriptive tests* describe something. *Relational tests* establish a relation between variables. *Causal experiments* find cause and effect patterns.
ANALYSIS	After experiments are performed and data is gathered, analysis is used to ascertain the validity of the hypothesis.

Table 9 – Steps in the Scientific Method

NOTABLE WORK: Novum Organum (Bacon, 1620)
PERSON: Francis Bacon
SYMBOL: SD. A question mark iconifies the exploration embodied by this periodic idea.
DATE: 1620
STORY: On September 3, 1928 Alexander Fleming had staphylococci in Petri dishes in his lab that was contaminated with a fungus. Alexander Fleming observed that staphylococci were killed by the mold. Applying the scientific method, he hypothesized that the mold could kill bacteria. To test his hypothesis, he grew mold in a pure culture. He found that it produced a substance that he called *"mold juice"* which killed disease-causing bacteria. He identified the mold as being from the genus Penicillium. On March 7, 1929, Fleming named the substance that the mold released *penicillin*. Eventually, the Penicillium Notatum mold was cultivated into the world's first antibiotic which revolutionized medicine (Hughes, 1977).
RELEVANCE TO YOU: How can you apply the scientific method to your situation? You can apply the principles of the scientific method even if you are not a scientist, detective, engineer, or philosopher. Activities great and small all require some thought, planning, and decision. The principles of the scientific method are to ask questions, create a hypothesis, gather evidence, determine if that hypothesis is true, and devise tests to ascertain its validity. Those basic steps find a wide variety of applications.

Suppose you want to troubleshoot a problem with your home appliance, such as a washing machine. You might start by gathering data. You observe what works and what malfunctions. You notice a pattern to the failures. Based on your observations, you hypothesize there is a faulty lid switch. You formulate a driving question. You hypothesize that the lid switch is not triggering properly and thus not starting the machine. You do some more investigation to test your prediction. You can watch videos or read articles of others who have also experienced malfunctioning lid switches. After you replace the component, you can confirm or deny your hypothesis. You might also hire a repairman to fix the faulty appliance. The repairman is also likely to walk through the steps of the scientific method to find a plausible explanation for the malfunction.

Chapter 22 – ANALYSIS

DESCRIPTION: Analysis is the processing of evidence and data to make sense of the information that has been gathered. The statistical analysis of data is the basis of modern scientific research. Today, data analysis propels scientific progress. Statistical analysis methods are used to evaluate the outcomes of an experiment, such as an *analysis of variance* (ANOVA), or a *t-test* (Aczel & Sounderpandian, 2005). These indicate a statistical degree of confidence in a hypothesis. A sense of truth is gauged from these tools. Analysis of variance (ANOVA) are statistical models with estimation procedures to analyze the differences in a sample data set. ANOVA was developed by statistician Ronald Fisher in 1921 (Fisher R. A., 1921). The ANOVA is based on the law of total variance, a variable is partitioned into components attributable to different sources.

Mathematical analysis gained prominence in the enlightenment. It was the basis for modern astronomy, chemistry, geology, and physics. The development of calculus by Isaac Newton and Gottfried Leibniz paved the way for scientific analysis to model and predict the motion of objects and planets (Boyer, 1959). Calculus is the mathematical study of continuous change. Differential calculus is concerned with instantaneous rates of changes. Integral calculus focuses on the accumulation of quantities and areas under curves.

NOTABLE WORK: Philosophiae Naturalis Principia Mathematica (Mathematical Principles of Natural Philosophy) (Newton, 1687)
PERSON: Isaac Newton
SYMBOL: AN. Raw data passing through a magnifying glass and resulting in ordered data symbolizes analysis.
DATE: 1687
STORY: Some of the most interesting stories in science involve a scientist solving a mystery through analysis. One such story celebrates Henrietta Swan Leavitt who created a means to measure the distance to other stars. She analyzed starlight coming from variable stars whose brightness fluctuates. She determined that a pulsating Cepheid variable star changes in brightness with a well-defined period and amplitude (Leavitt & Pickering, 1912). Her analysis would eventually revolutionize astronomy. In 1913, Ejnar Hertzsprung calculated the distance to 13 Cepheids which had become a cosmic measuring ruler, a standard candle (Hertzsprung, 1913).

In 1922, Edwin Hubble and Milton Humason used the Hooker Telescope to analyze the distances of over 40 Cepheids in spiral galaxies millions of light years away. Hubble's calculations revealed that the farther away a galaxy is, the greater its red shift. Starlight is red shifted when its source recedes away from the Earth. He discovered that the greater the separation between two galaxies the faster space expands between them (Hubble, 1929). His analysis concluded that space itself is expanding. That rate of expansion, 73 kilometers/second/megaparsec, became known as the *Hubble constant* (Riess, et al., 2018). A megaparsec is 3.3 million light-years. In 2001, the Hubble telescope conclusively verified these measurements (Freedman, et al., 2001). The insights of Hubble led to the development of the big bang theory. Hubble is regarded as one of the most important astronomers in history.

RELEVANCE TO YOU: News, project data, social media, and websites may inundate you with too much data to process. Information overload is a common problem in the age of information. Too many choices and data can overwhelm you. Analysis swoops in to save the day. Analysis allows you to make sense of a jumble of disparate information. Analysis reduces a mountain of data to a few gemstones of meaningful results, relationships and trends. Insightful conclusions result from analysis. Statistics can isolate meaningful patterns in data. Analysis can reveal diamonds in the rough allowing you to make progress in your endeavors. In scientific projects, analysis provides a probabilistic confidence level that a proposed hypothesis is true.

You can employ statistical methods to help you analyze data and make decisions. *Descriptive statistics* pertains to the collection, presentation and description of sample data. These include calculating the means, averages, and standard deviations in a set of data. For example, a census is a descriptive statistic which describes a population. *Inferential statistics* includes techniques to interpret the data, determine relationships among variables, to make decisions and draw conclusions. For instance, business analysts use inferential statistics to forecast market demands.

As an example of analysis in use, suppose you want to make a major purchase. You want to buy a new car. You are confronted with a bewildering array of choices. There are hundreds of vehicles to consider. When you consider the different combinations of condition, make, model, color and options the choices now get into the thousands. Analysis wrestles with the choices to catalyze decision-making. You can list all the attributes of a car that are important to you and rank them. Then, you can then use a selection method such as Best fit, Devil's Advocate, the Matrix Method (Pugh, 1981), Weighted matrix Method, or Feasibility Focus to finalize on a selection (Lehrer, 2010). You can learn more about these decision-making techniques in my book, the Four Elements of Thinking (Cheung, The Four Elements of Thinking, 2019).

Chapter 23 – SYSTEM

DESCRIPTION: A system is defined as a group of interacting, interrelated, or interdependent elements that form a complex whole (Webster's New World Dictionary, 1984). The term system derives from the Latin word *systema*, meaning a whole concept made from several parts or members. A system is bounded in time and space. It is surrounded and affected by the environment that it inhabits. A system is also characterized by its structure, purpose and function (Gharajedgaghi, 2005).

In 1824, Nicolas Sadi Carnot published *The Reflections on the Motive Power of Fire* (Carnot, 1824). He was a French mechanical engineer, scientist and the father of thermodynamics. Carnot studied the effect of heated water vapor in steam engines. He delineated a heated steam engine as a system whose purpose was to do mechanical work. His book laid the foundations for thermodynamics and described the second law of thermodynamics. He was the first to theorize on the maximum efficiency of heat engines. Carnot concluded that motive power is due to the transfer of heat from a hot body to a cold one. Later, Rudolf Clausius and Lord Kelvin formalized the second law of thermodynamics and defined the concept of *entropy* (Clausius, 1867). Other pioneering scientists who studied systems include Ludwig von Bertalanffy, Kenneth Boulding, Ralph Gerard, James Miller, George Klir and Anatol Rapoport.

There are three types of systems: open, closed and isolated. An open and closed system can have energy inputs and outputs. An *open* system can take in material inputs external to the system and can have material outputs. An example of an open system is a natural wildlife ecosystem. A *closed* system recycles materials within the system but blocks external material inputs. An aquarium, or a sealed biosphere dome exemplifies a closed system. An *isolated* system has neither energy inputs nor outputs. Isolated systems are used for theoretical purposes. For example, they are useful in constructing mathematical models of the planets or to study atomic models.

Daniel Kim described 10 basic tools of systems thinking (Kim, 1994). A *double-Q diagram* is a brainstorming tool to capture thoughts in a structured manner. *Behavior-over-time* graphs capture the behavior of one or more variables over time and shows their inter-relations. *Causal loop diagrams* show how variables are interrelated to identify reinforcing and balancing feedback. *System archetypes* are recurring common patterns and structures highlighting organizational dynamics. *Graphical functional diagrams* relate the effect of one variable against the full range of another variable. *Structure-behavior pairs* are basic dynamic structures that are the building blocks for developing models. Examples include exponential growth, S-shaped growth, and oscillations. *Policy structure diagrams* are a conceptual map for decision making focusing on factors used at decision points. *Computer models* map relationships through simulations and analyze policies. *Management flight simulators* use computer simulations to connect consequences to decisions. *Learning laboratories* promote practical experimentation with reflection and discussion.

NOTABLE WORK: *The Reflections on the Motive Power of Fire* (Carnot, 1824)
PERSON: Nicolas Leonard Sadi Carnot
SYMBOL: SY. The solar system is representative of this periodic idea. The icon shows the sun, earth and mars from our solar system.
DATE: 1824
STORY: Arthur Tansley was the Sherardian Professor of Biology at Oxford University. In 1935, he published an influential book entitled, *The Use and Abuse of Vegetational Concepts and Terms* (Tansley, 1935). In this book, he introduced the term *ecosystem* which is widely used today. He defined it as the system resulting from the interaction of all the living and non-living factors of the

environment (Tansley, 1935). Tansley emphasized the significance of material transfers between organisms and their environment. He regarded ecosystems as basic units of nature (Cooper, 1957). In biology, an ecosystem is an interconnected ecological community of organisms and plants along with the environment they live in (Willis, 1997). Scientists study biomass, competition, distribution, diversity, and population within an ecosystem. Scientists scrutinize ecosystem processes such as production of organic compounds, pedogenesis (soil formation), nutrient cycling (the food web), and niche construction (altering the environment) (Molles, 2012). A coral reef is an example of an aquatic ecosystem. A forest exemplifies a terrestrial ecosystem.

RELEVANCE TO YOU: The concept of a system helps you think about your environment. For example, your co-workers collaborating on a project could be considered a system. Your workspace or desk can be considered an open system. Your home can be considered an open system that consumes energy and expels waste. Your family and local community can be thought of as an open system. A local community takes in material and energy inputs from the larger society and produces material and energy outputs. Your appliances, such as your refrigerator, can be considered an open system. The human body is an open system.

Thinking about things in terms of systems can help you understand the world. It can help you tackle problems. Seeing the world through systems can help you think about your environment. The boundaries of a system define a problem space. You can observe or manage system inputs and outputs at its boundaries. You can define a system as the basis for modeling it. To understand a system, define its inputs, outputs, environment, structure, purpose and function.

Systems can adapt and grow. It can interact with its environment. Through synergy, a system can be more than the sum of its parts displaying emergent behavior. The world is an intricately intertwined and interconnected set of systems. Systems are characterized by interrelated elements that serve a purpose. System thinking looks at the whole system rather than concentrating on individual components (Gharajedgaghi, 2005). A grasp of systems thinking allows you to shape and affect its inputs and outputs.

The study of systems allows you to predict its behavior. People study systems to understand their dynamics, constraints, conditions and principles. I did my Ph.D. in operations research. It is study of optimizing systems (Winston, 1994). To optimize a system, you need to be able to understand and characterize it. You need to understand the flows and bottlenecks within the system. To optimize performance, you need to understand where and how elements arrive and move through a system.

When you first encounter a problem, identify the key elements. When you observe events look for patterns in related events. Differentiate between independent events and events that form a larger pattern unfolding over time. The patterns help you identify the underlying structures. Those structures allow you to delineate a system. Feedback loops create reinforcing and balancing processes and are often found within systems. Feedback loops govern system behavior over time and influence its underlying structures.

For example, Mary Xie wants to understand a problem with a malfunctioning system at work. She defines the environment, structure, purpose and function of the system in order to comprehend it better. Then, she observes the inputs and outputs of the system for a week noting the issues and logging them. The finds a pattern of related events and discusses the issue with her co-worker. She decides to employ a behavior-over-time graph, one of the 10 basic systems thinking tools. So, she graphs the behavior of her observation variable of the system over time and isolates the problem.

Chapter 24 – CLASSIFICATION

DESCRIPTION: In biology, taxonomy is a science that names, defines and classifies groups of organisms based on shared characteristics. The taxonomic ranks are domain, kingdom, phylum, class, order, family, genus, and species (Urry, et al., 2016). For example, humans are classified under the animalia kingdom, Chordata phylum, Mammalia class, primates order, Hominidae family, homo genus, and homo sapiens species. Complementary areas of study include phylogenetics, cladistics, systematics, economic taxonomy, and Bloom's taxonomy. *Phylogenetics* studies the evolutionary relationships among individuals by evaluating observed heritable traits (Baum & Smith, 2012). *Cladistics* categorizes organisms into groups, or clades, based on common ancestors and shared characteristics, also called synapomorphies (Williams, 2020). *Systematics* maps relationships using evolutionary trees (Rieppel, 2019). *Economic taxonomy* proposes industry classifications for economic activity including Pavitt's Taxonomy (Archibugi, 2001), standard industrial classification, and the international standard of industrial classification among others (Day, 1955). *Bloom's taxonomy* is a categorization of learning objectives in an educational setting (Bloom, Krathwohl, & B., 1969).

Early systems of taxonomy were based on arbitrary criteria including the system from Carl Linnaeus based on sexual classification (Dickinson, 1967) set forth in his book *Systema Naturae* (Linnaeus, Systema Naturae, 1735). John Ray compiled an encyclopedia of plants in his book *Historia Plantarum*, marking one of the first major scientific classification efforts (Ray, 2016). The publication of *On the Origin of Species* (Darwin, 1859) by Charles Darwin led to classification systems based on evolutionary relationships. Later, the development of molecular genetics and statistics created phylogenetics based on cladistics, rather than morphology alone.

NOTABLE WORK: On the Origin of Species (Darwin, 1859)
PERSON: Charles Darwin
SYMBOL: CL. A classification pyramid structure symbolizes this idea.
DATE: 1859
STORY: How would you go about indexing all of life on Earth? The *catalogue of life* is an ambitious project devoted to cataloging all living organisms on Earth. In June 2001, two organizations, the Species 2000 and Integrated Taxonomic Information System (ITIS) collaborated to produce the Catalogue of Life. The Catalogue integrated data from 168 taxonomic databases individually maintained by institutions around the world. The aggregated database catalog contains a 1,837,565 living and 5,719 extinct species (Roskov, et al., 2019). This is an impressive example of the classification periodic idea in action.

In 1889, in Paris, the international zoological congress convened to establish international rules to name animals. Consequently, the international code of zoological nomenclature (ICZN) became the widely accepted convention. It set forth the rules for the formal scientific naming of animals. The ICZN establishes the usage of binomial nomenclature. It also governs how to resolve naming conflicts, and how scientific literature should cite names (Ride, et al., 2020).

RELEVANCE TO YOU: Classification is how we make sense of the world around us. The organization of information produces knowledge. Patterns from data leads to understanding. For example, you have a mental classification for a tree. When you encounter a tree you have never seen, you already know a lot about it. The classification of information is a key step in comprehension. It serves to collect your thoughts and illuminate a path forward. When you categorize relevant information, you can see how elements are related.

You can study the usage of classification systems in taxonomy. That work may inspire you to adopt classification concepts in your project. Systems of classification look for shared characteristics or common ancestors. Are there similar patterns or characteristics you can use for your project?

Science tries to comprehend the natural world. To start, scientists observe commonalities. You can consider classification questions to guide your thinking. What are common characteristics that are applicable in your project? How can you cluster similar things together? Is there a hierarchy or ancestry between elements that you can identify? Where are there similarities between elements in your problem? You can organize information based on time, space, resources, people, form and function. Scientists gather specimens, make careful observations and classify organisms based on attributes, morphology, and DNA. In biological classification the taxonomic rank is domain, kingdom, phylum, class, order, family, genus, and species. Is there a "big picture" idea that can serve as your domain? Next, are there major branches that might serve as the kingdom and phylum? As you gather and organize information for your project, see if you can identify the "leaves", which correspond to the species in the taxonomic rank. The leaves are the individual elements for your situation.

For example, in October 2020, I taught a class on the Internet of Things (IoT). I had to investigate companies that made IoT products. I researched a lot of information about IoT products and services. I organized the data into the four main domains of IoT – consumer, commercial, industrial and infrastructure IoT. Then, I fit the other research that I gathered as branches under those domains. This helped me organize and structure the class that I developed.

Chapter 25 – SCIENCE PERSONAL RELEVANCE

This chapter collects and summarizes the personal relevance of each of the science periodic ideas. The methods and ideas that are used to perform scientific work are some of the most enduring and useful ideas mankind has ever devised. You can meaningfully employ these ideas as you study a subject, tackle a problem, or work on a project even if you are not a scientist. Modeling, experimentation, measurement, feedback, the scientific method, and analysis are tools for your mental toolbox. Standards, elements, classification, and systems are ways to define and think about a project, a problem, or a study.

The following table summarizes the personal relevance of science periodic Ideas. It can also be found in the appendix for quick reference.

SCIENCE IDEA	ID	PERSONAL RELEVANCE
STANDARDS **4236 BCE**	ST	Standards provides you with rules or guidelines as criterion to measure against. You can use them as standards of assessment, conduct, criterion, instruction, or practices. Standards of assessment allow you to test for outcomes.
MEASUREMENT **2900 BCE**	MS	Measurements allow you to synchronize with others to schedule meetings. It allows you to coordinate positionally to meet at a location. It establishes a uniform system of weights and measures aligning your tasks and activities with others.
ELEMENTS **360 BCE**	EL	Elements coaxes you to think about the atomic parts of your project. You can combine or permutate the elemental components of your project to unveil new avenues of thinking and exploration.

The Periodic Table of Ideas

SCIENCE IDEA	ID	PERSONAL RELEVANCE
FEEDBACK **250 BCE**	FB	Feedback gives you a mechanism to maintain performance or to control a system or process. Through trial and error, feedback encourages you to learn from your mistakes. Social feedback allows group members to adjust behavior. Biological feedback gets you to listen to the signals that your body tries to tell you.
MODEL **216 BCE**	MO	Models assist in your ability to visualize and learn about a problem or project. You can use Models to represent phenomena and processes to aid in your understanding.
EXPERIMENT **1021**	EP	You can use experiments to make a discovery, test a hypothesis, demonstrate a known fact, or determine the efficacy of an idea. You can also use experimentation to test a claim or assertion.
SCIENTIFIC METHOD **1620**	SD	The five steps of the scientific method allow you to refine a hypothesis to explain phenomenon. This method is the basis of how scientific knowledge is developed and can help you think about any subject or problem.
ANALYSIS **1687**	AN	Analysis gives you the tools to process your collected data from an experiment or project. Descriptive statistics characterizes data. Inferential statistics interprets data and draw conclusions. Analyses helps you make sense of gathered information by using statistical methods.
SYSTEM **1824**	SY	A system is characterized by its environment, inputs, outputs, function, purpose and structure. Defining a system allows you to frame a problem in its environment. Delineating an interdependent complex whole allows you to analyze and work with the system.
CLASSIFICATION **1859**	CL	Classification gives you insights on how to categorize information. By identifying shared characteristics, you can organize information. Organized data can aid in comprehension or to plan a project.

Table 10 – Periodic Science Ideas Personal Relevance

PART IV – TECHNOLOGY IDEAS

Chapter 26 – TECHNOLOGY IDEAS

The products of technology have transformed society and revolutionized the way we live and interact with the world. The eight main areas of technology are agricultural, biotechnology, communications, construction, manufacturing, medical, power, and transportation. *Agricultural technologies* use machines and materials to produce the food and natural products needed to maintain life (Marie, 2018). *Biotechnology* uses organic processes for industry often through the genetic manipulation of microorganisms to produce biological products including antibiotics and hormones (Thieman & Palladino, 2018). *Communications technologies* allow for a means of sending or receiving information at a distance (Moran, 2010). *Construction technologies* are used to erect structures on the sites where they will be used (Blankenbaker, 2012). *Manufacturing technologies* develop and use systems and process to convert materials into products in a factory (Kalpakjian & Schmid, 2013). *Medical technologies* use machines and systems to treat diseases and maintain our health (Snedden, 2008). *Power technologies* are systems and processes that convert, transmit and use energy (Webber, 2019). *Transportation technologies* use devices and systems to move people and cargo from an origin point to a destination (Fricker & Whitford, 2004).

Technology has created what would have been miracles to our forefathers. Through the millennia, technology has transformed every aspect of our everyday lives. Agriculture produces a cornucopia of food. Biotechnology has allowed us to understand life at its most fundamental level. Communications technologies allow people on the opposite ends of the planet to talk to each other in real-time. Networking has given rise to the internet and the world wide web. Social media has revolutionized our relationship with society itself. Construction technologies have produced modern metropolitan skylines. Manufacturing and medical technologies have vastly improved our quality of life. Power systems produce a bounty of energy. Transportation technologies whisk us anywhere on Earth in a few hours. It has also allowed us to send starships into space. Computers and information technologies empower all other technologies and are vast industries themselves.

The following table summarizes the periodic technological ideas sorted by date of introduction. It can also be found in the Appendix 4. The candidate technology ideas can be found in Appendix 8.

TECHNOLOGY IDEA	ID	DESCRIPTION
TRANSPORTATION TECHNOLOGY 4700 BCE	TT	Tepe Pardis. Transportation technologies use devices and systems to move people and cargo from an origin point to a destination. Its design factors include cargo, control, delivery, location, origin, positioning, speed, and steering. Transportation technologies include all types of vehicles from bicycles to spaceships.
PROTOTYPING 375 BCE	PO	Archytas. A prototype is an early model in advance of a release of a product created to test a concept. Prototyping allows designers to gain practical knowledge from an actual working system rather than a theoretical one.
COMPUTATION 1833	CP	Charles Babbage. A computer is a machine that can perform sequences of arithmetic, computational, or logical operations through a computer program. Computers control industrial and consumer devices assisting us in a wide variety of tasks.
COMMUNICATIONS 1837	CM	Sir William F. Cooke and Sir Charles Wheatstone. Communications technologies allow for a means of sending or receiving information at a distance. They are systems that can encode, store, retrieve, manipulate, transmit or receive information. The telegraph, telephone, cellular phone are examples of communication technologies.
ROBOTICS 1921	RO	Karel Capek. Robots are machines that can mimic human actions or substitute for humans in performing a task. Robots engage in walking, lifting, tasks, conversation, and

TECHNOLOGY IDEA	ID	DESCRIPTION
		cognition.
ARTIFICIAL INTELLIGENCE 1943	AI	Warren S. McCulloch and Walter H. Pitts, Jr. Artificial intelligence encompasses machines or computers that can perform cognitive functions often associated with the human mind, such as learning and problem solving.
NETWORKING 1953	NW	George Valley and Jay Forrester. Networking connects elements in a system together and brings them into contact with each other. It allows them to connect, share information, and operate together.
VIRTUAL REALITY 1957	VR	Morton Heilig. Virtual reality (VR) technologies create an immersive experience that can simulate the real world or an imaginary environment. Augmented reality (AR) is an interactive experience of a real-world environment where real world objects are enhanced by computer-generated information.
SOCIAL MEDIA 1978	SM	Ward Christensen and Randy Suess. Social Media technologies empower people to connect and share with others through the creation of virtual communities. Social media technologies are interactive applications that allow users to generate and share content through blogs, comments, posts, reviews, and videos.
PERSONALIZATION 2011	PZ	SRI International Artificial Intelligence Center. Personalization inventions customize or tailor something to an individual. A simple example are garments that are tailor-made to fit to an individual. Customized software applications allow us to unleash our creativity and express ourselves. Personal assistant software improves your productivity.

Table 11 – Periodic Technology Ideas

Chapter 27 – TRANSPORTATION TECHNOLOGY

DESCRIPTION: Transportation technologies use devices and systems to move people and cargo from an origin point to a destination (Fricker & Whitford, 2004). Vehicles are examples of transportation technology, including automobiles, bicycles, rockets, boats, planes, trains, and subways. The idea also encompasses any innovation that can move. For example, an ambulatory robot, or a mobile appendage of a robot. The development of transportation technology entails many factors including cargo, control, delivery, location, origin, positioning, speed, and steering. Transportation technologies have become the backbone of a modern society.

    Transportation technologies move people and deliver cargo from one place to another. Cargo ships and standardized intermodal containers are the basis for modern international trade. 90% of worldwide non-bulk cargo is transported by container ships (Ebeling, 2009). Trucks move containers from international ports to local destinations moving 70% of all freight in America (American Trucking Associations, 2020). Vehicles deliver people and things from an origin to a destination.

    Transportation technology is as old as the wheel and has become an integral part of society. These technologies find applications in all areas of human activity from scientific endeavors to economic projects. Each new development in vehicular technologies have inaugurated major social change. The wheeled carriage and cart allowed people to move more cargo than they could carry by hand (Piggott, 1992). Trains were an integral part of the industrial revolution (Stearns, 2012). Ships and container shipping move most of the cargo around the world (Ebeling, 2009). The invention of automobiles transformed society and greatly increased the mobility of the average person (Parissien, 2014). Airplanes and helicopters have revolutionized transportation whisking people and cargo from any point on the earth to another in a matter of hours (Grant, 2017).

NOTABLE WORK: Tournette, Potter's wheel (Potts, 2012)
PERSON: Tepe Pardis, Iran (Mesopotamian society)
SYMBOL: TT. A wheel, the quintessential aspect of many vehicles, represents the transportation periodic idea.
DATE: 4700 BCE
STORY: In 1955, former trucking company owner Malcom McLean partnered with engineer Keith Tantlinger to create the modern intermodal shipping container. McLean purchased the Pan-Atlantic Steamship company, later known as Sea-Land. Tantlinger was a seasoned engineer who had started to work on the development of containers in 1949. The result was an 8-feet (2.44 meter) tall by 8-feet wide and 10-foot (3.05 m) long box of corrugated steel. Cranes could easily lift them with a twist-lock casting mechanism on top of each of the four corners. This ingenious design allowed ports to easily and quickly process containers. On April 26, 1956 the *SS Ideal X* left from Port Newark, New Jersey bound for Houston, Texas. It carried 58 trailer-truck bodies, the first shipping containers, which would eventually revolutionize international trade. Five days later, those 58 containers arrived in Houston. They were then loaded onto trucks which hauled them to their final destinations. The resultant expansion in international trade allowed the United states to import four times as many varieties of goods in 2002 as it did in 1972 (Levinson, 2016). Today, a modern containership can hold 3,000 containers. Cranes whisk 40 boxes per hour off and on the ship in a synchrony of container movement. Computers choreograph the intricate dance of the containers as they arrive at port. Previously, the shipping container goods were manually loaded known as break-bulk shipping. It could take up to 3 weeks to unload and load a ship. Now, within 24 hours, a cargo ship can disgorge thousands of containers, take on an equal amount and is on its way to a new destination (Levinson, 2016).

RELEVANCE TO YOU: The periodic idea of transportation technology is about travel and mobility. Mobility gets you to consider *where* something will be important in a project. Is location relevant to your problem at hand? If so, you can travel to get first-hand observations of the project. To comprehend the world around you, you need to explore it. Go and travel and see the world. Observe other cultures and peoples. I have traveled to 30 countries on six continents, and those are some of my most precious life memories. My travels have provided valuable insights into human cultures, history, and society.

Transportation technologies gives us access to goods and resources from anywhere on the Earth. Markets and products benefit from regional specializations. Consider how your project may benefit from this cornucopia. Rather than creating something from scratch, perhaps there is already a product or component that you can order and have shipped to you? Transportation technologies coordinate the movement of goods. For example, modern airplane manufacturers have sub-assemblies built in disparate locations then brought together for final assembly. The ability to move goods from one place to another opens options for your project. Access to markets with secondhand goods may also create opportunities for creative solutions. For example, online auction houses, such as eBay, would allow you to find caster wheels for your home project. Moving resources to you, coordinating them, and moving resources between elements are three ways you can make use of the Transportation technology periodic idea.

In today's modern society, people are more mobile than ever. We can reach nearly anywhere on the earth in a matter of hours. Moreover, we can communicate with people in remote regions instantaneously. We can see and get reports of events anywhere in the world with news streams at our fingertips. We travel to explore, to meet friends and connect with family. Traveling creates memorable experiences as you encounter different cultures and regional attractions.

Chapter 28 – PROTOTYPING

DESCRIPTION: A prototype is an early model in advance of a release of a product created to test a concept (Hallgrimsson, 2012). The word prototype derives from the Greek word *prototypon*, which means "primitive form". It is used in engineering, software and technology development to evaluate a potential design. This allows analysts to study a working model in order to enhance a design or refine a proposal. Prototyping allows designers to gain practical knowledge from an actual working system rather than a theoretical one. Prototypes help designers evaluate the form, function, material, processes and specifications for products (Hallgrimsson, 2012). 3D printed models, clay sculpts, movie shorts, virtual reality simulators and wind tunnels are examples of prototypes. By looking at what succeeded and failed, prototypes can illuminate how to make better designs. Progress is made by conquering setbacks and addressing failures.

There are five basic categories of prototypes (Warfel, 2009). The first kind is a *functional prototype* which incorporates the form and function of the design allowing the creators to gain practical experience with the design. A *proof-of-concept* is created to study a specific aspect of a proposed design. A *user experience prototype* is a model used to gauge how effective people will interact with it. A *visual prototype* concentrates on the form of the design in shape, color, texture, and dimension. These are important where the appearance of the product is vital. A *working prototype* by contrast has nearly all the functionality of the final product in order to gain practical knowledge. In software development, an alpha or beta grade product is a software release that has limited functionality. It allows testers and evaluators to give the developers feedback on how to improve the software (Stackowiak & Kelly, 2020).

NOTABLE WORK: Flying pigeon, a steam-powered artificial self-propelled flying prototype device (Gellius, 1927).

PERSON: Archytas (435-347 BCE)

SYMBOL: PO. A cog on an engineering drafting grid captures the spirit of the prototyping idea.

DATE: c. 375 BCE

STORY: A television show that frequently used prototypes was MythBusters. It was a memorable program dedicated to testing the validity of myths. After a historic 14-year run, the show ended on March 6, 2016 (Discovery Channel, 2020). They attempted to verify the validity of 1,015 myths using the scientific method with 2,950 experiments. As Jamie Hyneman and Adam Savage put on their thinking caps, they would apply the scientific method to explain a myth. They studied information related the myth, defined a problem statement to test the myth and proposed a hypothesis. Then, they concocted an experiment to test their hypothesis. As they reasoned and discussed about a problem, the viewer could follow along in their thought process. Then, they built interesting prototypes to test their hypothesis. They would sometimes each manufacture a different prototype and test them against each other as a contest to see which one worked better. Next, they would iterate and improve based on what they had learned (Savage & Hyneman, 2010). They demonstrated that thinking about a problem in a scientific manner and performing scientific experiments could be fun as well as enlightening.

RELEVANCE TO YOU: You can employ the prototyping concept by considering where you can use them in your project. The uncertainties and unknowns in your problem shows where you can use prototypes. If you need to verify if something will work, see if you can think of a prototype. How could you construct a mock-up? For example, suppose you are due to give a presentation. You can perform a dry run to identify potential issues and get practice. 3D printed models, clay sculpts, storyboards, and virtual reality simulators are examples of prototypes that you might find useful. For example, if you have an idea to manufacture a science fiction themed spice rack you could 3D print one first.

Prototypes are a tool in your creativity toolbox to experiment with and learn from. Prototypes allow you to try out new avenues of thinking and gain experience with a project. When you wrestle with a problem using a prototype, you will gain insight into what works and what fails.

Experience allows you to make good judgments when a similar conundrum presents itself again. To make the best use of your experiences, it helps to keep a journal of your activities. Make notes to remind yourself of the lessons that you have learned. Prototyping is an iterative process. You design a prototype to see where problems exist so that you can course correct. When a similar situation ambushes you, experience offers solutions. For example, suppose you want to 3D-print a gift. Your first print has cracks. You solve the issue by adjusting the extruder temperature (Geeetech Blog, 2016). Next time, you know what to do before it ruins your project.

You can also research what other people have done with similar problems. Throughout history, people have experimented and learned through prototyping. See if you can build upon the experiences of others. Where have others failed and why did they fail? In the 3D printed gift example, you discover that others have stumbled over common 3D printing problems including warping, elephant foot, pillowing, stringing and ghosting (Geeetech Blog, 2016). Failure is a potent teacher because the mind remembers failures more often than successes. Prototypes allow you to fail in small steps on the way to success.

Chapter 29 – COMPUTATION

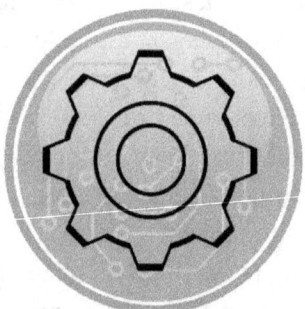

DESCRIPTION: Computers underpin modern society. Mankind has tamed daunting mathematical and statistical challenges using computers (Garfinkel & Grunspan, 2018). A computer is a machine that can perform sequences of arithmetic, computational, or logical operations through a computer program. Computers control industrial and consumer devices that assist us in a wide variety of tasks from daily chores to interplanetary exploration.

The evolution of computers has a storied history. Mechanical devices during the industrial revolution were used as guides in Jacquard looms (Hobsbawm, 1962). Charles Babbage conceived of the concept of a programmable computer and is considered the father of the modern computer (Halacy, 1970). In 1833, he conceived of the *analytical engine* wherein programs and data were fed in via punch cards much like the Jacquard loom. The analytical engine also had a printer, curve plotter and bell to serve as output. In 1941, the first electro-mechanically programmable, fully automatic digital computer was invented by Konrad Zuse called the *Z3* (Zuse, 1993). During World War II, at Bletchley Park, the British developed the *Colossus* to break the German Enigma encryption machine (Copeland, 2010). Colossus was the first electronic digital programmable computer. The principle of the modern computer was proposed by Alan Turing in

his seminal 1936 paper, *On Computable Numbers* (Turing, 1936). In 1945, John Von Neumann proposed a design for a computer that incorporated a processing unit, control unit, external mass storage, memory, and input/output mechanisms. This is now referred to as the *Von Neumann architecture*. It still serves as the basis of modern computer designs (Von Neumann, 1945). In 1974, the introduction of the *Altair 880* by Micro Instrumentation and Telemetry Systems (MITS) ushered in the era of the Personal Computer (Laing, 2004). In 1975, Bill Gates and Paul Allen founded Microsoft which introduced Microsoft Disk Operating System (MS-DOS), Windows and the Office suite (Laing, 2004). Microsoft revolutionized personal computing because they made the computer accessible and easy to use.
NOTABLE WORK: Analytical Engine, a mechanical general-purpose computer
PERSON: Charles Babbage
SYMBOL: CP. A gear superimposed on a circuit board represents this idea.
DATE: 1833
STORY: Search. Without search, the internet would be a big digital paperweight. Larry Page and Sergey Brin, while at Stanford University, created Google as a research project (Brin & Page, 1998). It allows users to search for information on the internet by inputting keywords and using operators. They started with their page rank algorithm which based the relevance of a webpage on the number and quality of other webpages that linked to that page (Battelle, 2006). Google was registered in 1997 and incorporated in 1998. Google has now indexed the 30 trillion pages of the internet and supports 100 billion searches every month (Koetsier, 2013). Internet users employ computation to search and sift through the vast amount of information on the internet which would otherwise be mysterious and unmanageable.
RELEVANCE TO YOU: Computers and computation surround you and is thoroughly embedded in nearly all aspects of society. Computers are used in control systems, and circuits for any kind of electronics that you might use. If you have a calculator, clock, computer, internet modem, microwave, printer, radio, remote, smart phone, television, or watch you are using the periodic idea of computation. Computers have blended into the background of our lives. They have become mental furniture.

How can you employ computation to make your life easier? A computer application can likely assist in your project task or problem. If you want to manage your weight, there are programs which can track your diet. Spreadsheet programs can help you analyze data and perform statistical analysis. Training programs can help you master a subject and retain information. Language training programs can teach you to become fluent in a foreign language. There is a Computer application for nearly every project you can think of.

Applications can connect you with people and information. According to Statista, the top 10 most popular smartphone applications as of July 2020 were Facebook, YouTube, Google maps, Gmail, Google search, Facebook messenger, Amazon mobile, and Google play (Clement, Reach of most popular U.S. smartphone apps 2020 , 2020). The most popular apps were in the social communication category followed by gaming and entertainment programs.

A productivity app is software that allows you to get more done in less time. These apps improve our time management skills or provide useful tools to increase our efficiency. According to CloudApp, the top 10 productivity apps in 2020 are Calendar, HelloSign, Hootsuite, HubSpot, LastPass, Lucidchart, Slack, Trello, Toggl track, and Zapier (Martin J. , 2020). *Calendar* is an app that can help you plan your time. *Toggl track* is a time tracking app that manages time blocks on your calendar. *HelloSign* is a legally binding electronic signature software. *Hootsuite* is a social media management app. *HubSpot* tracks your sales leads. *LastPass* manages your passwords. *Lucidchart* is a software tool to create flowcharts and online diagrams to visualize ideas. *Slack* is a team collaboration tool offering persistent chat rooms and sharing team content. *Trello* is a project management program. *Zapier* integrates your other tools together. These are just some examples of how the computation periodic idea can improve your life and increase your effectiveness.

Chapter 30 – COMMUNICATIONS

DESCRIPTION: Communications is at the heart of any modern society. Communications technologies are systems that can encode, store, retrieve, manipulate, transmit or receive information. They allow people to collaborate, organize, and socialize. Examples of communication devices include cell phones, computer networks, optical networks, radio, satellite systems, and television.

Modern communication technologies started with telegraphs and telephones developed in Victorian times (Standage, 2014). Information transmission before the telegraph included beacon fires, cannon, drums, flags, guns, lights, couriers, mirrors, and signal towers. In 1837, the first commercial electric telegraph was established by William Cooke and Charles Wheatstone. The telegraph transmitted data by sending coded electrical pulses through dedicated wires. Using Morse code, the telegraph delivered a telegram nearly instantaneously on the London and Birmingham Railway. The first worldwide electric telegraph networks were celebrated upon inauguration during the Victorian era (Standage, 2014). In 1876, the landline telephone, invented by Alexander Graham Bell, was demonstrated in Boston (Grosvenor & Wesson, 2016). Radio, television broadcasts, Sirius satellite radio, and fax machines debuted in the decades that followed. Cellular wireless networks started service in 1981 heralding mobile person-to-person communications (Wong, 2012). Wireless networks now connect every society on the planet.

Computer networks began humbly as the ARPANET in 1969 which blossomed into the modern internet (Abbate, 2000). In 1989, Tim Berners-Lee at CERN, invented networked hypertext which was the key to the creation of the World Wide Web (Abbate, 2000). Now, smart mobile phones can access the internet delivering the entirety of Mankind's knowledge into the palm of your hand on demand (Wong, 2012).

NOTABLE WORK: Improvements in Giving Signals and Sounding Alarms in Distant Place by means of Electric Current transmitted through metallic Circuits (Patent)

PERSON: Sir William F. Cooke and Sir Charles Wheatstone

SYMBOL: CM. The earth encircled by nodes of a communications network symbolizes this idea.

DATE: June 12, 1837

STORY: Claude Shannon is the father of Information Theory. His 1948 landmark paper was *A Mathematical Theory of Communication* (Shannon, A Mathematical Theory of Communication, 1948). Before Shannon, the word "*information*" might have referred to revelations gleaned from a printed newspaper. After Shannon, people thought of information in terms of bits and bytes. His revolutionary insight was that information could be a measurable entity. During World War II, he helped develop encryption systems. Shannon realized that encryption coding concepts could protect transmitted data from static and interference not just from malicious spies (Soni & Goodman, 2017). His work focused on the problem of how to optimally encode information that a sender wants to transmit. He calculated the maximum possible efficiency given an error-correcting method against the noise and data corruption in the channel. Shannon theoretically defined how much information you can send in a telecommunications link, or on a channel over the airwaves (Shannon & Weaver, The Mathematical Theory of Communication, 1971). Today, that is known as the Shannon limit. His insights shaped technologies that store, process, or transmit digital information. Information theory has found applications in art, biology, economics, linguistics, physics, and psychology.

RELEVANCE TO YOU: How can communications technologies make a difference in your life? How are they relevant to you? If you have a phone, a smart phone, an internet connection, or cable television you are connected to society. An internet connection is a gateway which connects you with billions of humans. A connection to society gives you a voice and lets you reach out and touch the lives of others. It allows you to partake in the public sphere. For more information see the public sphere periodic idea. A connection allows you to engage in social media and to join in on the conversation.

Fundamentally, you can use communication technologies in three ways. First, you can use them to connect to others. You can reach out and contact someone to discuss and deliberate. You can inform, inspire, and entertain. Secondly, communication technologies can facilitate collaboration with others. These technologies allow you to work with others to reach an objective. Finally, the communication periodic idea allows you to persuade others. You can rally a call to action, ask for help, or convince someone through reasoning.

People are naturally gregarious. Communication technologies allow us to connect and share the experiences of our lives. Dale Carnegie wrote *"there are four ways in which we have contact with the world: what we do, how we look, what we say, and how we say it"* (Carnegie, 1936). You can use the communications periodic idea to reach out to people to connect and collaborate. Recall from the computation idea that the most popular software programs were social communication applications. Let communication technologies help you collaborate and brainstorm with others. There are many periodic ideas that relate to groups and social interaction including social capital, public sphere and social media. All of these are enabled through communication technologies.

Chapter 31 – ROBOTICS

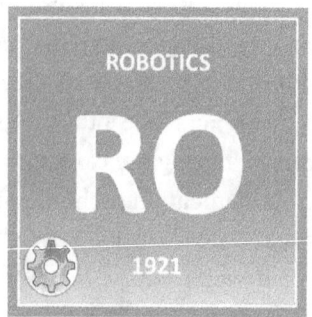

DESCRIPTION: Robots are machines that can mimic human actions or substitute for humans in performing a task. The word "robot" first appeared in the science fiction play Rossum's Universal Robots (Roberts A. , 2006). They have been employed in dangerous environments, manufacturing processes, in rescue operations, and simple household chores (Nocks, 2007). Robots can think, talk, lift, and walk among many other functions. The production of robotics incorporates mechanical, electronic, and information technologies. They are then infused with intelligence via software.

Robots find a variety of domestic, commercial and military applications. They perform jobs that are hazardous to people. They can defuse bombs, assist first responders in disasters, and explore shipwrecks. Robots are used extensively in various industrial production lines to precisely automate repetitive tasks. Robots march into environments that are lethal to humans. For example, they are used in space, underwater, extreme environments, and in disaster situations (Nocks, 2007).

Robots typically comprise of a power source, sensors, actuators, locomotion, manipulators, and a user interface (Lynch & Park, 2017). Sensors allow the robot to gain awareness of its environment. Actuators are the muscles of a robot. Examples of robotic sensors include acoustic, electromagnetic, infrared, optical, tactile, and ultrasonic. Locomotion are the things which allow a robot to move such as wheels. Manipulators are grippers or a mechanical hand which allows it to grasp objects. A robot may also have specialized appendages, tools, or devices to perform a specialized task. A user interface allows the robot to communicate to people or other machines. Examples of an interface include an electronic interface, gestures, remote controller, facial expressions, and speech.

NOTABLE WORK: Rossum's Universal Robots (Roberts A. , 2006)
PERSON: Karel Capek
SYMBOL: RO. A picture of a robot is used to depict this periodic idea.
DATE: January 25, 1921
STORY: Aido, designed by Ingen Dynamics, is a robot designed to help with household chores, handle schedules, connect to family medical devices, and keep your children company (Ingen Dynamics Inc, 2017). It will ship in 2021. It has a built-in projector and speaker. To serve as an entertainment system, it can project a video on a wall. Aido patrols your home to act as a security guard. Aido can create an interactive learning experience to teach you. It can recognize members of your household and adjust to individual preferences. It can serve as a home maker, companion, teacher, and assistant. It can control lightning, air conditioning, doors, and appliances. Industrial robots perform a narrow set of tasks for manufacturing. Aido makes the transition into the chaotic and dynamic environment of a home heralding a coming of age of home robotics.

RELEVANCE TO YOU: Before washing machines and dishwashers, the household chores of laundry and cleaning were time-consuming manual tasks. Automated appliances such as smart pressure cookers already have some aspects of a robot except mobility. So, the concept of machines assisting with household labor is not foreign.

The 1962 cartoon television show *"The Jetsons"* introduced us to the concept of a household general purpose robot in the form of *Rosie the robot* (Hanna & Barbera, 1962). Compared to a carefully designed factory setting, a home is a chaotic place with a jumble of household objects. Yet, many robots are now finding their way into the home. Robots excel in performing repetitive tasks and well-defined mundane chores. They can serve as personal companions, as a home security guard, as a babysitter, and as your child's friend.

You can find robots that can make a difference in your life. The *Roomba* produced by iRobot is a vacuuming robot which alleviates the chore of cleaning the floor. The Ubtech *Lynx* is a 16" tall programmable humanoid robot that was designed to entertain and educate (Ubtech, 2020). The Asus *Zenbo* is a smart mobile companion robot that entertains and assists (Asus, 2020). It can learn and adapt to household members, control household devices and act as a security system. The Zenbo can read to your children and keep them entertained, serving as a friendly babysitter. The *Landroid* by Worx is a quiet electric lawnmower robot that cuts your lawn (Worx, 2020). The *Dolphin Nautilus* developed by Maytronics is a robot that can vacuum, clean, and scrub a swimming pool (Maytronics, 2020). The *Budgee* created by Five Elements Robotics, gives you an extra set of hands to carry things around the house (Five Elements Robotics, 2020). It can follow you by using sonar sensing and accompanies you in running errands to help you carry stuff. These are just a few examples of how the robotics periodic idea might make a difference in your life.

There are a wide range of intelligent applications and robots. In 2020, I got a Hasbro smart R2-D2 robot. This scaled down version of the Star Wars astromech can explore, dance, patrol, and interact with you. Robots will help care for the elderly, carry heavy loads, perform personal tasks, adjust environment controls, execute information queries, provide entertainment, and relieve household chores. Robots can fill a spot in your home and heart.

Chapter 32 – ARTIFICIAL INTELLIGENCE

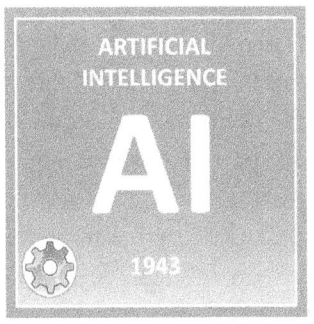 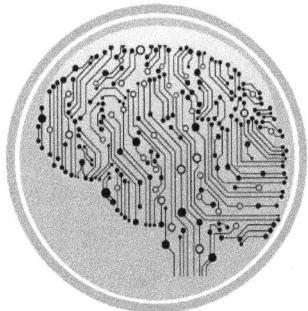

DESCRIPTION: Artificial intelligence (AI) describes machines or computers that can perform cognitive functions often associated with the human mind such as learning and problem solving (Russell & Norvig, 2009). The field of Artificial intelligence started in 1956 originating from a workshop at Dartmouth College (McCorduck, 1979). The first research work on AI defined the McCulloch-Pitts neuron (McCulloch & Pitts, 1943). Disciplines within artificial intelligence include the development of autonomous mobility, knowledge representation, learning, natural language processing, object manipulation, perception, planning, reasoning, strategic games, and systems operations (Russell & Norvig, 2009). Over the decades, many approaches have been used to advance AI including statistics, computational algorithms, and symbolic approaches. Along the way, numerous ideas have been employed in AI including Bayesian networks, deep learning, genetic algorithms, machine learning, statistical learning, and neural networks. Landmark accomplishments have been made including chess and go playing systems, self-driving cars, and the development of human speech recognition software.

Machine learning uses algorithms to improve through experience by building a model from training data (Bishop, 2006). Starting in 2012, Deep learning programs that filter data through self-adjusting neural networks have made promising progress on AI in speech and image recognition (Goodfellow, Bengio, & Courville, 2016). Training data is fed to a simulated neuronal network which strengthens connections between parts of the network. This allows it to interpret future data that it encounters better. For example, if you show a neural network many pictures of felines it can eventually recognize a cat in any photograph. Deep learning is now the dominant approach in machine learning.

General artificial intelligence, or strong AI, is the ultimate objective, where a machine intelligence can perform any cognitive task that a human can (Gupta & Nagpal, 2020). Weak AI does not attempt to perform a full range of mental tasks, but rather a more focused well-defined task. *Expert systems* emulate the decision making of a human expert. Developed in the 1970s, it was one of the first successful forms of AI (Gupta & Nagpal, 2020). Smart systems, cognition-enhanced applications, machine learning, expert systems, and intelligent advisors have already proved their value in human society.

NOTABLE WORK: A Logical Calculus of the Ideas Immanent in Nervous Activity (McCulloch & Pitts, 1943).

PERSON: Warren S. McCulloch and Walter H. Pitts, Jr.

SYMBOL: AI. A circuit board in the outline of a brain represents this periodic idea.

DATE: 1943

STORY: Artificial intelligence (AI) has made great strides recently. In 2017, Google DeepMind unveiled *AlphaGo Zero*. It surpassed the best Go game programs which had already defeated human Go world champions (Silver, et al., 2017). In 2017, Noam Brown at Carnegie Mellon University created the *Libratus Poker* AI (Poker Listings, 2017). The AI bested Dong Kinm, Jason Les, Jimmy Chou and Daniel McAulay, world-class poker players, at heads-up no-limit-hold'em poker.

In 2018, Google unveiled *Duplex*, a virtual assistant service that allows an AI program to book appointments for you. Duplex speaks in a flawless human voice that can negotiate alternate times for appointments (Leviathan & Matias, 2018). On the Google AI blog you can listen to recordings of Duplex making reservations (Leviathan & Matias, 2018).

Amazon's *DeepComposer* AI can embellish polyphonic compositions adding in a touch of rock, pop, jazz or classical around a baseline tune (Simon J. , 2019). It uses two AI networks, a generator and discriminator. The generator creates the music. The discriminator evaluates the output of the generator providing it feedback. Dr. Matt Wood demonstrated *DeepComposer* by providing a simple melody and the AI created the accompaniment including guitars, bass, drums, and synths (Wood, 2019). These are just a few of the many newsworthy stories at the forefront of AI.

RELEVANCE TO YOU: Intelligent software programs and applications have become woven into the fabric of society. Intelligent advisors, smart products, and cognition-enhanced applications probably already affect your life in subtle ways. They are involved in product development, manufacturing, delivery systems, utility control, and retailing. They are incorporated into the government, military, commercial, economic and financial systems that keep society running.

There are many smart software applications available to you which can keep you healthy, wealthy and wise. Intelligent applications can help you answer questions, diagnose health problems, learn new skills, recommend products, solve problems, and study a subject. Intelligent software applications, such as Google translate, can translate written languages and speech. Thus, they can assist you in communication and travel abroad. AI productivity applications can help you handle personal finances, manage your time, and schedule appointments for you. Take some time to explore the intelligent smart applications available to you. The computation periodic idea described many personal productivity applications that already exist. When fused with AI, these will become invaluable assistants to improve your personal effectiveness.

Chapter 33 – NETWORKING

DESCRIPTION: The periodic idea of networking concerns the connection of elements in a system together. Telecommunication networks link components and define protocols that allow them to efficiently interact. The internet is the best-known computer network. The concept of Networking connects elements together allowing them to share information and perform operations together (Huurdeman, 2008). Metcalfe's law asserts that the effect of a telecommunications network is proportional to the square of the number of connected users to the system (Hendler & Golbeck, 2008).

In a network, each element in the network is called node. The nodes are connected through data links. Data links are established through cables, fiber-optic connections or wireless transmission. Computers originate, route and terminate data. Protocols are prearranged methods to send information with structured payload headers and message bodies. The header specifies the intended destination and routing information. The allows routers to efficiently shuttle information from one node to another in the network. Computer networks support a variety of applications including data transmission, messaging programs, streaming digital audio-visual presentations, and the World Wide Web. The key aspects of a network are bandwidth, communication protocols, network scale, topology, traffic control mechanisms, and the transmission medium (Huurdeman, 2008).

The earliest computer networks were established during the cold war inaugurated by the U.S. military radar system Semi-automatic Ground Environment (SAGE) (Schaffel, 1991). Then, in 1960, the commercial airline ticket reservation system called Semi-Automated Business Research Environment (SABRE) was created. It coordinated 57,000 travel agencies linking them to two IBM 7090 mainframe computer systems. On average, an agent took 90 minutes to process a reservation. SABRE cut that time down to seconds (IBM, 2011). By 1964, it could handle up to 7,500 reservations per hour. It became the largest private real-time data processing system (Sabre, 2020).

Next, in 1969, the first four nodes of ARPANET connected universities with 50 kilobit per second connections (Sutton, 2004). Then, in 1973, *ethernet*, a distributed packet switching system for computer networks was invented (Metcalfe & Boggs, 1976). Ethernet helped to standardize network communication.

NOTABLE WORK: Semi-automatic Ground Environment (SAGE) U.S. Military Radar network (Redmond & Smith, 2000)
PERSON: George Valley and Jay Forrester
SYMBOL: NW. Three computers on a network symbolize this idea.
DATE: 1953
STORY: Marc Andreessen at the National Center for Supercomputing Applications (NCSA) launched the *Mosaic* web browser in January 23, 1993 (Andreessen, 2000). His 1-page technical release note heralded the beginning of web surfing. Mosaic featured an intuitive interface, bookmarks, icons, and multiple protocol support. It was the first browser to display text embedded with images (Berners-Lee & Fischetti, 1999). It was free to download which spurred its adoption. 5,000 copies were being installed each month; and by 1994, Mosaic had several million users. Microsoft licensed Mosaic to create its *Internet Explorer* web browser in 1995.

Sir Tim Berners-Lee invented the *World Wide Web* in 1989 while working at CERN near Geneva, Switzerland (Berners-Lee & Fischetti, 1999). He is currently the director of the World Wide Web Consortium which oversees the continued development of the Web. He proposed the world wide web as a network of hypertext documents. Browsers view them using a client–server architecture (Berners-Lee & Cailliau, WorldWideWeb: Proposal for a HyperText Project,

1990). The creation of the hypertext transfer protocol (HTTP) and the Mosaic web browser popularized the world wide web. The world wide web and the internet have become synonymous with computer networking.

RELEVANCE TO YOU: Some of the most influential technologies put people in touch with each other. Communications, networking, social media, and mobility make the world a smaller, more intimate place. These technologies work together to bring you closer to family and friends. Computer networking forms the backbone of the internet, allowing you to make the most of social media and communications technologies. Networking technologies are relevant to you because they allow you to connect with society in profound ways that were not possible in ages past. With networking, ideas and reports spread instantaneously around the world.

The periodic idea of networking connects elements together. You can personally benefit from the networking concept by finding ways to connect elements in your project. Social networking comes to mind when people are connected in a social web. Networking technology facilitates connections between elements in a project. These connections allow elements to share information and perform operations together.

As an example of the networking periodic idea, during the 2020 COVID19 pandemic, sequestered primary school students around the world had to take classes remotely. Using the networking periodic idea, teachers connected with students learning from individual streaming videos. Later, groups of families networked together to create learning pods by hiring a tutor. The students would attend the virtually taught class. The tutor would facilitate learning and help focus the students.

Chapter 34 – VIRTUAL REALITY

DESCRIPTION: Virtual reality (VR) technologies create an immersive experience that can simulate the real world or an imaginary environment (Bailenson, 2019). Virtual reality has been used for a variety of purposes including entertainment, education, training, tours, and commerce. Virtual reality systems use a headset or projectors to create a realistic visual environment and sounds to engage the senses (Bailenson, 2019). Some VR systems also engage the sense of touch through force feedback and haptic gloves. A person in a virtual reality simulation can look around the artificial world, move about and interact with virtual features or items (Harris, 2019). VR has been used in automobile design, flight simulation, guided meditation, medical applications, military training, museum tours, and video games. In 2016, there were 230 companies developing VR-related products. One popular product, the *Oculus Quest 2*, debuted in September 2020 (Oculus, 2020).

Augmented reality (AR) is an interactive experience of a real-world environment where the objects in the real world are overlaid and enhanced by computer-generated information (King, 2016). AR may also engage multiple senses including audio, visual, haptic, somatosensory and olfactory. An *augogram* is a computer-generated image superimposed on the view of the real world to create an AR experience. For example, an AR system could overlay historical data as you come across city landmarks. Another AR example is an overlay that points out the location of inventory items as you stroll the aisles in a warehouse.

A Mixed-reality (MR) system merges the real world with a virtual world to create a new environment. Physical and digital objects co-exist and interact in real time to create an immersive experience. Mixed reality is a hybrid of augmented reality and virtual reality facilitating many creative interactive applications and visualizations.

NOTABLE WORK: Sensorama, an interactive theater cabinet multimedia multi-sensory device (Albusberger, 2017)
PERSON: Morton Heilig
SYMBOL: VR. A virtual reality user represents this idea.
DATE: 1957
STORY: In 2017, a movie called *Marjorie Prime* debuted at the Sundance Festival (Almereyda, 2017). It was based on a play of the same name by Jordan Harrison. Set in the year 2050, an 85-year old Marjorie, portrayed by actor Lois Smith, exhibits the onset of Alzheimer's disease. Her daughter Tess (Geena Davis) hires a service called *Prime* designed to assist patients through interactive holographic projections of family members. They help Alzheimer patients rebuild memories by recounting their own life stories back to them. At the start of the movie, an interactive hologram of her late husband Walter, played by actor Jon Hamm, listens to stories of Marjorie's life. She enjoys listening to Walter prime recall her experiences. Throughout the movie, interactive holographic family members are used to comfort others. Near the end of the movie, the granddaughter of Tess, now an adult, interacts with Walter Prime, Marjorie Prime and Tess Prime reliving old memories. This innovative movie illustrates just one interesting potential application of mixed reality technology.
RELEVANCE TO YOU: A virtual representation serves as a proxy for something else. You can test, investigate, experiment and gain experience with a substitute proxy more accessible than the real thing. For example, a flight simulator allows you to experience flying airplane in lieu of an actual jet. A virtual reality (VR) tour of the Uffizi gallery may inspire creativity without traveling to Florence, Italy.

For your project, ask yourself if you can you use a substitute. Could you use a facsimile instead of the real thing? Is there a substitute that does not cost as much, or does not consume a limited resource? Could an image suffice? How could you display the elements of a project with AR details? Where can you use a rendition or replica instead of the real thing? What virtual visualizations could you employ? Could a proxy serve instead of the actual thing? Can you use a digital representation? Can you create a virtual construct? Can you utilize a computer simulation for your project? The use of VR, AR, or MR may enhance or advance your project.

Virtual reality simulations allow you to create prototypes to gain experience. When you tackle a project, try to employ a proxy, or virtual reality instead of the real thing to make progress. If you use a representation instead of the real thing it can facilitate experimentation. VR prototypes can help you visualize a problem before you turn a concept into reality.

You can use VR, AR and MR in a variety of applications to learn and explore. For example, you can take virtual tours of museums, famous places, or destinations you would like to visit. You can explore a place otherwise impossible for you to get to, such as the Moon or Jupiter. You can use VR to relive historic events, such as the 1969 moon landing. You can use VR for educational purposes to learn more about a subject. It has commercial and retail applications. For example, you could take a tour of a home before you buy or rent. You could make a virtual trip before you embarked on the real expedition. In VR, you could experience the world vicariously from the perspective of another person. Virtual reality systems can deliver memorable experiences or enhance an experience. As seen in the 2017 movie, *Marjorie Prime*, VR may eventually allow you to have virtual conversations with loved ones and family members even after they have passed away. You can use VR as therapy to overcome fears. There are a variety of VR, AR and MR applications that you might find interesting to try. They can entertain, educate, and guide. Let VR work for you and see how it can fuel your interests. See if you can use it creatively in your next project.

Chapter 35 – SOCIAL MEDIA

DESCRIPTION: *Social media technologies* are interactive applications that allow users to generate and share content through blogs, comments, posts, reviews, and videos (Van Dijck, 2013). Social Media technologies empower people to connect and share with many others. Prior to these, only broadcast technologies, such as radio and television had this capability. People are social by nature. We yearn to connect with others. Individuals find their humanity in connecting with society. People connect with others that share a common cause or purpose forming groups in the process. Social media technologies facilitate sharing and collaboration through the creation of online communities. People share their life experiences and insights on these platforms to connect with others.

Social networks are woven through an intricate web of connections and groups. Social media sites include Baidu, Facebook, Instagram, LinkedIn, Pinterest, QQ, QZone, Reddit, Snapchat, Twitter, Tumblr, WeChat, and YouTube among many others. As of November 2019, Facebook had 2.45 billion users (Clement, Number of monthly active Facebook users worldwide as of 3rd quarter 2019, 2019) connecting about a third of humanity together. YouTube has 2 billion users who watch 1 billion hours of video daily (YouTube, 2019).

Social media has unleashed creativity because individuals can express themselves and create content rather than just consume broadcast content from corporate sources (Kaplan & Haenlein, 2011). People create content in the form of blogs, forum posts, photos, portals, product reviews, and streaming videos (Agichtein, Castillo, Donato, Gionis, & Mishne, 2008). We share our loves, grief, joys, and frustrations using Social media as a medium. The modern mantra is "like" and "subscribe".

NOTABLE WORK: First public dialup Computerized Bulletin Board System (CBBS) (Scott, 2005)

PERSON: Ward Christensen and Randy Suess

SYMBOL: SM. Two conversation bubbles represent this idea.

DATE: February 16, 1978

STORY: YouTube has created two generations of celebrities and social influencers who have lucrative full-time careers making personal videos. PewDiePie and Felix Kjellberg make commentary videos about internet memes and video games. Kjellberg is a Swedish gamer, who lives in the United Kingdom, and has 102 million subscribers. He has made over 4,000 videos and each of his videos commands millions of views (Kjellberg, 2020). The Dude Perfect team command 48 million subscribers with just 223 videos (Cotton, Cotton, Toney, Hilbert, & Jones, 2020). They are famous for compilations of improbable trick shots and famous athletes that make guest appearances. Perhaps more surprising are the young content creators of the next generation. The *Like Nastya Vlog* has 44.9 million subscribers. They are video logs of a Russian-American girl named Stacy who plays with toys and goes on adventures with her family. Her videos regularly elicit millions of views, and some even have hundreds of millions of views. The South Korean dance track *Gangnam style* by Psy was the first viral video to clock more than one billion views on YouTube (Carlson D. , 2012). Numerous YouTube videos have climbed to over a billion views. At the summit, the music video *Despacito*, commands over 7 billion views (Fonsi, 2017). Malcolm Gladwell in his book the *Tipping Point* outlined how things go viral (Gladwell, 2002).

RELEVANCE TO YOU: Social Media platforms have connected billions of people together. Social Media platforms have allowed people to share their defeats, dreams, frustrations, ideas, and victories. Social network sites, such as Facebook, let you connect with your classmates, family, and friends. Peer-to-peer video and image sharing sites such as *YouTube* (YouTube, 2020), *Twitch.tv*

(Twitch.tv, 2020) and *Instagram* (Instagram, 2020) allow us to share our life experiences through videos. *LinkedIn* is a social network sites that allow you to connect with business contacts, and professionals (LinkedIn, 2020). Conversational social media applications such as *Snapchat* (SnapChat, 2020) and *WeChat* (WeChat, 2020) provide a platform for people to engage in a continuous, real-time conversations. *Twitter* is a microblogging service where its 321 million active users post short messages known as tweets (Twitter, 2020). *Pinterest* is a social media website designed to share ideas, recipes, creations, and life hacks (Pinterest, 2020). *Reddit* is a social media site that allows people to engage in discussion on a variety of topics including books, news, fitness, music, science and shows (Reddit , 2020).

Of the concepts in the Periodic Table of Ideas, social media may be one of the most profound for the future of humanity. Social media platforms bring people together into groups; those groups come together to form a planetary consciousness. It has enlarged the public sphere to include societies everywhere. When you partake in the conversation, you will expand your horizons. With social media you can explore new ideas and partake in interesting projects. It empowers you to become part of something greater than yourself. Take some time to connect to people and reach out on the various social media platforms to enrich your life.

Chapter 36 – PERSONALIZATION

DESCRIPTION: Personalization in a technological sense focuses on inventions which are customized or tailored to an individual. An example is a garment that is tailor-made to fit to an individual. In the modern era, where everyone owns the same mass manufactured things, we crave novelty, unique experiences, hand-crafted goods, and customization. Another example of personalization technology are 3D printers which have allowed people to design unique items. Applications that allow us to unleash our creativity and express ourselves will thrive.

Customized software applications or smart wearables can serve as personal assistants. They can track your diet, fitness regimen, health, and sleep patterns. Software assistants can help schedule your appointments, take notes, handle bills, and personal finances. They can handle many mundane tasks freeing you up to focus on more important matters and thereby improving your productivity. Time management applications allow you to track your time usage and plan your day efficiently. For example, *Calendar* and *Toggl* are popular time management software applications. Financial assistants allow you to optimize your resources. There are numerous intelligent personal assistants today including Siri, Google Assistant, Microsoft Cortana, Amazon Alexa and Lyra.

Personalized technology individualizes a product. These technologies will customize things to individually fit your needs. For example, smart watches and smart clothes can provide feedback and monitor your personal health. In all walks to life, the shoe will be a perfect fit.

Newborn technologies start with a focus on technical specifications and functions. Eventually, a mature technology becomes personal and customized. For example, cellular telephones went from expensive technological curiosities to indispensable individual expressions of identity. Today, people get personalized covers, monograms, and fingerprint security for their phones. They infuse their phone with personalized photo backgrounds, photo albums and unique ringtones.

NOTABLE WORK: Siri (Apple.com, 2020)
PERSON: SRI International Artificial Intelligence Center
SYMBOL: PZ. A person shown adjusting slider preference bars captures the essence of this idea.
DATE: October 4, 2011
STORY: Fingerprints are unique identity markers that everyone carries on their fingertips. Fingerprint security technologies use either optical scanning or capacitance scanning to identify a print (Ramotowski, 2012). With optical systems, a charge coupled device (CCD) generates an image of the fingertip much like a digital camera. A capacitance scanner uses electrical currents to create an image of a fingerprint ridges and valleys (Das, 2014). Fingerprinting technology and facial recognition systems are two examples of personalization technology applied to a security application.

Another thing that is unique to everyone is their DNA. Your DNA has 3.2 billion amino acid base pairs. The nucleobases of adenine-thymine and guanine-cytosine are the building blocks of your DNA (Urry, et al., 2016). DNA is the most personalized and unique thing to you.

In 1953, Francis Crick and James Watson identified the molecular structure of DNA at the Cavendish Laboratory (Watson & Crick, 1953). The X-Ray diffraction data acquired by Rosalind Franklin allowed Crick and Watson to deduce the double-helix structure of the DNA molecule. Today, DNA testing is frequently used to learn about ancestry, family history, genetic heritage, health risks and family planning. Numerous companies provide genetic analysis including CRI Genetics, 23andMe, and AncestryDNA. These companies exemplify the personalization periodic idea.

RELEVANCE TO YOU: When you look at the people around you, you realize we all own the same things. In an era of mass manufacturing, we all essentially have the same mass-manufactured appliances, clothes, furnishings, homes, and vehicles. Yours might be blue and mine is orange. Mass production enables you to enjoy a lifestyle only available to the nobility of former times. However, the result is that we crave uniqueness. We seek adventures that build our identity. In a cookie-cutter world, it is hard to stand out. Humans derive satisfaction from creative endeavors. We want to be unique, express ourselves, and bestow our sense of individuality to the world (Lieberman, 2006).

The modern citizen craves uniqueness. How is this relevant to you and how does this relate to the personalization periodic idea? Armed with the knowledge that distinct things stand out, consider how your experiences and life are unique from others. How can you differentiate yourself to your customers? What unique experiences separate you from the herd? What unique interests, qualities, and skills make you different than everyone else? What dreams do you have that other people might find interesting? For example, I have traveled to 30 countries on six continents. Those experiences differentiate my life from others and have created wonderful and precious memories for me.

The personalization periodic idea addresses the craving for uniqueness and identity. For example, if you make a tailor-fit product for a specific individual you have utilized the personalization concept. I usually have one unique story that I associate with each of my friends. These unique experiences with my friends make them special to me. When socializing, I often recount them with others. In turn, they appreciate that we shared that experience. Effectively, these stories personalize that relationship.

Chapter 37 – TECHNOLOGY PERSONAL RELEVANCE

This chapter collects and summarizes the personal relevance of each of the technology periodic ideas. Technological advancements have revolutionized society. They have transformed the way we interact with other people and society at large. The products of technology provide you with a variety of tools that can improve your personal productivity and propel your projects to success. Technology is infused into our daily lives. If we search, technological solutions will often present themselves to us creating new opportunities. The technology periodic ideas all have personal relevance. They can assist us in reaching our goals.

The following table summarizes the personal relevance of technology periodic ideas.

TECH IDEA	ID	PERSONAL RELEVANCE
TRANSPORTATION TECHNOLOGY 4700 BCE	TT	Transportation technologies allow you to move people and cargo from an origin point to a destination. It is a means by which you can deliver or obtain resources for your projects.
PROTOTYPING 375 BCE	PO	Prototyping allows you to test a concept and gain practical knowledge. You can verify if an idea will work, find new avenues of exploration and gain experience with a problem.
COMPUTATION 1833	CP	Computer applications assist you in a wide variety of tasks. They increase your productivity and help in accomplishing goals. Computational applications can help you in statistical analysis or calculating tasks. Many productivity apps can increase your personal effectiveness.

COMMUNICATIONS **1837**	CM	Communications technologies allow you to connect to others, engage in the public sphere, and link into social media. These technologies allow you to *connect*, *collaborate*, and *persuade*. You can connect to discuss, inform, and inspire. You collaborate to reach an objective. You persuade by a call to action, asking for help, or convincing someone.
ROBOTICS **1921**	RO	Robots can assist or perform your daily tasks and chores. They can provide companionship when you are lonely. Robots can assist in your projects and endeavors.
ARTIFICIAL INTELLIGENCE 1943	AI	Intelligent smart applications can assist in your endeavors and improve your personal productivity. A variety of smart applications have been developed to tackle complex problems.
NETWORKING **1953**	NW	Networking allows your computer(s) to connect, share information, and operate together. Networked elements in your project are the foundation for collaboration. Networking allows elements to share information and perform operations together.
VIRTUAL REALITY **1957**	VR	Virtual reality (VR) technologies empowers your ability to explore, prototype, and visualize. VR can create experiences that allow you to engage, explore, and learn in a VR environment.
SOCIAL MEDIA **1978**	SM	Social Media technologies allow you to connect and share with others in an online community. They allow you to generate and share content through blogs, posts, reviews, and videos. Social Media empowers you to reach a large audience.
PERSONALIZATION **2011**	PZ	Personalization allows you establish something unique to yourself. Customization creates something personally distinctive. Personalization caters to our craving for uniqueness. Personal assistant software improves your productivity.

Table 12 – Periodic Technology Ideas Personal Relevance

PART V – ECONOMIC IDEAS

Chapter 38 – ECONOMIC IDEAS

Economics is the study of the production, distribution and consumption of goods and services (Krugman & Wells, 2017). The periodic ideas in economics are central ideas in the operation of an economy. These ideas have withstood the test of time and appear in all modern societies. You will likely already have personal familiarity with many of these concepts. Most people have intimate experience with currency, credit, incentives, and markets. These concepts are part and parcel of our everyday lives. These pivotal ideas have played a critical role in the development and understanding of economies. Over the centuries, there have been many economists who have tried to make sense of the world through the lens of economic systems.

Economics is divided into two major branches: microeconomics and macroeconomics (Krugman & Wells, 2017). *Macroeconomics* considers the entire economy as a single system of production and consumption. The macroeconomic factors are capital, currencies, employment, inflation, investment, labor, public policies, and savings. It encompasses the concepts of business cycles, economic growth, fiscal policy, inflation, monetary policy, and unemployment. By contrast, *microeconomics* focuses on individual agents such as households, firms, buyers and sellers. Microeconomics includes concepts such as cost, efficiency, market failure, production, the public sector, specialization, supply and demand, and uncertainty (Krugman & Wells, 2017). Economic and political policy affect how people behave in society. These policies can steer the economic behavior of a society and thereby shape its character.

The candidate periodic ideas needed to satisfy several criteria. They needed to be cardinal economic ideas, historically prominent, and personally relevant. There were numerous candidate macroeconomic and microeconomic ideas considered. The final ten that were selected are concepts that have been pivotal in history, have persisted over time, and have personal relevance.

The following table summarizes the ten periodic ideas in economics. They are sorted by date of introduction.

ECONOMIC IDEA	ID	DESCRIPTION
MARKETS 3000 BCE	MK	Alfred Marshall. A market is a system where parties can exchange goods or services. Sellers offer wares or services in exchange for money. Markets serve as a mechanism to distribute resources and manufactured goods in society. The value of goods and services are established through transactions in the market.
CURRENCY 550 BCE	CU	Jack Weatherford. Currency is a medium of exchange or a system of money which can serve as legal tender. It is traded for its economic value. Currency has four purposes: as a medium of exchange, a store of value, a measure of value and a standard of deferred payment.
CREDIT 1494	CR	Luca Pacioli. Credit is the means which allows one party, the lender, to provide money or resources to another party, the debtor, for repayment later. Credit formalizes that reciprocity into a legally enforceable agreement which can extend to large groups of unrelated people.
DIMINISHING RETURNS 1766	DR	Anne-Robert-Jacques Turgot. Diminishing returns is the decrease in the marginal output in production as the amount of a single factor of production is incrementally increased. The first person assigned to a job is the most effective. Subsequent people added are less and less effective.
TRADE 1817	TR	David Ricardo. Trade is the action of buying and selling of goods and services for money or something of value. Barter is trading things without money. Modern traders generally negotiate through a medium of exchange, such as money. A system that allows for trade is a market.

The Periodic Table of Ideas

ECONOMIC IDEA	ID	DESCRIPTION
ECONOMIC CYCLE 1819	EC	Jean Charles Léonard de Sismondi. The economic cycle is the periodic boom and contraction in business cycles. It shifts between periods of economic growth and relative decline or stagnation. It is characterized by four repeating phases: expansion, boom, contraction, and depression.
MARGINAL UTILITY 1871	MU	William Jevons. Utility is the benefit from consuming a product. Marginal utility is the change in utility from an increase in the consumption of a good or service. *Cardinal utility* assigns a benefit value to subsequent units. *Ordinal utility* is concerned with the sequencing of additional units.
INCENTIVES 1914	IV	Jean-Jacques Laffont. Incentives are motivators that reward actions to produce a desired outcome. There are four types of incentives: financial, moral, personal, and coercive. *Extrinsic motivators* reward actions to yield a desired outcome. *Intrinsic motivators* are personal desires for self-improvement.
SOCIAL CAPITAL 1916	SC	Lyda Hanifan. Social Capital are factors of social cohesion that allows groups to function efficiently. These factors include cooperation, personal relationships, reciprocity, shared identity, shared norms, shared vision, shared values, and trust.
CREATIVE DESTRUCTION 1942	CD	Joseph Schumpeter. Creative destruction is a process through which something new brings about the demise of whatever existed before it. Capitalism and innovation create new products and markets even as they destroy the old ones.

Table 13 – Periodic Economic Ideas

Chapter 39 – MARKETS

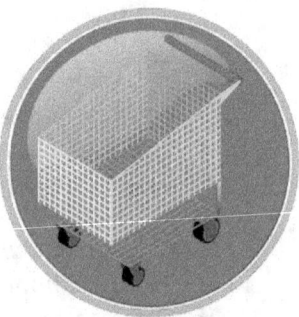

DESCRIPTION: A market is a system where two parties can exchange goods or services. Sellers offer wares or services in exchange for money. Markets enable trade which in turn, serves to distribute resources and manufactured goods in a modern society (Krugman & Wells, 2017). The value of goods and services are established through transactions in the market. Markets can spontaneously emerge, or they are deliberately created. Markets match consumer desire to producer opportunity.

There are different kinds of markets that vary in form, function, location, procedure, regulation, size and scale. *Black markets* are where goods or services are exchanged illegally. *Non-physical markets* include media markets (radio, TV), virtual markets (eBay), and artificial markets (carbon trading). *Virtual markets*, such as eBay, exchange goods using an online system where the buyer and seller never physically meet (eBay Press Room, 1995). *Consumer retail markets* include fairs, flea markets, stores, and supermarkets. *Business markets* include wholesale markets, labor markets, and trade fairs. *Financial markets* exchange assets which include bond markets, commodity markets, currency exchanges, and stock markets (futures markets). A market with one seller and many buyers is a *monopoly*. A market with a single buyer and multiple sellers is a *monopsony*. An *oligopoly* is a market dominated by a small number of sellers.

Many economic systems exist including *laissez-faire economics* (trade free of economic intervention), *market socialism* (social ownership of production in a market economy), and a *socialist market economy* (public ownership and state-owned enterprises in a market economy). Economic policies relate to fiscal policies or monetary policies. *Fiscal policies* are concerned with government actions for taxation and spending. *Monetary policies* deal with central banking actions with the money supply and interest rates. Economists studies markets through microeconomics and macroeconomics. Microeconomics is the study of individuals upon markets. Macroeconomics is the study of the performance and operation of an entire economy in aggregate (Krugman & Wells, 2017).

NOTABLE WORK: The Principles of Economics (Marshall, 1890).
PERSON: Alfred Marshall
SYMBOL: MK. The shopping cart is used to symbolize shopping and represents this periodic idea.
DATE: 1890
STORY: Ancient open-air markets sprung into existence in Assyria, the Arabian Peninsula, Babylonia, Egypt, Greece, and Phoenicia. The first market traded goods sometime around 3,000 BCE. A network of markets around the Mediterranean and Aegean seas caused trade to flourish in a variety of goods (Mehdipour & Rashidi, 2013). In 550 BCE, ancient Greek markets clustered around the types of goods sold. In 100 CE, the ancient Romans created Trajan's market housed in a four-level building. It has the distinction of being the earliest permanent retail storefront (Coleman, 2006). In the 11th century, Medieval Europe markets orbited monasteries, castles and royal estates. Rulers awarded market charters for the right to establish a market in exchange for a fee. These locations created demand for goods and simultaneously offered protection. Annual fairs punctuated regular weekly markets for necessities (Casson & Lee, 2011). Eventually, markets sprang up all around the world in Africa, the Middle East, the Orient and Meso-America.

In the 1960's the first virtual, on-line market was introduced. International Business Machines (IBM) created the on-line transaction processing (OLTP) system for processing financial transactions. In an on-line market, information technology companies act as intermediaries connecting buyers and sellers. Centralized electronic markets are hubs that provide services to consumers. Decentralized ones have participants directly in contact with each other. Now, numerous on-line electronic market places exist including auction sites (eBay, Alibaba), shopping malls (eCRATER, Shopping.com, Shopzilla, PriceGrabber), retailers (Amazon), classifieds (Craig's List, gumtree), legal services (Avvo), hand-crafted retailing (etsy), job placement sites (Freelancer, Monster), service request sites (taskrabbit, thumbtack), e-learning (Udemy), and medical care services (ZocDoc).

RELEVANCE TO YOU: Markets are one of the most fundamental ideas in economics. How are they relevant to you? Most people interact with markets frequently to buy groceries, sundry supplies, and clothes. Your job most likely involves some sort of market that produces or consumes goods and services. Markets are the principle way societies employ to move goods and deliver services. They are such an integral part of society that you probably do not often think about them. Markets are a social tapestry that blends into the background of our lives. Whether you are at home, play, or work you are likely employing a market of some sort, either directly or indirectly.

Consider the following questions. What resources do you need to complete your project? A market matches a producer to a consumer. Is there something you need to buy? Is there an opportunity here to sell something? Is there an idea you have that is looking for a consumer? Where could you find a relevant marketplace? Fundamentally, a market pairs the desire of a consumer with an opportunity for a producer.

Are there extraneous things that you can share or sell? You can shed second-hand stuff at online markets, and classified sites, such as Craig's list, where you can post the things you wish to jettison. Having sold many things on eBay, I can attest that it is an efficient way to slough off extraneous stuff. Peer-to-Peer marketplaces allow households to share idle or underused resources. Peer-to-Peer services such as Uber (Uber, 2020) and Airbnb (Airbnb, 2020) have given rise to the sharing economy.

Chapter 40 – CURRENCY

DESCRIPTION: Currencies are a medium of exchange or a system of money as legal tender and traded for their economic value. Typically, these are circulating bank notes and coins. Money has four purposes. First, it serves as a medium of exchange. It is a store of value; and it is a measure of value. Finally, it is a standard of deferred payment (Martin F. , 2015).

Digital currencies, underpinned by the blockchain concept, have developed as a system of money independent of banks. Online systems of payment, such as PayPal, uses money or credit serving as an intermediary between users for convenience and security (Martin F. , 2015).

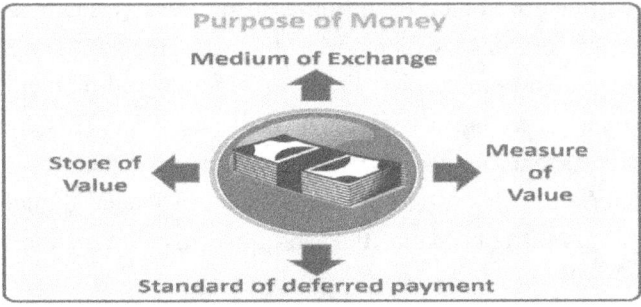

Figure 3 – Purpose of Money

NOTABLE WORK: The History of Money (Weatherford, 1998)
PERSON: Jack Weatherford
SYMBOL: CU. A stack of paper cash represents this idea.
DATE: 550 BCE
STORY: Money might have been one of those inevitable ideas that arises to facilitate social interaction, barter, trade and cooperation. The concept of money originated in ancient Egypt. The Sumerians kept a system of receipt to track grain production (Kramer, 1988). The Mesopotamian shekel was a unit of weight. In Asia, Cowrie shells were used. In the west, coinage first developed in Lydia with the Lydian lion electrum trite made of a gold and silver alloy in 600 BCE (Goldsborough, 2013).

Paper money was easier to transport than metal coins, less risky to move, enabled interest calculations, and facilitated stock redemption (Ferguson, 2008). Promissory notes were used in China from 118 BCE as a precursor to banknotes due to the insecurity and impracticality of transporting large sums of coinage. Flying cash, or *feiquian*, was a promissory note used during the Tang Dynasty (618-907). Marco Polo introduced the concept of the promissory note to Europe. Woodblock printing developed in China in the 11th century. Then, paper money was introduced during the Song dynasty. By the 13th century, the Chinese government issued paper currency. Money has been pivotal in history in the development of economies, societies and culture.

The development of computer technologies allowed money to be represented digitally. By 1990, most money transferred between central banks and commercial banks was in electronic form. By the 2000s, most money existed as digital currency in the database of a bank. Digital currency facilitates transactions and payment management.

Cryptocurrencies have evolved that are independent of centrally controlled government-issued currencies. Digital cash (digicash) in 1990 (Chaum, 1982) and eGold in 1996 were the forerunners of modern digital currencies. The invention of block chain, a distributed bookkeeping that was fungible and tamper resistant, caused the development of private decentralized trust networks. This spurred the creation of alternative currencies such as Bitcoin, Dogecoin, Ethereum, Litecoin, Monero, and Peercoin (Martin F. , 2015). Bitcoin, the most popular digital peer-to-peer cryptocurrency, was introduced in 2008 and was invented by the reclusive Satoshi Nakamoto (S., 2015).

RELEVANCE TO YOU: The idea of currency is probably already so familiar to you do don't give it a second thought – it has been seamlessly woven into your life. Currency is a means to an end. We define what is meaningful to us and decide what careers and passions to pursue. Money gets you what you need, the essentials. For example, we need food, clothing and shelter to function in society. After that, money serves as a basis for a meaningful life. It can help you facilitate your dreams.

Focus on your dreams and what you wish to accomplish. Meaningful things in life often require you to break down your aspirations into bite-sized chunks. Develop a roadmap to get you there a step at a time. Money can facilitate the completion of project tasks. Money allows you to acquire the equipment and resources needed to advance a project.

You can save, plan and budget to realize ambitious long-term goals. Money management is a basic life skill. Develop a simple strategy that balances your household income against your expenses. Consider what you need, what you want, and save the rest. You can allocate funds to long-term goals under your "wants" category. Try to pay off debts. Invest your savings wisely. For example, suppose you have a desire to visit another country within two years. The trip requires a certain amount of funds. Estimate the costs and break that down into 24 monthly payments. Then, contribute to that objective each month.

Chapter 41 – CREDIT

DESCRIPTION: Credit is the means which allows one party, the lender, to provide money or resources to another party, the debtor (Bertola, et al., 2008). The borrowing party promises either to repay or return those resources (or other materials of equal value) later. Credit formalizes that reciprocity into a legally enforceable system and extends it to potentially large groups of unrelated people. The resources provided may be financial (e.g. granting a loan), or they may consist of goods or services (e.g. consumer credit). Credit has now come to encompass any form of deferred payment. Through credit, one party provides resources to another for repayment later. It is a formal, legally enforceable reciprocity (Bertola, et al., 2008). Credit is an engine of creative growth in an economy because small business and entrepreneurs with a great idea can obtain the capital necessary to launch their enterprise. The periodic idea of credit revolutionized commerce. It is one of the most important economic ideas ever conceived.

NOTABLE WORK: Summa de Arithmetica, Geometria, Proportioni et Proportionalita (Everything that is known about arithmetic, geometry, proportions and proportionality) (Pacioli, 1494).

PERSON: Luca Pacioli

SYMBOL: CR. A credit card is used as the icon to symbolize credit.

DATE: 1494

STORY: In 1494, Luca Pacioli first described the double-entry bookkeeping system in use during the Renaissance by Venetian merchants, traders and bankers (Pacioli, 1494). That system of debt and credit he defined is still in use by modern bookkeepers. In this system, debits and credits are processed simultaneously such that the assets equal the sum of the liabilities and equity. The invention of credit was a vital idea to a national economy. Practically everything you are surrounded with was first funded through credit. In a modern economy, brilliant ideas from budding entrepreneurs and inventors require capital to turn them into reality. Today, there are many types of credit including bank credit, consumer credit, investment credit, international credit, public credit and real estate. Credit fuels a productive economy.

In 1889, Edward Bellamy first described the concept of a credit card in his book *Looking Backward 2000-1887* (Bellamy, 1889). The concept became reality in September 1958 when Bank of America mailed 60,000 homes in Fresno, California a small piece of plastic called the *BankAmericard*. This was the first successful modern credit card. The trial coaxed consumers to start using a card that formerly few merchants would accept. Conversely, retailers began to accept a strange card from consumers but from a recognizable town bank (Nocera, 1994). This experiment conquered initial reluctance and eventually evolved into the ubiquitous Visa credit card network. As a testament of its success, revolving debt ballooned from $1.5 billion in 1958 to a staggering $944 billion in 2018 as it fundamentally changed the way consumers thought about money, credit and debt. Many companion ideas soon followed including the concepts of annual percentage rate, banking licenses, basis points, credit insurance, credit rating, credit default, credit default swap markets, installment loans, mutual credit, revolving credit, risk-return spectrum, secured collateralized credit, subprime lending, and unsecured non-collateralized credit.

RELEVANCE TO YOU: You are probably already familiar with consumer credit which include credit cards, mortgages, personal loans, retail loans, and vehicle financing. People commonly use credit to purchase everything from groceries to vehicles and homes. The place you are living in was likely to have been funded with credit either when it was built or purchased. Credit facilitates the purchase of capital expenditures, such as a vehicle, more manageable through monthly installments. However, credit is not without its dark side. Predatory lenders and payday loan centers try to exploit those in dire straits charging exorbitant interest rates.

If you are considering a new project, credit may play a role in turning that project into reality. Venture capitalists seek to apply their resources to a worthy cause and newborn projects require funding. The lender takes some risk if the project fails to get off the ground. The people who set forth on the adventure are often given guidance from the more experienced venture capitalists. While any project may fail, many of the best ideas in history at one point were just ventures. The beginning is a very delicate time (Herbert, 1990).

Managing your credit can play a vital role in your success in life. It is important to get a credit card just to build up your credit rating. This is relevant because when you apply for credit to purchase a vehicle, home, or business your odds increase of securing the necessary funds. Credit allows you to magnify your economic presence. This happens because for a fraction of the loan you are leveraging your capital investment. For example, a family purchases a home and puts a down payment which is only a portion of the entire loan. They can immediately move into that home after closing. Without credit, they would have to pay for the entire value of the property all at once which would be impractical for most people.

Chapter 42 – DIMINISHING RETURNS

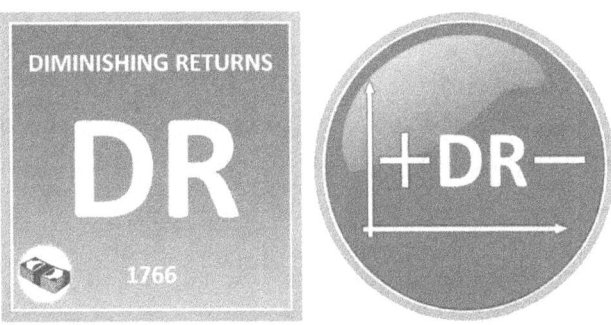

DESCRIPTION: In economics, diminishing returns is the decrease in marginal output in production as the amount of a single factor of production is incrementally increased (Mankiw, 2017). The first person assigned to a job is the most effective. Subsequent people added to that same job should theoretically improve efficiency. However, each person added is less and less effective as each new person increases the complexity of orchestrating the job and they start interfering with each other.

The concept was pioneered by Jacques Turgot, Adam Smith, Thomas Malthus and David Ricardo. Early economists only considered a single output in mind and that each unit of labor was identical. Modern economists consider other factors such as input quality, unit substitution, input complement and output co-production.

Liebig's law of the minimum is a concept from agriculture. It was proposed by Carl Sprengel in 1840 and popularized by Justus von Liebig (Liebig, 1840). It states that growth is dictated not by total resources available but by the scarcest resource. Growth is governed by a key limiting factor.

To illustrate the concept of diminishing returns, consider in software development, throwing more developers at a project will not get it done faster. In his 1975 book, *The Mythical Man-Month*, Fred Brooks observed that at some point adding more people to a software project paradoxically delays the project instead of speeding it up (Brooks, 1975). The concept of diminishing marginal returns is one of the most pivotal ideas in modern economic theory.

NOTABLE WORK: Reflections on the Production and Distribution of Wealth (Turgot, 1766).

PERSON: Anne-Robert-Jacques Turgot

SYMBOL: DR. The symbol for this idea is that of a graph with total input (time, effort, resources) in the horizontal X-axis (abscissa) plotted against the total output (work output) in the vertical Y-axis (ordinate). The "+" represents a productive region where added input yields productive output. Thus, it pays to invest here. The "DR" represents a region of diminishing returns where each added input leads to a decreasing rate of output. The "-" represents negative returns where additional input results in decreased overall output.

DATE: 1766

STORY: A story to illustrate the diminishing returns concept is drawn from my personal experience. I was a software development engineer working on Magnetic Resonance Imaging (MRI) and Ultrasound systems at General Electric Medical systems in Milwaukee, Wisconsin. Later, I worked on wireless base station software at Alcatel-Lucent (now Nokia). I have worked closely with project managers and worked on large-scale projects with millions of lines of code. I have observed first-hand that adding more people to a project will not necessarily improve development, test, or integration schedules. Inexperienced developers can add software that introduces faults. Counterintuitively, too many experienced architects can cause fruitless debates. Dividing one coherent task into separate jobs creates interdependencies. Then, when something breaks, no one wants to take responsibility because ownership is diluted. Experienced project managers eventually learn the proper number of people to assign to a project task. Before reaching a point of diminishing returns, it does pay dividends to add more people and resources to a project task. Too few workers make a large project insurmountable. The key is to know when adding too many developers to a task starts hindering progress.

RELEVANCE TO YOU: The concept of diminishing marginal returns finds applications in all walks of life, whether you are a clerk or the president of a country. The concept is useful in any area from household chores to rocket science. When you are performing a task, at first, more resources, time, effort, money, and people are vital. The early phase of a project requires many resources to launch the enterprise. Investment in this "productive" period is useful and necessary.

Eventually, a point of diminishing returns is reached where additional resources thrown at the project tasks will no longer help. This has been codified into the idiom "*too many cooks spoil the broth*", meaning too many people managing an activity can ruin the result. Each of the cooks adds an ingredient to the soup which in the end tastes awful. Too many directors, each tugging in a different direction results in a project going nowhere. It is captured in the phrase, "*perfection is the enemy of completion*" which implies that additional effort in refining a solution towards absolute perfection impedes progress because it consumes precious time and resources while adding little real value. Often, it is more beneficial to just complete a task to the best of your ability, and then launch. Then, afterwards observe how it performs and iterate.

There are times, of course, where it is imperative to get as close to perfection as possible. For example, if you are shooting for the Moon and you know you will only get one shot at it. If lives are at stake, the team should dedicate adequate time to analysis and conduct meaningful experimental trials. Thus, it is important to recognize the point of diminishing returns in order to maximize your time, effort and resources balanced against concerns for security and safety.

Chapter 43 – TRADE

DESCRIPTION: The definition of trade is the action of buying goods and services or exchanging a thing for something else (Webster's New World Dictionary, 1984). It is at the heart of economics. The concept of trade is older than recorded history. The earliest form of trade was bartering where two parties exchanged goods or services for other goods and services without the use of money (Bernstein, 2009). Modern traders generally negotiate through a medium of exchange, such as money. Trade is fundamental to commerce.

Trade in ancient times was personal, intimate, and individual. Goods moved to market by water because the Phoenicians developed an extensive maritime trade network around the Mediterranean (Bernstein, 2009). By 1000 BCE, caravans of camels linked Africa, Asia, Arabia, Egypt, and Phoenicia. By the 1st century CE, the silk road connected Asia to western Europe. Trade grew throughout the middle ages (476 CE to 1492 CE) because Genghis Khan protected the silk road. This period was known as the *Pax Mongolica* (Bernstein, 2009). Trade had become networked and international.

David Ricardo argued in favor of industry specialization and free trade. Nations should concentrate resources on industries where they have a comparative advantage (Ricardo, 1817). The colonial era saw the rise of joint stock companies with trading companies as powerful as nations (Micklethwait, 2005).

The World Trade Organization annually publishes the World Trade Statistical Review. In 2018, WTO Members merchandise exports totaled a staggering $32 trillion USD (World Trade Organization, 2018). The top 10 traded commodities were apparatus, electronics, fuel, iron & steel, machinery, organic chemicals, pharmaceuticals, plastics, precious stones, and vehicles. Today, trade is efficient, impersonal, and global.

NOTABLE WORK: On the Principles of Political Economy and Taxation (Ricardo, 1817).
PERSON: David Ricardo
SYMBOL: TR. Two arrows encircle a sphere representing the earth with national flags from many countries.
DATE: 1817
STORY: Starting on July 14, 2005, Kyle Macdonald made a series of extraordinary trades (Macdonald, 2007). The out-of-work Kyle started with one big red paperclip. He made 14 trades over the course of a year. The first few trades were unremarkable. The red paperclip was traded for a fish-shaped pen. The pen exchanged for a hand-sculpted doorknob. The doorknob switched hands for a Coleman camp stove. However, the next series of trades were quite remarkable. In December 2005, he traded an "instant party" (keg of beer and Budweiser sign) for a Ski-doo snowmobile. Two exchanges later, on January 7, 2006, he traded a two-person trip to Yahk, British Columbia for a box truck! He upgraded the box truck for a recording contract, a year's condo rent, an afternoon with Alice Cooper, then a KISS snow globe. Corbin Bernsen, a movie director and avid collector, traded for the KISS snow globe for a movie role.

Bert Roach was the Economic Development Officer for the town of Kipling, Saskatchewan, Canada. With petitioning from Bert, and after some negotiation with the Kipling Council, Kyle Macdonald made his last trade on July 12, 2006. He traded his movie role in *Donna on Demand* for a two-story farmhouse on 503 Main Street in Kipling (Macdonald, 2007). Kyle is in the Guinness book of world records for the best internet trade (Guinness World Records Ltd, 2019). After his success, Kyle attracted worldwide attention from many media outlets including the BBC, CBS news, CNN, and the Wall Street Journal.

RELEVANCE TO YOU: You might not have the trading prowess of Kyle Macdonald. However, the typical person is engaged in trading on a frequent basis.

People regularly buy food, clothing, and necessities. To do so, they trade money for goods and services. They exchange money for financial, health care, legal, medical, and utility services.

Bartering is the art of trading a thing you have for something you want. Aside from straight-forward purchases, to put this periodic idea to use, think outside the box. If there is something you need, maybe you can trade away something you don't need for it. Alternatively, you might trade away your skills, knowledge, or services in exchange for the money, goods, or services of another.

The idea of renting an underutilized spare bedroom sparked peer-to-peer hosting services, such as Airbnb (Airbnb, 2020). Trading idle time of an automobile led to the development of ride-sharing services, such as Uber (Uber, 2020). In a sharing economy, you may trade your gardening skills for the plumbing skills of another. You may also have some talent, skill or knowledge that you can trade for money, goods or services.

Kyle Macdonald started with a series of mundane trades with ordinary household objects. He then executed a set of unusual trades with unique things. In some cases, he found the right person at the right time to close a successful trade. Opportunity favors those who are at the right place at the right time. Finding a trading partner to carry out an exchange is facilitated by online trading sites such as Craig's list and Priceline. Spotting an opportunity engenders successful trading. Artful trading creates opportunities. If you peruse an online auction house, such as eBay (eBay Press Room, 1995), you will come to realize that in a marketplace of billions, you can sell almost anything. Moreover, people will buy almost anything.

Consider three items in Kyle Macdonald's trade sequence. The hand-sculpted doorknob, an afternoon with Alice Cooper, and the movie role. The doorknob may seem unremarkable at first. In the modern era of mass manufacturing, we all essentially own the same things. In the post-industrial society, we all wear the same mass-manufactured clothes, own the same kitchen utensils, and drive the same cars. Consequently, the common person lives like a king of ancient times. However, another side effect is that we crave uniqueness. We want to own unique belongings such as the hand-sculpted doorknob from Kyle's trade. We seek adventures that build our identity. We want to meet celebrities, such as Alice Cooper. We want to have unique experiences, such as a movie role in *Donna on Demand*.

Chapter 44 – ECONOMIC CYCLE

DESCRIPTION: An economic cycle is characterized by four repeating phases: expansion, boom, contraction, and depression (Krugman & Wells, 2017). In the *expansion phase*, the economy grows and expands. This blossoms into a boom where the economy is in overdrive, jobs are plentiful, and goods are in high demand. In *boom times*, companies increase production to meet growing consumer demand. Eventually the economy *contracts*, jobs are lost, and investors shrink away. To remain competitive, companies cut costs, automate, offshore, and outsource. This results in reduced profits, lay-offs and contraction of the economy. Finally, it stagnates into a recession or *depression*. Eventually, the lowered prices increase demand and improved profits which causes the economy to rebound. These cycles of boom and bust repeat themselves (Sismondi, 1819).

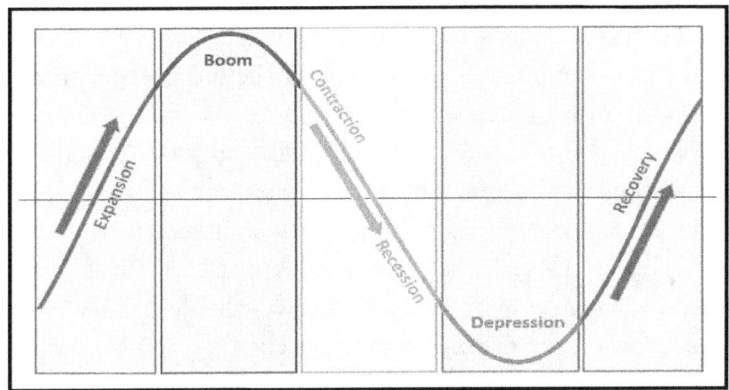

Figure 4 – The Economic Cycle

NOTABLE WORK: *Nouveaux Principes d'économie politique* (Sismondi, 1819). New Principles of Political Economy.
PERSON: Jean Charles Leonard de Sismondi
SYMBOL: EC. The symbol for Economic cycles is a flower of curved arrows. The green arrow corresponds to the expansion phase of cycle. The blue arrow represents a boom. The yellow arrow represents a contraction and the red arrow stands for a depression.
DATE: 1819
STORY: The creation of the world wide web fueled a technology-led boom during the 1990s in the United States of America (USA) (Lowenstein, 2004). The world wide web transformed communication and commerce. Consequently, the 1990s saw a sustained period of economic growth, job creation, low inflation, increasing productivity, and a rising stock market. This was the longest period of economic prosperity and continuous expansion in the USA where GDP increased continuously for almost ten years. During this period, 80% of the world's venture capital was funneled into Silicon Valley, California. This capital created a legion of dot.com companies. However, the speculative stock market burst on March 11, 2000 and was dubbed the dot com bubble (Cassidy, 2009). During this time, many on-line companies failed and shut down. By the end of 2000, most internet stocks had declined 75% in value wiping out $1.75 trillion in value (Kleinbard, 2000). Eventually, the internet companies regained their footing to deliver an array of useful services. Decades later, in 2019, California still attracted 54% of venture

capital dollars. Home to Silicon Valley, it commanded $11.5 billion USD out of a total of $21.1 billion in venture capital.

RELEVANCE TO YOU: Things come and go, ebb and flow. Whatever industry or market you work in may experience down-turns before it experiences upward growth again. The key is to capitalize on opportunities when things are going well; and prepare for winter before things turn cold. Many industries experience cycles that are like the seasons. In the spring of the economic cycle, businesses blossom. In the summer during the boom, sales heat up. In a bull market, people can develop an irrational exuberance. This is what causes stock market bubbles and dot com crazes. However, markets may over-extend themselves. In the fall, the market loses steam. Commerce slows down because companies cut-back and consumers reduce spending. And in the winter, a recession settles in and markets freeze up.

Economic cycles are characterized by consumption, employment rates, prices, interest rates and investment. The consumption of consumer goods is greatly affected by fluctuations in the economic cycle. Fluctuations in profitability affect prices, interest rates and investments. During an expansion, business investments increase to meet a growing market demand. Recession or expansion spreads from one industry to another until it affects an entire economy. During a recession, production is decreased as businesses contract. Due to international trade, countries are interwoven through industry, trade and markets. Consequentially, recessions or expansions in one large economy tends to spread around the world.

Armed with this knowledge, you can act. During an expansion you should seek opportunities as markets are on the march. At the height of a boom, you should find plentiful opportunities. As the boom troughs, you should watch for signs of a contracting economy. Prepare for a recession before it happens. Reallocate resources to anticipate an economic downturn. Increase your savings. During a recession or depression make the most of your preparation and savings. As the economy rebounds with a recovery, seek new opportunities.

Chapter 45 – MARGINAL UTILITY

DESCRIPTION: In economics, utility refers to the benefit derived from using a product. Thus, the marginal utility of a good is the change in the utility from an increase in the consumption of a good or service (Moscati, 2018). The first unit of a resource has high value. Each subsequent unit represents the marginal utility of a good or service. For example, to a nomad living in a desert, a cup of water brings great benefit because it helps keep him alive. The second cup of water he gets may still have a lot of benefit. However, the 1,000th additional cup of water has little benefit or is wasted. The law of diminishing marginal utility states that consuming the first unit of a good yields more utility than the second and subsequent units, with a continued reduction of usefulness for additional units.

Economics defines two terms related to the benefit of subsequent consumed units: cardinal utility and ordinal utility (Moscati, 2018). *Cardinal utility* assigns a numerical value to the benefit of subsequent units; whereas, *ordinal utility* is only concerned with an ordering of the series. In the water for the nomad example, suppose the second cup of water had a benefit value of 12 and the third cup had a benefit value of 6. Cardinal utility cares about the qualitative benefit values assigned to the cups of water, 12 and 6. Ordinal utility is only concerned with the ordering of the three cups in first, second and third place.

In his famous work, *The Wealth of Nations*, Adam Smith describes the Paradox of Value. He uses an example comparing water to diamonds (Smith A. ,

1776). Water paradoxically has a lower value than diamonds even though water is more vital to human life. Thus, you would expect that water should have a higher value than diamonds, yet it does not. The explanation of this paradox is that water is much easier to obtain than diamonds. Consequentially, the marginal cost of water is lower than diamonds. Other related concepts include the concept of *Veblen goods* (where demand increases as price increases), *Giffin goods* (where consumption rises with price), theory of value (explaining how goods are priced), and elasticity of demand (responsiveness of demand to price change) (Moscati, 2018).

NOTABLE WORK: Theory of Political Economy (Jevons, 1871).
PERSON: William Jevons
SYMBOL: MU. The symbol is of a battery with a full charge. The marginal utility of energy when empty is high, eventually leading to zero marginal utility when the battery is full.
DATE: 1871
STORY: Consider two simple stories to illustrate the concept of marginal utility. My friend, Steve Chew has a family of four. Suppose he is preparing for a trip to an amusement park and sees an advertisement. If he buys four tickets, he will get a fifth ticket for free. However, since Steve has only four people in his family, the fifth ticket has zero marginal utility. There is great benefit to the first four tickets since he has four in his family. Thus, he would waste the fifth. However, if the fifth ticket was in the form of a voucher that did not expire, and Steve determined that he could eventually use the fifth ticket, it would have positive marginal utility.

As another example, Steve uses Vitamin D (calciferol) supplements. Vitamins have a recommended daily value (RDA) and a tolerable upper intake level (UL) which varies for children and adults (Cooperman, 2019). The RDA for Vitamin D for an adult under the age of 70 is 15 micrograms (600 IU) per day and the upper limit is 100 micrograms (4,000 IU). The first 15 micrograms have a positive marginal utility as it benefits his health. The next 15 has minimal marginal utility. Intake beyond 100 micrograms has negative marginal utility as the body cannot use that much Vitamin D. In fact, prolonged excessive vitamin D intake leads to a vitamin overdose that results in nausea, vomiting, kidney damage, bowel irregularities, and heart rhythm abnormalities (Cooperman, 2019). In 2016, 63,930 cases of vitamin toxicity were reported to the USA poison control center (Gummin, et al., 2017).

RELEVANCE TO YOU: Marginal utility asks: "how much is enough?" and "can you have too much of a good thing?" There is only so much you need. However, there is no limit to desire. If you are working on a project or task, consider that the initial seed resources are likely to make a big difference. At first, additional resources will help the cause. Eventually, further additional resources are likely to make less of a difference than those first few seed resources.

Consider some questions to help you think about Marginal Utility. Is your time better spent harnessing new activities or new directions? Does it make sense to put some effort into figuring out how to organize better, or make more efficient use of incoming resources? Where will your energies make the most difference? Are you starting to waste resources and time?

Suppose you are working on a project that requires multiple sessions to complete. For example, you might want to clean, design, paint, study, or write. In this case, imagine you are tackling a cleaning task. You get cleaning supplies for the job. The first bottle of cleaning fluid is vital. You decide to get an additional bottle in case you run out. That second bottle has some marginal utility. The second bottle is enlisted should the first bottle become lost, leaky, or expended. A third and fourth bottle would only add a little more value. Sometime, in the future, you might need to open them. However, the 100th bottle would only take up space and create clutter. This example illustrates diminishing marginal utility with the reduced usefulness of additional bottles of cleaning fluid.

The concept of marginal utility applies to many types of problems and in multiple dimensions of a task. Projects needs resources: money, goods, people, services and time. We consume goods, services, and resources for a variety of purposes. Take some time to consider just how many resources you need to get a project task done and launch with that. The more accurately you can identify the exact resources you need, the less you will squander to diminishing marginal utility.

Chapter 46 – INCENTIVES

DESCRIPTION: Incentives are motivators that reward actions to encourage a desired outcome. Incentives come in a variety of forms including benefits, bonuses, enticements, rewards, recognition, and trophies. From an economic standpoint, there are four types of incentives: coercive, financial, moral, and personal (Mankiw, 2017). *Coercive incentives* use punishment, force, or imprisonment to get people to comply. For example, incarceration is a coercive incentive to deter crime. *Financial incentives* promise a monetary reward to inspire people to action. For example, a bounty awarded to the first person to finish a project task. *Moral incentives* induce people to behave in a way that is seen as socially proper, virtuous, or admirable. Moral incentives speak to a person's self-esteem or responsibility. For example, assisting with the elderly is a moral incentive. Coercive, financial, and moral incentives are *extrinsic motivators* because they originate from a source external to a person. *Personal incentives* motivate someone intrinsically based on their desires, tastes, and values. When people find activities meaningful, they do them even if there is no compensation.
NOTABLE WORK: The Theory of Incentives: The Principle-Agent Model (Laffont & Martimort, 2002).
PERSON: Jean-Jacques Laffont, David Martimort
SYMBOL: IV. The trophy symbolizes incentives as a widely recognized icon of achievement and accomplishment bestowed upon an individual.

DATE: 1914 (Henry Ford's $5 per day wage)

STORY: In 1861, the German company Krupp, led by Alfred Krupp, pioneered social services for their workers. Krupp incentives included subsidized housing, schooling, health and retirement benefits which was unusual for its time (James H. , 2012). He inspired the chancellor of Germany, Otto von Bismarck, to introduce government social services.

Later, on January 5, 1914, Henry Ford offered a $5 per day wage to qualified employees of his Ford Motor company. This more than doubled the $2.34 rate of most of his workers in nine-hour shifts (Ford & Crowther, 1922). A typical worker in the USA made $11 per week at the time. He reduced turn-over at Ford by using unprecedented financial incentives. Previously, turn-over was high. In 1913, he had to hire 52,000 people just to maintain a work force of 14,000. The cost of training, searching for new employees, and down-time of the production line was costly. Through incentives, Ford created a long-term, productive, loyal, and skilled work force. This was a famous business decision related to incentives. This combination of the mass production of consumer goods coupled with high wages is now called *Fordism* (Thompson F. , 2005). Ford was a vanguard in welfare capitalism where companies offered new benefits and social incentives to their employees. Subsequently, many companies arranged cultural activities, created social clubs, gave medical benefits, offered educational initiatives, sponsored sports teams, and subsidized housing for their workers. All of these are extrinsic incentives that engendered loyalty and a desire for their company to succeed. In the early 20th century, the Ford Motor Company, International Harvester, Pullman Car Company, Standard Oil, and United States Steel pioneered incentives such as educational opportunities, medical benefits, paid vacations, pensions, and recreational facilities (Brandes, 1976).

There are other famous examples where incentives were masterfully employed. In 1962, John F. Kennedy delivered a speech at Rice University tugging at personal incentives and national pride (NBCLearn, 1962 (2015)). His space program vision mobilized a nation to land a man on the moon. The 2011 USA Occupy Wall Street movement (White, 2011) and France's 2018 Yellow Vest demonstrations (French: *Mouvement des gilets jaunes*) are examples of movements based on moral incentives appealing to economic equality and fairness.

RELEVANCE TO YOU: Incentives can motivate you and they can motivate others. By their nature, incentives are personal. Financial and coercive incentives compel you through your primal instincts of self-preservation and survival. Moral incentives appeal to your sense of social dedication and virtue. Personal incentives speak directly to your values and desire for self-actualization. Incentives have been woven into the tapestry of society. For example, governments use financial incentives to steer society. Whether you work alone or with a group of people, learning to use incentives can get people working together harmoniously. Incentives have been used by parents throughout recorded history to get children to cooperate and behave. Financial, moral or personal incentives tend to solicit more enthusiasm than coercive incentives. Honey and carrots are better motivators than vinegar and beating sticks.

Consider an important task that you are working on. What financial incentives you can use to motivate people? For example, you could offer a monetary bonus for the completion of a key task delivered on time. To motivate people with moral incentives ask yourself what is virtuous about the project? How does it help people or society at large? People will join a cause because it is virtuous or morally right. For example, a project that donates to a charitable cause engenders support.

Personal incentives speak to what a person finds meaningful. Personal incentives appeal to an innate desire to love, to learn and to leave a legacy. To motivate people through personal incentives, consider their values, dreams and aspirations. People spend time freely with their families, on their hobbies and pet projects. Why? Because they are motivated by personal incentives. You can motivate yourself with incentives to elicit your best performance.

Chapter 47 – SOCIAL CAPITAL

DESCRIPTION: Social Capital are factors of social cohesion that allow groups to function efficiently (Halpern, 2004). They are the things that keep groups together and working harmoniously over the long haul. Social Capital factors include cooperation, personal relationships, reciprocity, shared identity, shared norms, shared vision, shared values, and trust. These factors apply to any kind of group including families, companies, and associations. A team within an organization typically shares a vision, an identity, and has built up trust over time. They know how to cooperate and reciprocate. This is also true of effective families. In his book *Social Capital*, David Halpern indicated that social capital is important because it affects the economic performance, crime, education, and the effectiveness of a state (Halpern, 2004). Effective social capital improves the productivity and effectiveness of a group through cooperation and communication.

NOTABLE WORK: The Rural School Community Center (Hanifan, 1916). It is the first occurrence of the term *social capital* describing community enrichment through social investment.

PERSON: Lyda Judson Hanifan

SYMBOL: SC. The overlapping circles with silhouettes of people show interconnectedness.

DATE: 1916

STORY: On September 12, 1962, President John F. Kennedy delivered a speech to 40,000 people at Rice University in Houston, Texas USA (Kennedy, 1962). Historians refer to this as the "*We choose to go to the moon*" speech. The speech described an ambitious vision of a landing a man on the moon before the end of their decade. It was a pivotal 17 minutes and 28 seconds that altered the course of human history. It rallied a nation and stirred a sense of pride and commitment. It focused and mobilized America's space program. On July 20, 1969, Apollo 11 astronauts Neil Armstrong, Michael Collins, and Edwin "Buzz" Aldrin, Jr. landed the Lunar Module, Eagle, on the Moon's surface. Neil Armstrong proclaimed "*that's one small step for man, one giant leap for mankind*" (NASA, 2007) as he stepped onto the Moon's surface.

Kennedy's vision provided many social capital hooks to latch onto including a shared vision, optimistic values and national identity. That vision propelled an interest in mathematics, science and engineering. Kennedy's vision resonated with and inspired 500,000 engineers, industrialists, pilots, researchers, scientists, and workers that turned that dream into a reality. It created social cohesion that resulted from social capital. These pioneers were united in a common cause. Kennedy's dream became theirs.

Michael D'Antonio wrote a memorable account of America's space program in his book *A Ball, A Dog and a Monkey: 1957 – The Space Race Begins* (D'Antonio, 2008). The ball referred to Sputnik; the Dog referred to the Russian astro-canine Laika, and the Monkey the American astro-simian Gordo. Eventually, the space exploration program produced numerous spinoff technologies including artificial limbs, baby formula, camera phones, CAT scans, dust busters, freeze dried foods, insulin pumps, LASIK, memory foam, scratch resistant lenses, shock absorbers, solar cells, and wireless headsets (NASA, Spinoff Technology Transfer Program, 1976-2019).

RELEVANCE TO YOU: Unless you are a hermit, isolated from human contact, social capital plays a role in your life. Humans are social creatures; and we need to interact with other people. Society depends upon an intricate web of relationships to produce and deliver the goods and services you regularly use. A typical person has a huge cast of people that dance across their life's stage including assistants, clerks, co-workers, doctors, family, friends, grocers, and neighbors.

Think of social capital as a bank account. However, instead of depositing money, you deal with social currency. You make deposits of trust, social cohesion, and shared identity. Sympathy, goodwill, and cooperation build up the account. When you break a trust, cause social disruption or stray from the group, you make withdrawals from the social capital bank account. Social capital builds interest over time and pays dividends through trust, friendship, loyalty and cooperation. When you take the time to understand someone, really listen to their dreams and values you build up social capital. Make some deposits into your social capital bank account with people in your social network today.

Time is the most precious commodity you have. When you spend time with someone, you make memories together. You build up a sense of shared identity. When you find a middle ground or reach a compromise with a person, you make a deposit in your social capital bank account with them. Social capital is about building trust over time between individuals in a group. This allows them to weather the storms that life throws at them.

Think of a team, family or group that functions well. What makes them hum together? Anything you identify relates to social capital. Their members have developed a sense of trust through strong relationships. They share life goals, and value the same things which fosters cooperation and harmony. John Field, in his book *Social Capital*, describes how relationships can affect how people acquire information, learn skills, and find meaning in life (Field, 2005).

Chapter 48 – CREATIVE DESTRUCTION

DESCRIPTION: Creative destruction is a process through which something new brings about the demise of whatever existed before it. Capitalism and innovation create new products and markets even as they make old ones obsolete. Joseph Schumpeter defined *creative destruction* by writing *"the gale of creative destruction"* describes the *"process of industrial mutation that incessantly revolutionizes the economic structure from within, incessantly destroying the old one, incessantly creating a new one."* (Schumpeter, 2008).

Werner Sombart is credited with an early use of the term in his work *Krieg und Kapitalismus* (War and Capitalism) (Sombart, 1913). Sombart described a new spirit of creation that arises from creative destruction. For example, when firewood became scarce in Europe, it ushered in the invention of coal for heating as a substitute (Sombart, 1913).

The concept of creative destruction originated in economics but has since been applied to many disciplines. This term has found a home in diverse areas including architecture, art, literature and philosophy. In his book, *The Creative Destruction of Manhattan 1900-1940*, Max Page observed the process of urban renewal and modernization in New York City (Page M. , 2000). Philip Fisher highlighted creative destruction in literary works in his book *Still the New World,*

American Literature in a Culture of Creative Destruction (Fisher, 1999). Human ingenuity is constantly innovating which improves our quality of life and advances culture. However, creative destruction causes prior creations to become obsolete to make way for the new innovations.
NOTABLE WORK: Capitalism, Socialism and Democracy (Schumpeter, 2008).
PERSON: Joseph Schumpeter
SYMBOL: CD. A phoenix symbolic of the new rising from the ashes of the old represents this idea.
DATE: 1942
STORY: New innovations have sparked transformations in society and been a boon to consumers. However, along the road to progress there are casualties. Some examples in history of creative destruction came from the creation of the transistor, digital photography, and personal PC. In 1947, the invention of the transistor paved the way for new consumer electronics industries. However, it caused the demise of vacuum tube products from RCA and Zenith (Yenne, 1993). Bell laboratories invented the charge coupled device (CCD) which is an electronic image sensor that is the basis for digital photography (Janesick, 2001). This creative innovation caused the destruction of traditional film photography. Furthermore, Super8 movie cameras were replaced by digital video cameras. Email and phone texting replaced Fax machines which had superseded Telex (Coopersmith, 2015). The personal computer (PC) was developed by Apple and Microsoft (Wozniak & Smith, 2007). The invention of the PC spawned a new industry, but it shrunk the market for mainframe computers produced by IBM and DEC.

There are other examples of creative destruction in different markets. The development of the automobile displaced the horse and buggy (Parissien, 2014). The creation of the airplane replaced trains and steam ships for long distance personal travel. In the music industry, Compact Discs (CDs) replaced Vinyl records. Electric lighting superseded gas lighting which had overtaken candlelight (Stross, 2007). A variety of internet services have displaced traditional services (Abbate, 2000). For example, on-line travel websites replaced the travel agent. eBay, the on-line auction house replaced yard sales. On-line retailers, such as Amazon, supplanted much of the retail business from bricks and mortar stores (Abbate, 2000).
RELEVANCE TO YOU: Creative destruction is about innovation that displaces existing products, structures and systems. While this idea originated in economics, you can still apply the essence of the concept. You can utilize the idea to let go

of the old in order to make way for the new. To make way for new things to come into your life, you need to relinquish the old. This idea can apply to many aspects of community, business and life.

When necessary, your willingness to start over may foster long term success. Fresh beginnings can create new opportunities. Old projects can clutter your mind and home. Take some time to clear away the past to make way for new projects. Clearing away the growth from prior interests makes space for new projects to flourish and blossom.

In a fast paced, modern industrial society, innovation spurs progress. Technology advances and product innovation generate a tsunami of new goods. The periodic idea of creative destruction can key you into the shifting trends caused by product disruption. See if you can spot those markets that are being disrupted by creative destruction. What product debuts are likely to upset existing incumbents? What markets look like they are becoming phased out? One obvious example is personal computers. Just as you purchase a computer, another more advanced model is already on the horizon. When you can spot these trends, you can act with foresight. For example, instead of getting the latest model, you may buy one a generation behind at a more affordable price. This would let you upgrade more frequently to try to keep pace with innovation. Creative destruction lets you navigate around market landmines and ride creative currents.

Take an inventory of your interests and values. Your introspection will reveal what is important to you. Focus on projects that matter to you. When you take on a new project or hobby, consider if you need to let an old one go.

Chapter 49 – ECONOMIC PERSONAL RELEVANCE

This chapter collects and summarizes the personal relevance of each of the economic periodic ideas. The economic periodic ideas are embedded into the consciousness of society. They have become indispensable tools in our lives. They allow the cogs of society to function efficiently. Currency, credit, markets and trade develop an economic footing for your projects. Diminishing returns and marginal utility maximize the use of your resources. Incentives and social capital motivate group cohesion and effectiveness. Creative destruction lets you identify new innovations that are in the process of disrupting markets. These timeless economic concepts are personal, valuable, and pervasive. If you familiarize yourself with them, they can be effective allies on your way to success.

The following table summarizes the personal relevance of the economic periodic ideas:

ECONOMIC IDEA	ID	PERSONAL RELEVANCE
MARKETS 3000 BCE	MK	Markets allow you to exchange goods or services with others. You can buy resources that you need. Through a market, you can adjust and balance resources for your projects. Markets can guide you to find customers for your idea and producers for your needs.
CURRENCY 550 BCE	CU	Currency helps you attain necessities and facilitates your dreams. Money management is a basic life skill. Develop a financial strategy to balance your income against your expenses. You can save, plan and budget to realize your long-term goals. Break down large projects into manageable tasks. Money allows you to get the resources to complete those tasks.

ECONOMIC IDEA	ID	PERSONAL RELEVANCE
CREDIT 1494	CR	Credit can allow you to get the resources necessary to start a new project. Managing your credit is vital to your success in life. It is used as a gauge of financial standing by lenders.
DIMINISHING RETURNS 1766	DR	You need to recognize the point of diminishing returns in order to maximize your time, effort and resources. As you continue to add resources to a project, those subsequent resources have decreased effectiveness in accomplishing the goal.
TRADE 1817	TR	You can employ the concept of trade to buy and sell goods and services for money or something of value. You can barter to trade things without the use of money. If there is something you need, you may try to obtain it by trading away something you don't need.
ECONOMIC CYCLE 1819	EC	The economic cycle suggests that you recognize that there are periods of boom and contraction which shift between growth and decline. You need to capitalize on opportunities in times of prosperity and yet prepare for recessions before they happen.
MARGINAL UTILITY 1871	MU	Marginal utility suggests that there is only so much that you need. You should consider how many resources you need for a project and launch with that. You can add in a safety buffer for contingencies, but do not go overboard. Marginal utility asserts the excess resources will just sit idle.
INCENTIVES 1914	IV	Incentives motivate individuals and groups. Extrinsic motivations originate from external sources. Intrinsic motivations compel you based on your personal desires and values. Financial, moral, and personal incentives get you to excel. Financial and coercive incentives connect to your primal instincts of self-preservation and survival. Moral incentives appeal to your sense of social dedication and virtue. Personal incentives speak to your values and desire for self-actualization.

The Periodic Table of Ideas

ECONOMIC IDEA	ID	PERSONAL RELEVANCE
SOCIAL CAPITAL 1916	SC	You can use social capital to create social cohesion in a group. You can build trust and friendship to engender cooperation and reciprocity. Finding a shared identity, shared vision, shared norms and shared values develops interpersonal relationships.
CREATIVE DESTRUCTION 1942	CD	Creative destruction suggests that, if necessary, you let go of the old to make way for the new. Sometimes, to make way for new things to come into your life, you need to relinquish the old. New chapters in your life can flourish when old ones close. Creative destruction lets you navigate around market landmines and ride creative currents.

Table 14 – Periodic Economic Ideas Personal Relevance

PART VI – BUSINESS IDEAS

Chapter 50 – BUSINESS IDEAS

A business is a profit seeking enterprise engaged in commerce, manufacturing or a service (Webster's New World Dictionary, 1984). It is the activity of making a living or making money by producing, buying or selling products and services. The ultimate purpose of business is to fulfill the needs and wants of the public efficiently. The periodic business ideas will explore some of its most enduring, influential, and recurrent ideas. These include the concept of a company, division of labor, managerial capitalism, the multi-divisional form and intellectual capital. Business ideas underpin efficient economies.

Companies have changed culture, finance, politics, science, and technology. They have been instrumental through thousands of years of human history. The first business arrangements date back to 3,000 BCE in Mesopotamia (Bertman, 2005). The earliest limited partnerships date back to ancient Roman companies (*societates publicanorum*) and guilds (*corpora*) (Fleckner, 2020). The Dutch East India Company (Verenigde Oostindische Compagnie) was the first company to issue bonds and shares of its stock to the public (Parthesius, 2010). In the USA, there are 5.6 million firms with 89% of those companies having fewer than 20 workers (Small Business & Entrepreneurship Council, 2016).

Today, businesses cater to the needs of a worldwide public. They make a difference even to those in remote locations. Businesses manufacture goods, deliver products, and provide services that cater to the needs and demands of the public. Today, multinational businesses span the globe to bring value to communities. They improve the standard of living and transform the lives of billions of people in the process of doing business. People depend on businesses to provide for their necessities and manufactured goods. Governments deliver services built a platform of basic consumer products such as automobiles, buildings, computers, foodstuffs, and office products.

The periodic business ideas are distilled from among hundreds of concepts. Division of labor, multi-divisions, and managerial capitalism were landmark milestones in business history. Companies and intellectual capital are the foundation of modern capitalism. These concepts have endured the test of time and propelled enterprises to success.

The following table summarizes the periodic business ideas. They are sorted by date of introduction.

BUSINESS IDEA	ID	DESCRIPTION
COMPANY 1602	CO	Dutch East India Company. A company is a legal entity composed of an association of people for commercial or industrial purposes. Three ideas underpin the modern company: joint stock ownership, limited liability, and the company as a legal personality. Examples of companies include voluntary associations, business enterprises, and financial firms.
DIVISION OF LABOR 1690	DL	Sir William Petty. The division of labor is the separation of tasks in an organization or group. Assigning people to specialized tasks optimizes individual talent thereby improving group efficiency. Specialists in a group with unique capabilities complement other people with different skills.
MULTI-DIVISIONS 1920	MD	Alfred P. Sloan, Jr. The multi-divisional form (M-Form) is an organizational structure where a diversified company is separated into semi-autonomous units. The M-form frees top management from the minutia of daily operations and allows them to concentrate on corporate strategy, market positioning, and resource allocation among divisions.
MANAGERIAL CAPITALISM 1977	MC	Alfred D. Chandler, Jr. Managerial capitalism relates to corporations that employ professional managers. Professional managers set objectives, organize activities, motivate teams, measure outcomes, and develop people in an organization. Managerial capitalism superseded patrimonial family-run capitalism.
INTELLECTUAL CAPITAL 1991	IC	Thomas Stewart. Intellectual capital are the intangible assets of a company. They are the nonphysical and nonfinancial assets that command value. They are typically classified into three categories: human capital, structural capital and relational capital.

Table 15 – Periodic Business Ideas

Chapter 51 – COMPANY

DESCRIPTION: A company is a legal entity composed of an association of people for commercial or industrial purposes (Micklethwait, 2005). Examples of companies include voluntary associations, business enterprises, and financial firms. Companies have changed culture, finance, politics, science, and technology. It is a concept that has been influential on the world's stage for thousands of years of human history.

The first business arrangements date back to 3000 BCE in Mesopotamia (Bertman, 2005). Ancient Greeks formed business partnerships with venture-funded contracts. The earliest limited partnerships were ancient Roman companies (*societates publicanorum*) and guilds (*corpora*) (Fleckner, 2020). In 1602, the Dutch East India Company (Verenigde Oostindische Compagnie) was the first company to issue bonds and shares of its stock to the public (Parthesius, 2010).

Companies have become the cornerstone of modern capitalistic societies. Three key ideas underpin the concept of a modern company (Micklethwait, 2005). The first key idea is *joint stock ownership* whereby shareholders can trade shares of company stock (Courtney, 2012). The second idea is the *limited liability* concept. In this notion, the owners are not personally liable for the debts or

liabilities of a company. The third concept is that of the company as a legal personality, essentially an artificial person in the eyes of the law.
NOTABLE WORK: First issued shares of stocks and bonds
PERSON: Dutch East India Company (Dutch: *Vereenigde Oostindische Compagnie* or VOC)
SYMBOL: CO. An icon of a corporate office building represents this periodic idea.
DATE: 1602
STORY: As the industrial age gave way to the information age, service companies became more prominent than manufacturing companies. Steve Jobs and Steve Wozniak introduced the *Apple I* personal computer on April 1, 1976 (Dorf & Byers, 2005). The personal computer industry flowered in the 1980s. Companies that catered to the personal computer, such as Microsoft, bloomed. In 1989, Tim Berners-Lee at CERN proposed the hyperlink concept which blossomed into the World Wide Web (Abbate, 2000). This spurred the creation of online companies, such as Amazon (Amazon.com, 2020) and eBay (eBay Press Room, 1995), which deliver products and services over the internet.

As the internet matured, online services thrived. In the 2000s, social media companies, such as Facebook, created a virtually connected culture (Van Dijck, 2013). In the 2010s, peer-to-peer service companies, such as Airbnb (Airbnb, 2020) and Uber (Uber, 2020) came into existence. The service industry encompasses educational, financial, human, health, hospitality, and retail services. Information technologies underpin the service industry. Service companies play a more prominent role than manufacturing in the information age. Biotechnology, nanomaterials, 3D printing, artificial intelligence, and robotics companies will usher in the next revolutionary era (Schwab, 2017).
RELEVANCE TO YOU: Companies are woven into the tapestry of society. They provide for your food, clothing and shelter. They are so vital to our livelihoods that it is hard to imagine life without them. Companies have become commonplace and blend into the backdrop of our lives.

Companies synergize with many other periodic ideas. There are numerous companies each dedicated to science, technology, and finance. There are even ones that concentrate on philosophical matters such as ethics, aesthetics, virtues, and values. Special interest companies or nonprofit organizations can assist you in any endeavor you want to pursue. They can help you fund, develop, or promote your projects making your dreams come true.

Companies unite people under a common purpose. At the heart of a company are the people who bring their talents and skills together to achieve a goal. They are a means to organize people and rally resources to accomplish an end. There are specialized companies that can help you accomplish tasks as a step towards reaching your ultimate objective. A bit of searching may reveal a niche organization that is tailored to your needs. Whether at work, home or play companies can help you learn and provide the tools you need to finish a project.

If you have an idea, it is now easy for you to become a provider to other people. Through market portals, such as Amazon (Amazon.com, 2020) and Etsy (Etsy.com, 2020), you can promote and sell your products to reach out and help people. Crowd funding sites such as Kickstarter (Kickstarter.com, 2020) allow you to launch new ideas. They provide the platform and support you need to turn ideas into reality.

Companies provide opportunities for people to engage in. By doing so, people feel like they contribute to society. It offers them a chance to take part in something bigger than themselves. Organizations allow people to make a difference to society at large. Corporations can influence society through innovation. Their products create new markets and inaugurate progress. Consumer companies have specialties in health care, retail distribution, retail products, services and transportation. Enterprises dedicated to these endeavors improve society and provide for the needs of the people.

Chapter 52 – DIVISION OF LABOR

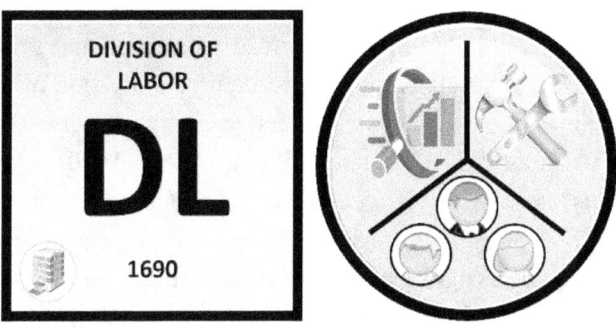

DESCRIPTION: The division of labor is the separation of tasks in an organization or group of people. This concept allows people in a society with unique capabilities and skills to make optimal use of their talents (Durkheim, 1893). Specializations allow people to complement other people with different knowledge and abilities. Assigning people to specialized tasks optimizes individual talent thereby improving overall group efficiency. Together, they form a collective greater than the sum of its parts. For example, organizations that assign economists to financial tasks benefit the most from their expertise. The division of labor allows people to better fulfill the needs of the group. In a company, the division of labor allows employees to focus on specific functions. For example, people may specialize in finance, research, production, or management.

In a hunter gatherer society, some people were hunters who could catch game while others specialized in gathering food. Agriculture allowed 20% of the people to produce enough food for all. This freed up the remaining 80% of society to specialize. When cities first developed, the division of labor allowed people to pursue vocations in agriculture, crafts, military, or services. Plato's book, *Republic*, claimed that a state is best established through the division of labor with specialties of a farmer, builder, weaver and craftsman (Plato, Republic, 1992). These jobs represent the basic elements needed to establish a state in ancient times.

From 1764 to 1840, during the industrial revolution, the division of labor allowed workers to concentrate on a focused set of tasks (Stearns, 2012). This reduced the training time required to produce the same overall amount of output. The division of labor allowed industrial factories to transition from highly skilled craftsmen to a less skilled workforce. It increased the total output and trade of an industrial society. This resulted in an expanded workforce and improved national prosperity. Complex industrialized processes required a division of labor.

Sir William Petty was the first modern writer to observe the effectiveness of the division of labor in Dutch shipbuilding (Petty, 1690). Classic shipyards would build ships as complete units, finishing one before starting another. By contrast, the Dutch organized people into teams, each working on focus tasks for successive ships. People assigned to atomic tasks would discover efficient methods to optimize their jobs. Thus, Dutch shipbuilding superseded its rivals. By 1672, the Netherlands was the foremost maritime power in the world (Swart, 1969). This is now known as the *Dutch Golden age* (Hetscheepvaart Museum, 2020).

NOTABLE WORK: Political Arithmetick (Petty, 1690)
PERSON: Sir William Petty
SYMBOL: DL. A whole divided into three sections each representing a different specialization symbolizes the division of labor concept.
DATE: 1690
STORY: The fast food industry has become an iconic staple of modern life. McDonald's pioneered the industry. Dick and Mac McDonald opened their restaurant in 1948. They invented the *Speedee* Service system which streamlined their operations through limiting the number of menu items. The menu featured 15 cent hamburgers, shakes and fries. In 1954, Roy Kroc was a milkshake mixer salesman, and visited the first McDonald restaurant. He was stunned by the speed and effectiveness of their operation. Their limited menu allowed them to focus on delivering quality with quick service (McDonald's, 2020).

In 2016, *The Founder*, a movie adaptation of the origins of McDonald's debuted (Hancock, 2016). Actor Michael Keaton portrayed Ray Kroc who is awestruck by McDonald's fast service, high quality food, disposable packaging and friendly atmosphere. During a memorable scene 20 minutes into the movie, the McDonald's described to Ray how they developed their procedures. They went to a tennis court and used chalk to draw out their stations including the drinks, front counter, fryer, frying area, garnishes, griddle, and ice cream. They divided the work into 16 stations each dedicated to a specific task. They had their employees choreograph the motions and practice their job functions. After observing people work, they rearranged the stations with economy of motion in mind. The result was a symphony of efficiency. Their *Speedee* system magically produced a meal in 30 seconds instead of 30 minutes that a typical restaurant took. The movie was a visual spectacle of how to think about the division of labor. It portrayed in a practical, real-life example the benefits of applying the division of labor.

RELEVANCE TO YOU: A modern society has many specialists that fulfill the various functions to make it operate smoothly. As such, it may behoove you to find a professional for your situation. In any group, company or organization, there are experts that have specialized knowledge related to their job function. With a little investigation, you may find talented people who can help you. If you belong to a group or organization, find someone who can give you advice in their area of expertise. For example, if you have some difficulty with a computer task, perhaps there are experts who can lend you advice? If you want to design or analyze a complex process, attempt to break it down into simpler stations and parts.

For example, when I renovated my bathroom, I happened to volunteer for Habitat for Humanity. This organization remodels and builds homes for those in need. I discovered that many specialists volunteer to help for that organization. I met retired electricians, plumbers, and craftsmen. I learned a lot by observing them in action which I later put to good use in my home renovation project. You can find specialists that can help with your project. Additionally, you can learn just about anything from peer-to-peer video services, such as YouTube (YouTube, 2019), by watching skilled specialists ply their craft. You can learn everything from rocket science to knitting.

At work, you may find it beneficial to divide a complex task into more manageable parts. If you want to accomplish something, you can assign specific tasks to specialists or focus teams. At home, you will find that many tasks are amenable to dividing up. Many hands make for light work. Furthermore, you can find professionals that can assist you in home repairs, chores, home improvements, and other projects. At play, there are experts in nearly every hobby, passion, and sport that you can imagine. You can take lessons from expert musicians, hobbyists, and artists. You can learn from enthusiasts who are willing to share their knowledge so that you can improve your skill.

Chapter 53 – MULTI-DIVISIONS

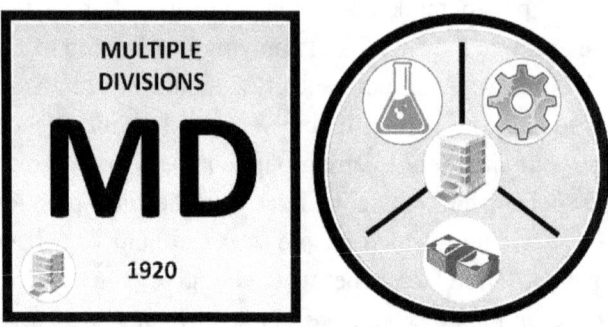

DESCRIPTION: The multi-divisional form (M-Form) is an organizational structure where a diversified company is separated into semi-autonomous units. Alfred Chandler in his book, The Visible Hand: The Managerial Revolution in American Business (Chandler, 1977), claimed that large diversified enterprises should organize into a multi-divisional firm. This business structure frees up top management from the minutia of daily operations and allows them to concentrate on market positioning, and resource allocation among divisions (Micklethwait, 2005). The central office focuses on strategic decisions, while the separate divisions focus on their market operations. This form is well suited to international corporations. The multi-divisional form simplifies information-processing and decision-making when diversification creates operational complexity.

In the 1920s, after World War I, the United States grew in population and urbanized. World War I thrusted the United States onto the world stage. As a result, it grew into an industrial powerhouse. American firms expanded into disparate markets. This business strategy is now known as diversification. In this period, several companies transitioned to multi-division businesses including Dupont, General Electric, General Motors, Standard Oil, US Rubber, and US Steel (Micklethwait, 2005). Alfred Sloan propelled General Motors to success by creating divisions. These divisions included Buick, Cadillac, Chevrolet, Oldsmobile, and Pontiac (Sloan, 1965). Each brand focused on a different consumer market ranging from entry level to luxury cars.

While rare in the early twentieth century, by 1960, the M-form had become widely accepted as the best form of organizational structure for complex and diverse industrial enterprises. After the transition to an M-form, firms displayed greater productivity and profits compared to companies that still clung to a unitary form (U-Form) (Chandler, 1977). The Multi-divisional form allows companies to efficiently expand, adding new businesses dynamically. The M-form combined the advantages of branding and economy of scale of a large company while retaining the flexibility of a small firm. Central management sets an overall strategy while each arm acts autonomously to seek success in its own market.

NOTABLE WORK: My Years with General Motors (Sloan, 1965)
PERSON: Alfred P. Sloan, Jr.
SYMBOL: MD. The symbol for this idea is an M-form dividing a company into three segments representing different market specialties.
DATE: 1920 with the first Multidivisional Companies
STORY: Drawing from my personal experience, I have spent my entire career in global multi-divisional companies. I have worked at General Electric (GE), Lucent technologies, Alcatel-Lucent, and Nokia. As an engineer at General Electric Medical systems, I worked in the Magnetic Resonance Imaging (MRI), Computed Tomography (CT) and Ultrasound divisions. The MRI division operated like a large company, while the Ultrasound division was run more like a startup. This was necessary because many of the Ultrasound competitors were small nimble manufacturers. The divisional form allowed GE to setup different businesses each with their own character.

In the wireless divisions of Alcatel-Lucent and Nokia, it was apparent that the M-Form was instrumental in focusing that business arm. It allowed the wireless division to concentrate research & development, specialize its workforce, tailor the sales force, and master the peculiarities of that market. The division would create engaging trade show exhibits and produce high quality products in that industry. This would have been impossible if the company was one monolithic (U-Form) corporation. In a U-form, basic functions such as sales must cater to a broad spectrum of business lines.

RELEVANCE TO YOU: The multi-divisional form propelled corporations to success in the twentieth century. The M-form has a proven track record in the business arena. What is the best way to organize thousands of people? At the turn of the 20th century, it was unclear how to best arrange a large organization. Today, with a long pedigree of success, the M-form seems obvious and common sensical. Creating divisions allows organizations to specialize and adapt to changing markets.

How might you employ this periodic idea? The essence of the M-form idea is to divide resources into specific focus areas. The concept suggests that you group people and resources into autonomous teams. Even if you do not head a vast international conglomerate, you can use the essence of the multi-division form idea in a variety of applications. For example, suppose you want to plan a wedding. The accommodations, caterer, coordinator, deejay, florist, photographer, officiant, and venue are essentially divisions each in service of a common wedding goal. Each division is specialized, acts autonomously, and gets strategic orders from the bride and groom. Other examples include divisions for party planning, house chores, and personal projects.

At home, when you organize a space for a home office, you may divide your work area based on activities. For example, computer work, financial matters, reading, writing, and project tasks are ways you might group things in your home office. This grouping allows you to concentrate on a specific task.

At work, if you are part of a company, it is likely to be organized into separate divisions. You can take advantage of this by utilizing the knowledge of specialized professionals from other divisions. Perhaps, you can hand off part of your project task so you can focus on your specialty.

At play, with your extra-curricular activities, you can view the divisions as learning, training, and reviewing. In learning, you need to acquire knowledge and competence. In training, you need practice to develop experience and ability. In reviewing, you need to assess and analyze. For example, if your hobby is photography, the divisions might be learning about the basics, practicing portrait photography, and reviewing your project work.

Chapter 54 – MANAGERIAL CAPITALISM

DESCRIPTION: Managerial capitalism is a concept where corporations employ professional managers. According to Peter Drucker, professional managers set objectives, organize activities, motivate teams, measure outcomes, and develop people in an organization (Drucker, 2010). Managerial capitalism developed during the twentieth century and superseded traditional patrimonial capitalism.

In patrimonial capitalism, the owners directly made all the decisions and performed all the management functions. Businesses before the managerial revolution were family owned and family run. That seems natural because the owners innately have a vested interest in its success. However, as companies grow, family firms thrust household members with no managerial experience into business positions without the proper training and experience (Micklethwait, 2005). Managerial capitalism uses professional managers to direct, organize, motivate, and develop employees. As a business grows to large size, it is impractical for a single person or family to retain complete control and handle advanced managerial functions.

Alfred Chandler won the Pulitzer Prize for History with his work, *The Visible Hand: The Managerial Revolution in American Business* (Chandler, 1977). In his magnum opus, he studied middle management in the corporate structure of large American firms. He described managerial firms such as Standard Oil, General Electric, US Steel and DuPont. He observed how managers improved productivity and lowered costs, resulting in higher profits. These gains in efficiency propelled modern American industry to success over family run firms in Europe. He postulated eight propositions in the areas of administrative coordination, economic activity, managerial hierarchy, managerial policy, and professional managers.

NOTABLE WORK: The Visible Hand: The Managerial Revolution in American Business (Chandler, 1977)
PERSON: Alfred D. Chandler, Jr.
SYMBOL: MC. An organizational chart with professional managers is used to symbolize this idea.
DATE: 1977
STORY: Alfred P. Sloan was the Chairman of the board of General Motors (GM) in 1937 (Parissien, 2014). He revolutionized business management (Sloan, 1965). Sloan separated the ownership of a company from the managerial control of a company. He made firms realize that owners cannot oversee every detail of a large business operation. They could not find the necessary management skills among immediate family members. Professional managers with formal business training would apply their organization skills and strategic insight to guide business operations. He established an executive committee to set a strategic vision and let competent managers realize that vision. After the Sloan revolution, credentials superseded lineage in importance (Micklethwait, 2005). Good managers marshal resources, spur innovation, and nurture the workforce.

    The managerial revolution produced advanced business schools. Wharton in 1881 (Wharton School, 2020) and Harvard (Harvard Business School, 2020) in 1908 pioneered the field. They transformed business education from mere secretarial and bookkeeping skills to include management theory, marketing, corporate finance and business policy. In 1931, Sloan sponsored a university-based executive education program, the *Sloan Fellows* at MIT. In 1950, a Sloan Foundation grant created the MIT School of Industrial Management aimed at producing competent managers (MIT Libraries, 2020). It became a world premier business school. In 1964, it was renamed the Alfred P. Sloan School of Management.

    By comparison, The Ford Motor company, in the 1920s, clung to a family-oriented managerial style (Ford & Crowther, 1922). Ford was a major rival auto maker in the USA to General Motors. In 1919, after a stockholder conflict with the Dodge brothers (Hyde, 2005), the Ford company became wholly owned by the Ford family. The family has retained operational control through a special class of stock ever since (Muller, 2010). Henry Ford wanted to administer the entire company by himself. He ignored the wisdom of management theory and disliked managerial structures. He drove away his most talented managers. As a result, Ford neglected consumer interests, innovative features, luxury options, and financing options. Ford lacked managerial oversight in his company with disastrous consequences (Micklethwait, 2005).

By 1929, Ford's share of the auto market had fallen from 61% to 31%. Meanwhile, General Motors' market share rose from 17% to 32%. Ford, famous for the invention of the assembly line, lacked the advantages of managerial capitalism. By 1962, GM had captured 50.7% of the USA auto market (Knoema, 2020). As of 2019, GM still commands a dominant 16.9% share of the auto market (Wagner, 2020).

RELEVANCE TO YOU: The idea of managerial capitalism propelled American businesses to success in the twentieth century. How can you put this periodic idea to work for you? At the core of the concept is the separation of ownership from control. It may seem counter-intuitive that you can own something and yet turn over the management of your project to someone else. In a sense, the owners who hatched the idea, let their chicks fly from their nest. Many small businesses start as a family-owned operation. The owners may struggle to find managers that they can rely on. It is scary to turn over control. It requires trust. Much like when a child leaves home for college, or summer camp, the parents worry. Managerial capitalism asserts that the owners cannot do everything. Managerial professionalism was successful because Alfred Sloan recognized the value of talented managers. He realized he was only one person with limited time at his disposal. He relied on a cadre of management experts and trusted them. He created a system to motivate and measure their performance. He created a managerial culture and set a vision. He clearly communicated his goals to let people know what was expected of them.

If you have a project in progress, perhaps there are experts that you may consider turning over part of the project to. Make use of professionals to make the best use of your time. Delegate project tasks where you lack expertise. Find a company that you can outsource parts of your project to. If you are part of a large organization, see if people can assist in work that you are not well suited to.

At home, you must trust that your children or your spouse is competent enough to perform a task. Trust in them. Divide chores among family members. Set your expectations and communicate that you are all working towards a common goal, a united family. Describe your goals so they know how to proceed. In your extra-curricular activities and hobbies, it may help to seek advice from others, or to turn over part of your project to a professional.

Chapter 55 – INTELLECTUAL CAPITAL

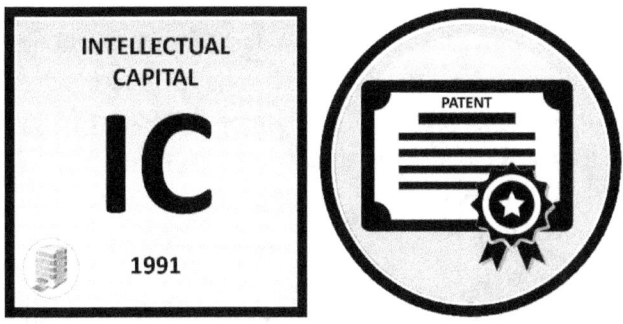

DESCRIPTION: Intellectual capital are the intangible assets of a company. They are the nonphysical and nonfinancial assets that command value. They are typically classified into three categories: human capital, structural capital and relational capital (Edvinsson & Malone, 1997). *Human capital* creates value for an organization through creativity, innovation, knowledge and experience. *Structural capital* maximizes the potential of human capital. It includes intangible facilitators such as patents, procedures, processes, techniques, and trade secrets. *Relational capital* is the value derived from relationships a business has with its customers and suppliers. Those relationships produce value through goodwill and intangible efficiencies. Furthermore, reputation and market clout engender brand loyalty from customers. Thomas Stewart argues that knowledge not natural resources, machinery or financial capital is the most important competitive advantage that an organization has (Stewart, Intellectual Capital: the New Wealth of Organization, 2010).

In 1985, Microsoft shares were sold for ten times more than its book value (Sveiby, 1997). What could account for this difference? Intangible assets explain the discrepancy. Intangible assets include management skills, patents, proprietary processes, workforce creativity and experience (Stewart, Intellectual Capital: Brainpower, 1991).

Intellectual capital has existed since the first company. However, it was not rigorously studied until the 1980s. In 1991, Thomas Stewart, first referred to intangible assets as intellectual capital in Fortune magazine. Later, Karl Sveiby identified three categories of intellectual capital: *external structure, internal structure* and *employee competence*. These ideas encompass administrative systems, branding, employee skills, external customer relations, organizational structure, and patents (Sveiby, 1997). Nick Bontis divided intellectual capital into *human, structural* and *customer capital* (Bontis, 1998). Companies now view intellectual capital as a foundation for their success.

NOTABLE WORK: Intellectual Capital: Brainpower (Stewart, Intellectual Capital: Brainpower, 1991).
PERSON: Thomas Stewart
SYMBOL: IC. A patent is one of most widely recognized forms of intellectual capital. So, it symbolizes the intellectual capital periodic idea.
DATE: 1991
STORY: Patents, brands and logos are examples of intellectual capital. Looking at instances of noteworthy intellectual capital can help you recognize its potential. What is the most valuable patent that has ever been filed? Alexander Graham Bell produced the first landline telephone in 1876 (Grosvenor & Wesson, 2016). The patent for the telephone (United States Patent No. 174,465, 1876) is one of the most valuable patents ever awarded. The telephone is one of the most widely adopted inventions. In 2020, the GSMA reported that there are 5.2 billion mobile telephone subscribers (GSMA Intelligence, 2020). Innovators and scientists are human capital that create value for the world through their ingenuity.

Who has the most patents? Thomas Edison was one of the most famous inventors. He held 1,093 patents and established the first industrial research lab in the world (Stross, 2007). Now, many inventors have surpassed the remarkable achievements of Edison. The world's most productive inventors are: Shunpei Yamazaki who holds 5,640 patents, Kia Silverbrook who has 4,747, and Kang Guo Cheng who has 2,069 patents (United States Patent and Trademark Office, 2017).

Who are the most famous actors and actresses? Among them include Robin Williams, Denzel Washington, and Betty White. Actors create intellectual capital for movie studios through their thespian talent. What are some of history's most recognizable songs? Some famous songs include Michael Jackson's *Beat it*, and Survivor's *Eye of the Tiger*. Singers are human capital whose voice talent generate value for record companies.

What are the most recognizable brands and logos? Interbrand annually evaluates the value of brands based on brand management, customer relations, licensing, marketing, portfolio management, and return on investment. In 2019, they ranked Apple, Google, Amazon, Microsoft, Coca-Cola, Samsung, Toyota, Mercedes, Macdonald's, Disney, BMW, IBM, Intel, Facebook and Cisco as the top 15 most valuable brands. In 2019, Interbrand valued the Apple brand at $234 million USD and Google at $167 million USD (Interbrand, 2020).

RELEVANCE TO YOU: Physical things and modest finances bring stability and security in life. Material goods are necessary for survival and can facilitate your dreams. Intellectual capital in the form of human capital, structural capital and relational capital bring value to an endeavor. Those same intangible things can make a difference in your projects. Human capital is comprised of creativity, knowledge and experience. These are your tools which promote meaningful accomplishments.

What are the intangible things that give your life meaning? What experiences have you had that you cherish? What virtues do you value? What relationships have made a difference in your life? How can you effectively apply your creativity and knowledge? What skills have you cultivated that have brought you a sense of meaning and satisfaction? What of your accomplishments have brought you joy? The quality of your accomplishments, relationships and experiences that bring you happiness are a better yardstick of success than material wealth.

Your *human capital* emerges by applying your creativity, experiences, and knowledge. We all strive to live, to learn, to love and to leave a legacy. Your accomplishments, relationships, and experiences transcend material happiness. The skills and knowledge that you cultivate forms the foundation of your human capital.

A musician moves an audience emotionally through sounds. An author stirs a reader with words. An artist evokes the imagination through colors. A dancer expresses grace through movement and poise. These people develop an inner joy through their human capital immeasurable by money.

Forming bonds with people cultivates your *relational capital*. Compassion, caring, and commitment strengthens relationships. The relationships and friendships that you take a lifetime to nurture generate a sense of fulfillment.

Relational capital creates a sense of social harmony and belonging. It underscores your humanity.

Your *structural capital* are the discipline, habits, and techniques, that you employ to foster success. The methods by which you acquire a skill, develop competence, and master knowledge are the structural capital that make a lasting difference in your life. Structural capital allows you to maximize your potential. It empowers your human and relational capital.

The Periodic Table of Ideas 181

Chapter 56 – BUSINESS PERSONAL RELEVANCE

This chapter collects and summarizes the personal relevance of each of the business periodic ideas. A business is a profit seeking enterprise engaged in commerce, manufacturing, or a service. Businesses fulfill the needs and wants of the public efficiently. The periodic business ideas explore some of its most enduring, influential, and recurrent ideas. *Companies* are an association of people for commercial or industrial purposes. *Division of labor* separates tasks in an organization to optimize the use of the talents its people. *Managerial capitalism* employs professional managers to set objectives, organize activities, and develop people in an organization. The *multi-divisional form* separates a diversified company into semi-autonomous units. *Intellectual capital* is the human, structural and relational assets of an enterprise.

The following table summarizes the personal relevance of periodic business ideas.

BUSINESS IDEA	ID	PERSONAL RELEVANCE
COMPANY 1602	CO	You can use companies that can provide services and products for your project. You can reach out to associations, enterprises, or financial firms for their assistance or services. Companies can also provide opportunities for you to engage in and contribute to society at large.
DIVISION OF LABOR 1690	DL	You can use division of labor to assign people to specialized tasks to best utilize their knowledge and talents. Dividing a project into manageable parts facilitates people taking on its tasks. You can also look for specialists to help you.
MULTI-DIVISIONS 1920	MD	The multi-divisional form (M-Form) idea asserts that you should divide resources into specific focus areas. You can divide your project into separate divisions. Then, you can create autonomous teams or use specialists to manage those tasks.
MANAGERIAL CAPITALISM 1977	MC	Managerial capitalism suggests that you separate ownership from control of a project. For your project, see if there are experts that you can turn over project tasks to. When you delegate parts of a project where you do not have expertise, you can focus your time on where you do have competence.
INTELLECTUAL CAPITAL 1991	IC	Intellectual capital are the intangible assets that you have. Try to identify the intangible things that give your life meaning. You can then nurture and make the most of your human capital, structural capital and relational capital.

Table 16 – Periodic Business Ideas Personal Relevance

PART VII – PSYCHOLOGY IDEAS

Chapter 57 – PSYCHOLOGY IDEAS

Among the periodic ideas, the psychology ideas are some of the most intimate and personal. You are likely to find these powerful recurring ideas relevant to you. The word psychology has its roots in the Greek words *psyche* meaning "mind", and *logia* meaning "study". The American Psychological Association defines psychology as the study of mind, behavior, and the collection of behaviors, traits, and attitudes that characterize an individual (American Psychological Association, 2020).

Philosophy are the ideas about ideas. By contrast, psychology is the study of the human mind and behavior. It focuses on how we come to have philosophical notions and what that tells us about the workings of our minds. Science embodies knowledge about nature. Science progressed by applying scientific methods to philosophical questions to arrive at practical knowledge. By contrast, psychology wrestles with philosophical questions relating to cognitive processes, and human behavior. Psychology studies attention, behavior, creativity, decision making, language, memory, motivation, perception, problem solving, and thinking. Because these topics are intrinsically hard to study, the application of scientific methods was slow to transform philosophical speculation into practical knowledge.

The experimental lab established by Wilhelm Wundt at the University of Leipzig in 1879 inaugurated psychology as a scientific discipline. The first major concept in psychology was behaviorism. Then, it progressed to psychotherapy, cognitive psychology and the psychology of difference. Early psychologists found it difficult to study mental processes directly but easy to observe behavior. This gave rise to *behaviorism*. In 1913, John B. Watson formulated behaviorism asserting that personality is a product of conditioning and the environment (Watson J. B., 1913).

After behaviorism, psychoanalytic theory was created by Sigmund Freud and Josef Breuer which focused on the unconscious mind (Freud, 2012). Freud developed *psychotherapy* by observing patients and their case history. Afterwards, psychology shifted to a scientific study of mental processes because of advancements in communications technologies and computer sciences. Information processing models helped develop psychology theories. As a result, in the 1950s, *cognitive psychology* blossomed (Bruner, 1956). The *psychology of difference* is the study of personality and intelligence. The systematic study of personality traits was pioneered by Gordon W. Allport (Allport & Allport, 1921).

Psychology is used in practical applications such as institutions, government, and industry. Psychology helps us understand ourselves, others and our social interactions. Social psychology encompasses the study of attitudes, group dynamics, persuasion, social cognition, social influence, and interpersonal attraction (American Psychological Association, 2020). The results from psychology studies have become integrated into our culture and we now call them "common sense". Thus, the insights from the periodic psychology ideas will find relevance in your life.

The following table summarizes the periodic psychology ideas. They are sorted by date of introduction. This table can also be found in the appendix for quick reference.

PSYCHOLOGY IDEA	ID	DESCRIPTION
PERSONALITY TRAITS 1937	PT	Gordon Allport. Personality traits are characteristics or qualities that combine to form the distinct character of an individual. These traits motivate the essential drive and desires of a person. The big five personality traits are: agreeableness, conscientiousness, extraversion, neuroticism, and openness.
PROPINQUITY EFFECT 1950	PE	Leon Festinger, Stanley Schachter, and Kurt Back. The *propinquity effect* is the tendency of individuals to form close relationships with people they repeatedly encounter. The propinquity effect can arise from physical, psychological, or functional proximity. Similarly, the *mere-exposure effect* is a preference for something resulting from repeated exposure.
FIELD THEORY 1951	FT	Kurt Lewin. Field theory asserts that behavior is a product of the individual interacting with their environment. It describes behavior in terms of interrelationships between people and their psychological circumstances, social situation, and physical surroundings.
SOCIAL PSYCHOLOGY 1951	SP	Kurt Lewin. Social psychology is the study of how the thoughts, feelings, and actions of individuals are affected by the actual, imagined, or implied presence of other people. It includes the study of attitudes, persuasion, social cognition, social influence, group dynamics and interpersonal attraction.
COGNITIVE PSYCHOLOGY 1960	CY	George Armitage Miller and Jerome Bruner. Cognitive psychology is devoted to the study of mental processes such as attention, language, memory, perception, problem solving, creativity, and thinking. You have two attention systems: *exogenous* is reflexive, and *endogenous* is deliberate. You have short-term, working, long-term, procedural, semantic, and episodic memory. Perception interprets stimuli from our senses.

Table 17 – Periodic Psychology Ideas

Chapter 58 – PERSONALITY TRAITS

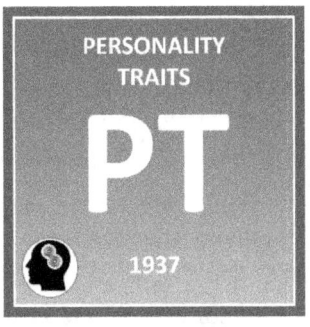

DESCRIPTION: The American Psychological Association defines psychology as the study of mind, behavior, and the collection of traits, attitudes that characterize an individual (American Psychological Association, 2020). Personality traits are the qualities that combine to form the distinct character of an individual. Early philosophers explained personality by humors and temperaments. Hippocrates suggested that there are four fundamental personality types: sanguine (pleasure-seeking), choleric (ambitious), melancholic (analytic), and phlegmatic (thoughtful) (Jones, 2006). In 1913, John B. Watson formulated behaviorism which asserted that personality is a product of conditioning and the environment (Watson J. B., 1913). Psychoanalytic theory was developed by Sigmund Freud and Josef Breuer which focused on the unconscious mind (Freud, 2012). Freud asserted that personality is composed of the id, ego and superego. These are motivated by instinct, reality, and morality respectively.

The first psychologist to systematically study personality was Gordon W. Allport (Allport & Allport, 1921). In 1936, Gordon Allport and Henry S. Odbert hypothesized that relevant personality traits are expressed in language (Allport & Odbert, Trait Names: A Psycho-Lexical Study, 1936). This is now known as the lexical hypothesis. They identified 17,953 words to describe personalities and eventually narrowed those down to 4,504 adjectives. Eventually, Allport concluded that personality is a combination of three categories of traits: cardinal, common and secondary (Allport G. W., Personality: A Psychological Interpretation, 1937). *Cardinal traits* are fundamental to a person, governing their entire approach to life. They motivate the essential drive, core needs and desires of a person. *Common traits* are general characteristics which are the building blocks of personality. Finally, *secondary traits* are contextual and situational. These traits express preferences and attitudes. Secondary traits round out the composite personality makeup of a person. Allport observed that personality is an assemblage of traits, motivations, and relationships. Following his research, traits became central to the study of personality in psychology. He pioneered the creation of what is now called trait theory. Psychologists no longer divide people into strict types, but instead acknowledge that people are a medley of personality traits working in synchrony.

In 1946, Raymond Cattell reduced the 4,504 adjectives identified by Allport and Odbert to 171 by eliminating synonyms (Cattell, Description and Measurement of Personality, 1946). In 1957, Cattell further narrowed these 171 down to just 16 dimensions of personality and created a personality assessment called 16 PF (Cattell, Personality and Motivation Structure and Measurement, 1957). These 16 factors were: abstractedness, aggressiveness, anxiety, assertiveness, dutifulness, emotional stability, independence, intellect, introversion, liveliness, open mindedness, paranoia, perfectionism, social sensitivity, tension, and warmth.

NOTABLE WORK: Personality: A Psychological Interpretation (Allport G. W., 1937)
PERSON: Gordon W. Allport
SYMBOL: PT. A person divided into interlocking puzzle pieces with each piece representing personality traits symbolizes this periodic idea.
DATE: 1937
STORY: In 1961, Ernest Tupes and Raymond Christal proposed the big five personality traits model (Tupes & Christal, 1961). The big five personality traits are: agreeableness, conscientiousness, extraversion, neuroticism, and openness. You can remember these with the acronym OCEAN or CANOE. Today, the big five traits model, also known as the five-factor model, is the most popular theory among psychologists. Each of the big five personality traits in the five-factor model contains six facets, each of which is measured with a separate scale. *Openness* is a measure of adventurousness, curiosity, and inventiveness. A person low in

openness is a creature of habit. They are cautious, consistent and crave familiarity. *Conscientious* people are achievers, dependable, disciplined, efficient, and organized. On the other end of the spectrum, those who are less conscientious are carefree, easy-going, freewheeling, and spontaneous. *Extraversion* is a quality of being energetic, gregarious, outgoing, and socially active. Introverts tend to be solitary and reserved. They tend to seek solo or small-group activities. *Agreeableness* is a sense of how compassionate, friendly, helpful, trusting, and warm someone is. Disagreeable people tend to be challenging, cold, detached, suspicious, and uncooperative. Those high in *neuroticism* are anxious, nervous, obsessive, and worriers. Those low in neuroticism are confident, emotionally stable, even keeled, and secure.

The following diagram shows the big five personality traits with their six facets:

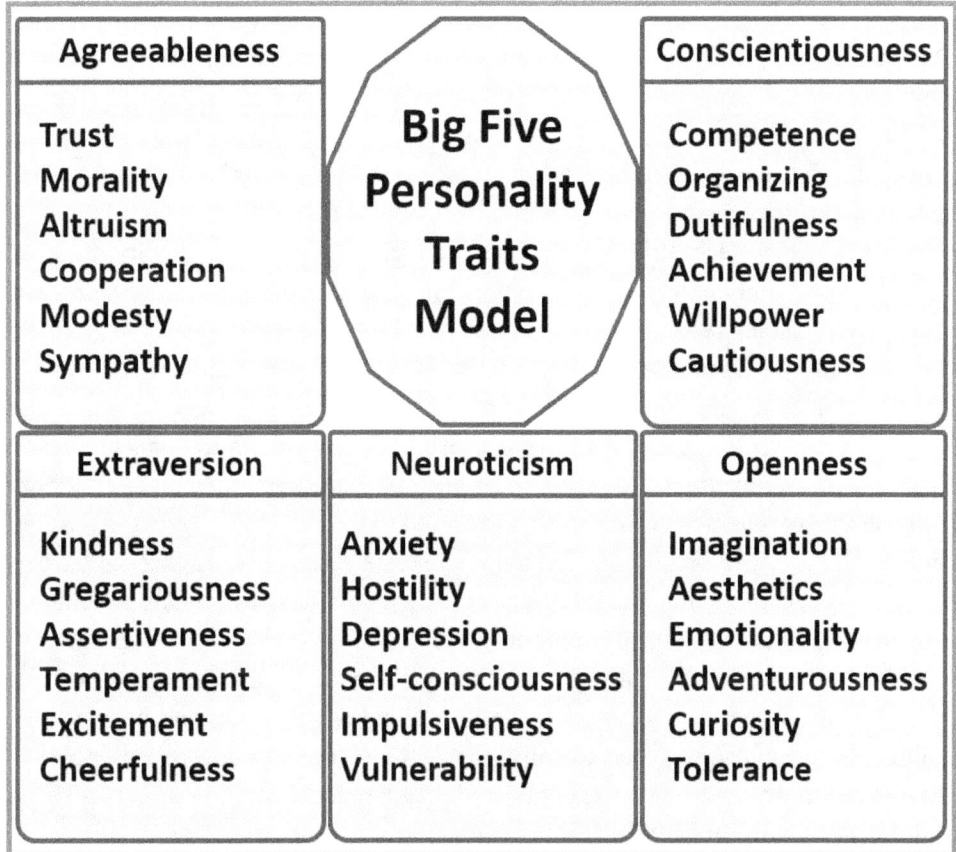

Figure 5 – Big Five Personality Trait Model with Facets

RELEVANCE TO YOU: Allport and Odbert suggested that we are all driven by the attitudes, habits, and sentiments embodied in our personality traits (Allport & Odbert, Trait Names: A Psycho-Lexical Study, 1936). An understanding of personality is a vital asset which helps you interact with people. Gordon Allport pioneered a systematic understanding of personality traits (Allport G. W., Personality: A Psychological Interpretation, 1937). The personality makeup of a person underpins their motivations and approach to life. Personality traits shape their sense of adventurousness, confidence, organization, security, and sociability. These traits guide their approach to their loves, desires, and drives. You can connect to someone if you get a sense of their personality characteristics. This understanding lets you to find common ground with someone. You can accommodate differences once you are sensitive to them.

Consider the big five traits. If a person is low on openness, ascertain their comfort zone and stay within it at first. Suggesting adventurous activities outside of their comfort zone, such as skydiving, will only alienate them. If someone is an introvert, do not drag them to a 20,000-person convention; instead, suggest a private affair. If you need to work with a person who is disagreeable, they may seem cold and uncooperative by your affable standards. However, if you realize that is part of their personality, you can start with a transactional style. Focus on business first and pleasantries later. If a person has a neurotic personality, they are prone to worry and anxiety. They may need reassurance from you to remain calm in the face of adversity.

Many professionals depend on a knowledge of personality traits. Skillful nurses and doctors have an innate sense of personality characteristics. It is part and parcel of their work. An effective bedside manner allows them to connect to their patients. Another example are writers who need to understand personality traits to craft believable characters and draft memorable stories. Movie directors use an understanding of personality and behavior to create realistic movie scenes. Actors can portray people with vastly different personality traits. Detectives employ personality psychology when questioning subjects. Investigators can connect with people to further their analysis. Psychologists and counselors need a deep understanding of personality traits in order to diagnose, connect and help people. Politicians and managers need to rally people. A comprehension of this periodic idea is vital to that end. At work, home, and play, an understanding of personalities traits will help you connect, collaborate, and motivate people.

Chapter 59 – PROPINQUITY EFFECT

DESCRIPTION: The American Psychological Association (APA) defines the propinquity effect as the tendency of individuals to form close relationships with people they repeatedly encounter (American Psychological Association, 2020). The word propinquity derives from the Latin word *propinquitas* which means *nearness*. The more frequently a person encounters another person, the more likely they will form a friendship or romantic relationship with each other. For example, classmates, co-workers and neighbors often form friendships. In social psychology, the propinquity effect is one of the main factors that contributes to interpersonal attraction.

The propinquity effect can occur from *physical proximity*. For example, next-door neighbors. It can also apply to *psychological proximity*. For instance, people with similar political beliefs possess a higher propinquity than those whose beliefs widely differ. These social preferences are reflected in idioms such as "birds of a feather flock together".

The propinquity effect was first described in 1950 by Leon Festinger, Stanley Schachter, and Kurt Back when they tracked friendship formation in the residents of the Westgate Apartments at the Massachusetts Institute of Technology (Festinger, Schachter, & Back, 1950). They also described how *"functional distance*" can result in propinquity from *positional relationships* and features of architectural design. For example, residents near an elevator or stairs were more likely to make friends with people who live on other floors of the building. The function of stairs and elevators determined which people crossed paths most often.

A similar phenomenon to the propinquity effect is the *mere-exposure effect*. The APA defines this as an increased preference for a stimulus or something consequent to repeated exposure to that stimulus or thing (American Psychological Association, 2020). The mere-exposure effect was described in 1968 by Robert B. Zajonc (Zajonc, 1968).This effect is likely to occur when there is no preexisting negative attitude toward the stimulus; and it is strongest when the person is not consciously aware of the contact.

For example, the Mona Lisa painting was elevated from obscurity to fame by the mere-exposure effect through its theft from the Louvre in 1911 (Sassoon, 2009). When Vincenzo Peruggia stole the Mona Lisa, it fueled the mere-exposure effect because the theft became a media circus inspiring many cartoons, parodies, postcards and songs. The two-year police investigation helped the Mona Lisa become one of the best-known artworks in the world.

NOTABLE WORK: Social Pressures in Informal Groups – A Study of Human Factors in Housing (Festinger, Schachter, & Back, 1950)
PERSON: Leon Festinger, Stanley Schachter, and Kurt Back
SYMBOL: PE. Interacting neighbors represent this periodic idea.
DATE: 1950
STORY: The propinquity effect will cultivate new friendships from people in your community, from your activities, work, or school. These relationships often arise from repeated contact with someone. In December 8, 2017, the New York Times ran an upbeat article about the development of an unusual friendship that formed between Spencer Sleyon and Rosalind Guttman (Proulx, 2017). Spencer was a 22-year old rapper from East Harlem, New York City and Rosalind a white woman who lived in a retirement community in Palm Beach, Florida. They were separated by 1,200 miles (1,900 km). They met through an online game called *Words with Friends*. Sleyon flew to Florida to meet Rosalind which garnered a positive reaction from social media. People appreciate that friendships can form despite demographic and geographic boundaries. The development of virtual reality, augmented reality, online communities, and social media technologies have allowed people to smash through the typical barriers to forming new friendships. Sleyon and Rosalind nurtured a friendship sparked by the propinquity effect.

RELEVANCE TO YOU: The propinquity effect and the mere-exposure effect suggest that we should cultivate relationships through increased contact with people. People are naturally social. We care about the things that we encounter frequently. We struggle to be concerned with someone you have never met, or a distant thing. Someone half-way around the world is less meaningful to you than your next-door neighbor. The exception is social media, tele-presence, and video telephony which reel a distant person into close proximity. We are all limited by time, with only the capacity to cultivate a limited number of relationships. The propinquity effect increases the relevance of something to you through repeated exposure. In this case, *familiarity breeds affinity*.

Many professionals employ the propinquity effect. For example, marketers know that frequent exposure to a brand endears you to it. Hence, retailers use promotions. Promotions get you to walk into their store. Thus, familiarizing yourself with the retailer. This exposure creates an opportunity to form a relationship with a potential customer. Politicians on the campaign trail drum up support through repeated exposure and advertisements. Marketing, commercials, and advertisements rachet up the mere exposure effect for a brand, store, or product. Salesmen reach out to clients in these different ways to create a sense of personal attention and support. This amplifies the propinquity effect in the minds of prospective clients. A psychologist gains the trust of their patients through regular sessions and active listening. A teacher who actively engages their students and provides support reaps the benefits of the propinquity effect.

How can you put the propinquity effect to work for you? Social networking can propel to you to success. The social webs that people form enrich their lives. These connections serve as the cornerstone to a happy and productive life. Often, it is not what you know, but *who* you know. People with the right contacts at an opportune moment forge their destiny. The propinquity effect develops your relationships with clients, customers, associates, and co-workers. It expands your social network. Repeated contact promotes a mere acquaintance to a friend.

There are many avenues to bump into people: through business transactions, conventions, meetings, and social gatherings. Modern technology also offers online and virtual opportunities to nurture the propinquity effect. Some examples include chat rooms, social media, virtual gaming, and online meeting applications such as Zoom. The propinquity effect creates the opportunity to develop a connection to someone. In modern society, we all need to connect with people; we depend on people. You must seize the opportunity to cultivate a budding relationship. You never know what doors a new friendship will open.

    The propinquity effect can expand a social network. Repeated exposure to a person presents a chance to connect. People who spent time with each other are naturally drawn together; it is human nature. I have over 600 friends in my social media network on Facebook. When I look through my friends list, I can attribute most of them to the propinquity effect. I met them through frequent contact in grade school, college, activities, work, or in my community.

Chapter 60 – FIELD THEORY

DESCRIPTION: The American Psychological Association defines field theory as an approach describing behavior through relationships between individuals and their psychological circumstances, social situation, and physical surroundings. That environment is known as the *field space*, or *life space*, and the interactions are forces with positive or negative valences (American Psychological Association, 2020). The idea of Field Theory was developed by Kurt Lewin in 1951 (Lewin, Field Theory of Social Science: Selected Theoretical Papers, 1951). Field theory asserts that behavior is a product of an individual interacting with their environment. The *life space* are the things in the environment that influence a person. There are helpful forces which assist people in reaching their objectives and hindering forces which impede progress. Lewin drew upon the concept of a field in physics in formulating field theory for psychology.

Lewin formulated a model of change management in a three-stage process (Lewin, Frontiers in Group Dynamics: Concept, Method and Reality in Social Science; Social Equilibria and Social Change, 1947). The first stage is called *unfreezing*, which involves dismantling an existing mind set and routines. Unfreezing is facilitated with a guiding vision and good communication. You should identify the urgency and need for change. The second stage is the *transformation*, where the actual transition to the new pattern occurs. In this stage, people relinquish familiar routines to adopt new skills. Replacing ineffective beliefs requires seeking new values. The final stage is called *freezing*, where the new practices and behaviors adopted during the transition are locked in. The new mindset becomes engrained. People internalize the new mindset. During the freezing stage, new practices are tested which will either reinforce the change or start a new change cycle. Today, this three-step process is the basic model for making change in organizations.

Lawrence Blair and Lyall Watson in the 1970s described the hundredth monkey effect in the book *Lifetide* (Watson L., 1979). Scientists studied macaque monkeys on the Japanese island of Koshima in 1952. They observed groups of monkeys learning a new behavior and how that new skill spread through the monkey population through observation and repetition (Amundson, 1985). Researchers concluded that once a critical number of monkeys were reached, the hundredth monkey, the newly learned behavior would quickly spread through the rest of the population. New ideas go viral with a critical mass of devotees.

NOTABLE WORK: Field Theory of Social Science: Selected Theoretical Papers (Lewin, Field Theory of Social Science: Selected Theoretical Papers, 1951)
PERSON: Kurt Lewin
SYMBOL: FT. A person stepping out into the world symbolizes this idea.
DATE: 1951
STORY: Many innovations have revolutionized project management. These ideas include benefits realization management, critical chain management, earned value management, iterative management, lean project management, and process-based management (Kozak-Holland, 2011). Each of these brought strategic advantages to their innovating organizations. Transitioning to these new processes required changes in mindset, and organizational culture. Groups that adopted these new techniques gained a competitive advantage in the marketplace. Many organizations used the three-stage change management process proposed by Lewin to make the transition.

For example, the Kanban lean project management of Toyota propelled it from a small company to one of the largest automakers in the world (Holweg, 2007). It was created by Taiichi Ohno to improve efficiency with just in time manufacturing. The concept was to identify the activities which add value and those which do not. Value-adding activities were encouraged. Activities that did not add value were eliminated. Taiichi Ohno identified seven forms of waste (Holweg, 2007).

In 2005, David Anderson, working at Microsoft, adapted Toyota's Kanban concept to software management. He socialized the idea through talks and his Kanban book (Anderson D. J., 2005). Eventually, agile software development became one of the most widely used methods for managing software projects (Denning, 2018).

RELEVANCE TO YOU: The most successful people and organizations learn to adapt to changing environments and circumstances. Field theory asserts that individuals affect their environment, and their environment influences them. Consider some life milestones: primary schooling, university, leaving home, getting married, working, having children, and retirement. One constant in life is change. Change management fosters the mindset and behaviors needed to transition from one stage of life to a new one.

Many environmental forces influence us to change including natural, political, social, and technological events. For example, the COVID-SARS-2 (COVID-19) pandemic of 2019-2021 caused people to social distance for health purposes. Stay-in-place isolation caused people to engage in new practices to cope.

New technologies cause us to change our behavior. Home appliances revolutionized chores. Smart phones have transformed the way we access information. Social media has revolutionized the way people interact. Video streaming and sharing have altered the way we consume news, learn, and entertain ourselves. Technology affects that way we connect to society, collaborate with others, and socialize.

People settle into beliefs, routines and habits. However, as we open each new chapter in our lives, we need to adapt to our new environment. Each chapter has a new story to tell with new actors, challenges, and plot twists. The practices and behaviors that worked for us as children need to transform as we enter adulthood. In organizations, the processes that worked well previously need to adapt to new changes in markets, society, and technology.

The Lewin three-stage process efficiently creates personal change. The first stage is *unfreezing* your former mindset; then applying the *transformation*, and lastly *freezing* into the new process. In the *unfreezing* stage, you will need to leave your comfort zone. In this stage, you will unravel your existing practices which paves the way for change. To escape an old mind set, you need to recognize and acknowledge that change is necessary. For example, if you want to alter a bad habit, find a reason why the change is good. Suppose you are over-weight and you would like to shed a few pounds. Picturing the resultant health benefits motivates the change. Changing customer demands, new competitors, shifting markets, and technological advancements require people to adapt to new situations. Next, in the *transformation* stage you will develop and adopt new processes. Organizations change their culture through leadership and perseverance. Leaders inspire people through a compelling vision which motivates change. The last stage is the *freezing* stage. The new processes are drilled until it becomes engrained into the culture. As people exercise the new methods, they reap the benefits which reinforces the new behaviors. You need to regularly practice new behaviors until they become routine. For example, if you want to implement a new diet, or adopt an exercise regimen you need to regularly train until it becomes second nature to you. If something did not work well, it may trigger a new change cycle. Groups, individuals, and families can use Kurt Lewin's three-stage process of change management to adapt to new environments.

Chapter 61 – SOCIAL PSYCHOLOGY

DESCRIPTION: Gordon W. Allport defined social psychology as the study of how the thoughts, feelings, and actions of individuals are affected by the actual, imagined, or implied presence of other people (Fiske, Gilbert, & Lindzey, Handbook of Social Psychology, 2010). Social psychology encompasses the study of attitudes, persuasion, social cognition, social influence, group dynamics and interpersonal attraction (American Psychological Association, 2020).

Attitudes are expressions of approval, disapproval, or favorability. Robert Cialdini defined six *persuasion* principles: authority, consensus, consistency, likeness, reciprocity, and scarcity (Cialdini, 2006). These principles speak to our sense of excellence, community, commitment, respect, cooperation, and preservation respectively. *Authority* figures convince people through facts and reasoning. *Consensus* nudges people to observe the behaviors of others to guide their own actions. *Consistency* suggests that accepting small voluntary commitments lead to larger pledges. The *likeness* factor suggests that we are influenced by people we like. *Reciprocity* is returning a gift or favor. *Scarcity* sparks interest if people perceive something is restricted or limited (Cialdini, 2006). Persuasion principles motivate people towards an objective. It is central to many disciplines including advertising, diplomacy, marketing, and public relations.

Social cognition is the perception, interpretation, and judgment of social interactions (American Psychological Association, 2020). It encompasses many concepts including automaticity, base rate fallacies, confirmation bias, memory schemas, priming, representative heuristics, primacy and recency (Fiske & Taylor, Social Cognition: From Brains to Culture, 1991). It is now the mainstream approach to social psychology. Social cognition investigates what people find memorable in social interactions.

Social influence is how people affect each other. People are influenced through social institutions, such as organized religion and political parties. These alter our attitudes, behavior, beliefs, and values (Aronson, 1972). Social influence also occurs through interactions with friends, family, and acquaintances. Socialization is the process by which we are inducted into a culture or society. The language we speak, our beliefs, and behavior are the product of social influencers (Aronson, 1972). Robert Cialdini explains that we internalize habits from reflexive, automated behaviors that are responses to conditioned stimuli (Cialdini, 2006). People react automatically and unconsciously to social stimuli.

Group dynamics arise from interactions within social groups and between social groups. These are called intragroup and intergroup dynamics. Kurt Lewin coined the term group dynamics (Lewin, Frontiers in Group Dynamics: Concept, Method and Reality in Social Science; Social Equilibria and Social Change, 1947). Group dynamics looks at collective decision making and how the group adopts new ideas. It is vital in comprehending social prejudice and discrimination (Forsyth, 2013). Community structures, language, and custom emerge from the interaction of individuals in a group. The whole is greater than the sum of the parts. The three factors that affect group cohesion are environmental, personal and leadership (Forsyth, 2013).

Interpersonal attraction are factors that cause people to establish relationships including romantic relationships. The factors that spark attraction are complementarity, familiarity, physical appeal, propinquity, reciprocal liking, reinforcement, and similarity. *Complementarity* allows people to find strength in diversity (Fiske A. P., 2000). People with different talents and interests can complement each other. *Familiarity*, the propinquity effect, and *reinforcement* increase attraction through frequency of encounters (Festinger, Schachter, & Back, 1950). *Reciprocal liking* causes people to appreciate those who like them (Montoya & Insko, Toward a More Complete Understanding of the Reciprocity of Liking Effect, 2008). Physical, social, cultural, and attitudinal *similarity* strengthens interpersonal attraction (Montoya & Horton, A meta-analytic investigation of the processes underlying the similarity-attraction effect, 2012).

Social psychology was pioneered by many luminaries. Kurt Lewin is the father of social psychology (Lewin, Field Theory of Social Science: Selected Theoretical Papers, 1951). Solomon Asch (Asch, 1951) and Erving Goffman (Goffman, 1959) created theories about conformity and cultural norms. In the 1960s, Melvin Lerner studied victim mentality and social justice (Lerner & Simmons, 1966). Stanley Milgram (Milgram, 1963) and Philip Zimbardo (Zimbardo, Haney, Banks, & Jaffe, 1972) performed authority figure experiments. Social psychologists have influenced other disciplines including anthropology, economics, politics, and sociology.

NOTABLE WORK: Field Theory of Social Science: Selected Theoretical Papers (Lewin, Field Theory of Social Science: Selected Theoretical Papers, 1951)
PERSON: Kurt Lewin
SYMBOL: SP. Two people facing each other, each with the cogs of their mind turning due to the presence of the other symbolizes this idea.
DATE: 1951
STORY: There have been many famous social psychology experiments. In 1951, Solomon Asch performed what are now called the conformity experiments (Asch, 1951). These studies demonstrated the power of conformity in small groups. Participants were asked to estimate the length of a line printed on a card which was a trivial task. The participants were nestled among actors purposely spouting incorrect answers. Consequentially, in 37% of the trials, participants conformed to the majority even though they were clearly wrong. Asch performed subsequent studies varying the number of actors and responses. His experiments illustrate the bandwagon effect which is a phenomenon where people adopt ideas to conform to the majority.

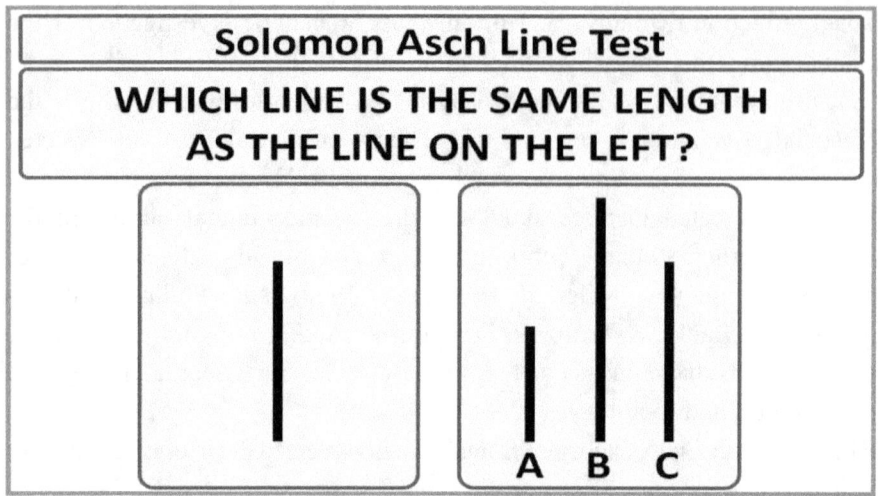

Figure 6 – The Solomon Asch Line Test Conformity Experiment

Stanley Milgram performed a famous experiment in 1961. He wanted to know how far people would go to obey an authority figure that conflicted with their personal conscience (Milgram, 1963). An experimenter commanded a participant to give what they thought were painful electric shocks to an actor. The actor was a confederate of the experimenter. Most participants continued to administer shocks to the actor despite their pleas for mercy. The fake electric shocks would have been lethal had they been real. The study showed that most people in a modern society are conditioned to obey an authority figure.

In 1971, Philip G. Zimbardo conceived of the Stanford prison experiment. 24 students were assigned to be either prisoners or guards (Zimbardo, Haney, Banks, & Jaffe, 1972). It was designed to study the psychological effects of perceived power. Zimbardo wanted to know whether the disposition of guards or the prison environment sparks social tension. Within a few days, the students who took on the role of guards became cruel, and the prisoners were miserable. Guards enforced authoritarian rules and subjected prisoners to psychological torture. The Zimbardo experiment was recreated in 2002 in a BBC documentary series where 15 men were randomly selected to be either a prisoner or guard. The eight-day experiment simulated a prison. This is now known as the BBC prison study.

RELEVANCE TO YOU: Social psychology lets you navigate tricky and turbulent social waters. It allows you to comprehend attitudes, group dynamics, persuasion, interpersonal attraction, social cognition, and social influencers. Social psychology topics are intimate and relevant to everyone.

Attitudes are expressions of approval, disapproval, or favorability. Understanding attitudes helps you realize how people approach the world. You can navigate social encounters with a sense for attitudes.

Group dynamics refers to effects that arise from group interactions including group decision-making, group performance, and deindividuation. It can arise from interactions within social groups and between social groups. Learning about group dynamics will help you understand how decisions are made and how ideas are adopted by a crowd. Language, custom and religions emerge from the interaction of individuals in society. The whole is greater than the sum of the parts. Understanding group dynamics allows you to bring out the best in other people. The ideas in social psychology which nurture individual relationships also apply to an assembly. One person who excels at group dynamics can make the whole crew more cohesive and function efficiently.

Interpersonal attraction are factors that cause people to establish relationships including romantic relationships. Your mastery of interpersonal attraction develops relationships. Recall, the factors that foster attraction are complementarity, familiarity, physical appeal, propinquity, reciprocal liking, reinforcement, and similarity. *Complementarity* refers to how well others serve as a counterpart for your weaknesses (Fiske A. P., 2000). In long-term relationships, your talents that complement another person serves to strengthen the bond. *Familiarity, the propinquity* effect, and *reinforcement* increase attraction through frequency of interaction (Festinger, Schachter, & Back, 1950). To improve your relationships, spend time with people because our most valuable assets are time and attention. Thus, sharing these shows you care. *Reciprocal liking* causes people to be attracted to those who like them (Montoya & Insko, Toward a More Complete Understanding of the Reciprocity of Liking Effect, 2008). If you take the effort to appreciate others, they often reciprocate. Social, cultural, and attitudinal *similarity* strengthens interpersonal attraction (Montoya & Horton, A meta-analytic investigation of the processes underlying the similarity-attraction effect, 2012). To foster better rapport, identify common interests you have with others. Interpersonal attraction results in enhanced social cohesiveness.

Persuasion is the act of influencing people toward the adoption of an attitude, behavior, or idea. Recall, Robert Cialdini championed six persuasion principles: authority, consensus, consistency, likeness, reciprocity, and scarcity

(Cialdini, 2006). These principles speak to our sense of excellence, community, commitment, respect, cooperation, and preservation respectively. Your powers of persuasion can guide people to a conclusion, change their attitude, or call them into action.

Social cognition studies how people judge, perceive, and remember other people. To that end, people typically use heuristics and schemas. Social cognition helps you understand what people find memorable in social interactions. A grasp of social cognition allows you to make a lasting impression on a person or a group. Furthermore, being memorable cements lasting relationships.

Social influence is the persuasive effects that people have on each other. People are influenced through culture, organized religion, political parties, and social institutions. These alter our attitudes, behavior, beliefs, and values (Aronson, 1972). Social influence also occurs through interactions with your community family, and friends. As we travel, we display our culture. As we converse, we exhibit our political preferences. Heralds champion ideas and causes. People tend to react automatically to social stimuli. Try to observe when you are affected by social influencers. Learning how to win friends and influence people propels you along the road to success.

Chapter 62 – COGNITIVE PSYCHOLOGY

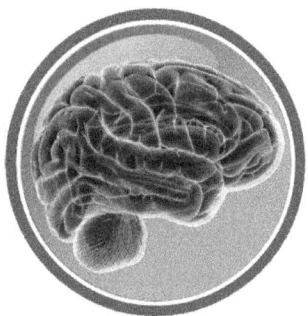

DESCRIPTION: Cognitive psychology is devoted to the study of mental processes including attention, creativity, language, memory, perception, and problem solving (American Psychological Association, 2020). It has been used in abnormal, educational, developmental, personality, and social psychology (Anderson J. , 2020). You have two *attention* systems. Exogenous control is reflexive; and endogenous control is deliberate. *Creativity* produces innovative, novel, original, and useful ideas. Cognitive psychology strives to understand how the mind processes *language*, acquires language and the components of language (Gibbs & Gerrig, 1988). Psychologists study short-term, working, long-term, procedural, semantic, and episodic *memory*. *Perception* is a cognitive process that understands the world through the interpretation of stimuli from our senses. Cognitive psychologists have made great strides in understanding the mental processes involved in attention, language, memory, and perception (Anderson J. , 2020). Guilford & Hoepfner determined that analysis, flexibility, mental fluency, originality, problem sensitivity, redefinition, and synthesis are characteristic of creativity (Guilford & Hoepfner, 1971).

The 1940s forged advances in computer sciences, communications systems, and information technology. This led to thinking about the brain as an information processor with cognitive processes (Anderson J. , 2020). In the 1950s, the cognitive psychology revolution superseded behaviorism which had focused only on observable behavior to draw conclusions. In 1960, George Armitage Miller and Jerome Bruner co-founded the Harvard Center for Cognitive Studies (Harvard University Department of Psychology, 2020).

The advent of cognitive psychology shifted the focus of study towards language, memory, and perception (Anderson J. , 2020). Jerome Bruner proposed that learning is a process. Learning occurs through active experience and participation. Bruner pioneered cognitive psychology with his landmark book, *A Study of Thinking* (Bruner, 1956). George Armitage Miller proposed that the mind has a working memory with limited capacity to hold approximately seven plus or minus two elements at a time (Miller, 1956). His work is one of the most frequently cited psychology papers. Miller created an information processing model of memory formation, and it is now referred to as "*Miller's law*". Herbert Simon asserted that the brain forgets irrelevant material in working memory to allow for more substantial information to accumulate (Simon, 1966). Robert Brown (Brown & Kulik, 1977) investigated *flashbulb memories* of shocking events.

NOTABLE WORK: Founding of Harvard Center for Cognitive Studies (Harvard University Department of Psychology, 2020)
PERSON: George Armitage Miller and Jerome Bruner
SYMBOL: CY. A picture of the human brain represents this periodic idea.
DATE: 1960
STORY: There are many interesting results from studies in cognitive psychology. In the 1950s, attention researchers studied air traffic controllers. Consequently, in 1953, Colin Cherry studied the ability to pick out one conversation amongst many and termed it *the cocktail party problem* (Cherry, 1953). In 1956, Donald Broadbent created the first study in attention where each ear is presented with different conversations (Broadbent, 1956). These are now called *dichotic listening tasks*. One famous attentional blindness experiment was performed by Daniel Simons and Christopher Chabris in 1999 at Harvard University (Simons & Chabris, 1999). Study participants were asked to count the number of ball passes between basketball players. As they focused on counting passes, participants failed to notice an actor in a gorilla suit strutting across the court.

Harry McGurk and John MacDonald demonstrated a speech perceptual phenomenon with an interaction between hearing and vision (McGurk & MacDonald, 1976). The illusion occurs when one speech sound is paired with the visual display of different sound. This results in perception of a third speech sound. Because the brain integrates sensory information, it alters what it hears based on what it sees. For example, a video of an actor saying, "bah" repeatedly is altered visually with them mouthing "gah". This will alter what you hear. However, if you close your eyes you will hear the actual sound "bah". This is now called the *McGurk effect*.

There are a few landmark memory studies. One experiment by Hermann Ebbinghaus demonstrated the primacy and recency effect (Ebbinghaus, 1913). This illustrates the *serial position effect* where information at the beginning and end of a list is better recalled than elements in the middle of the list. In different study, Lloyd and Margaret Peterson showed that short-term memory only lasts from 15 to 30 seconds (Peterson & Peterson, 1959). The Petersons performed an experiment where participants tried to recall three-letter strings. Another famous memory study was performed by Elizabeth Loftus and John Palmer, at the University of California in 1974. They showed how the use of verbs to describe a car crash can alter the memories of the accident (Loftus & Palmer, 1974).

RELEVANCE TO YOU: Psychology topics were selected for the periodic table of ideas because they are likely to be relevant to you. Cognitive psychology is a broad field with many interesting areas of study including attention, creativity, language, memory, perception, and problem solving (Anderson J., 2020).

Once you are aware of attentional blindness (Simons & Chabris, 1999), you can choose to widen your attention focus or choose to intentionally block out external stimuli. The cocktail party problem and *dichotic listening tasks* are tests designed to discover the limit of your ability to process information simultaneously. You should discover these limits for yourself. What is your ability to multi-task? Can you watch a movie while you read a book? Have you been at a party and try to listen to multiple conversations at the same time? I have found, with practice, I can listen to multiple conversations at the same time. On April 1, 2020, I had to attend two conference calls simultaneously. I was hosting one call while presenting on another call! You may not know what you are capable of until you try.

The serial position effect illustrates the idea of recency and primacy. The effect suggests that you are more likely to remember information at the start and end of a study session. Armed with that knowledge, you can improve your ability to learn. You can take breaks to create mental sprint sessions instead of running marathon cram sessions.

Short-term memory fades information unless it is refreshed. When you learn something vital, you should periodically review that data to reinforce it in your memory. Take good notes and review them weekly. Eventually that knowledge transfers to your long-term memory. Elizabeth Loftus and John Palmer demonstrated that the choice of verbs can affect your perception of an event, and even alter your memory of it (Loftus & Palmer, 1974). With this foreknowledge, you can dodge some of the effects of mind-altering verbs.

George Miller discovered "*Miller's Law*", that we have a working memory of seven plus or minus two items (Miller, 1956). To exploit this law, you can group information with memory retention techniques to better recall it. One method is the memory palace technique, also known as the method of loci (Yates, 1966). You imagine walking through a familiar building with distinct loci. To remember a set of items, you associate one item with one location. To recall the items, you stroll through the locations again and imagine the associations you made. For example, three locations in your home might be your kitchen, bedroom, and bathroom. To memorize grocery list items, you might associate bread with the kitchen location, apples with the bedroom, and milk with the bathroom.

If you dig, cognitive psychology offers many interesting nuggets of mental gold. With it you can improve your attention span, language aptitude, memory recall, observation skills, and critical thinking. For a systematic development of your thinking, you can read my book, *the Four Elements of Thinking* (Cheung, The Four Elements of Thinking, 2019).

Chapter 63 – PSYCHOLOGY PERSONAL RELEVANCE

This chapter collects and summarizes the personal relevance of the psychology periodic ideas. Among the periodic ideas, the psychology ideas are some of the most intimate and personal. *Personality traits* are a combination of qualities that characterize an individual. The *propinquity effect* asserts that people tend to form relationships with people that they encounter frequently. *Field theory* states that our behavior is a product of the individual interacting with their environment. *Social psychology* draws conclusions about human interactions including attitudes, group dynamics, interpersonal attraction, persuasion, social cognition, and social influence. *Cognitive psychology* studies mental processes including attention, creativity, language, memory, perception, and problem solving. Each of these dimensions of psychology are consequential and personal. The following table summarizes the personal relevance of psychology periodic ideas.

PSYCHOLOGY IDEA	ID	PERSONAL RELEVANCE
PERSONALITY TRAITS 1937	PT	Personality traits allows you to assess the motivations, drives, and desires of someone. People are driven by the habits, needs, and attitudes embodied in their personality traits. Thus, an understanding of personalities traits helps you collaborate, connect, and motivate people.
PROPINQUITY EFFECT 1950	PE	The propinquity effect cultivates relationships through frequent contact. You can take advantage of this effect through social networking. You can nurture relations by physical, psychological, or functional proximity. The *mere-exposure effect* is a preference for something resulting from repeated exposure. Armed with that knowledge, you can navigate through life better.
FIELD THEORY 1951	FT	Field theory suggests that we need to learn to adapt to changing environments and circumstances. Each new chapter you open in your life presents new actors, challenges, and plot twists. You can make changes through the Lewin three-stage process. First, *unfreeze* your mindset; next, *transform*; and then *freeze* into your new practice.
SOCIAL PSYCHOLOGY 1951	SP	Social psychology improves your social interaction skills. Your mastery of attitudes, group dynamics, interpersonal attraction, persuasion, social cognition, and social influence allows you to build rapport and create synergy with others.
COGNITIVE PSYCHOLOGY 1960	CY	With cognitive psychology, you can improve your attention span, creativity, critical thinking, language aptitude, memory recall, observation skills, and problem-solving competency. Awareness of the conclusions from cognitive psychology research can improve your mental aptitude. These include attentional blindness, dichotic listening tasks, the *McGurk effect*, *Miller's law*, and the serial position effect.

Table 18 – Periodic Psychology Ideas

Part VIII – CONCLUSION

Chapter 64 – CROSS FERTILIZATION & CREATIVITY

The periodic table of ideas span six disciplines: philosophy, science, technology, economics, business and psychology. They are grouped vertically on the periodic table of ideas into these six domains. The philosophy, science, technology, economics, psychology, business periodic ideas are color-coded with blue, red, orange, green, brown and yellow respectively. They are periodic because they show up repeatedly throughout history. You will discover that the periodic ideas have personal relevance in many situations. Whether you are trying to solve a problem, investigate a subject, or develop an idea, these concepts can assist. No matter what phase of a project you are working in, these ideas can provide inspiration and guidance.

The individual chapters on the periodic ideas each described how they might be of use to you. This chapter explains how the periodic ideas can work together. The periodic ideas can combine in different ways. For example, Artificial Intelligence can cross fertilize with other periodic ideas. Some examples include AI powered robots, cognitive networking, intelligent computation, intelligent personal assistants, smart communications, smart prototyping, smart social media, self-driving cars, and smart VR worlds. The periodic ideas also synergize within a domain. Atomic ideas combine to form molecular concepts with new characteristics. Concepts in the periodic table of ideas combine to form hybrids with emergent properties.

The periodic table of ideas are organized by domain. However, for your purposes, you may wish to group the ideas clustered by function. They could be grouped into the following functional categories: individual self-actualization, group dynamics concepts, mental tools and practical tools. In this kind of grouping, the periodic ideas work together across disciplines. The following diagram shows the periodic ideas arranged with these alternate groupings:

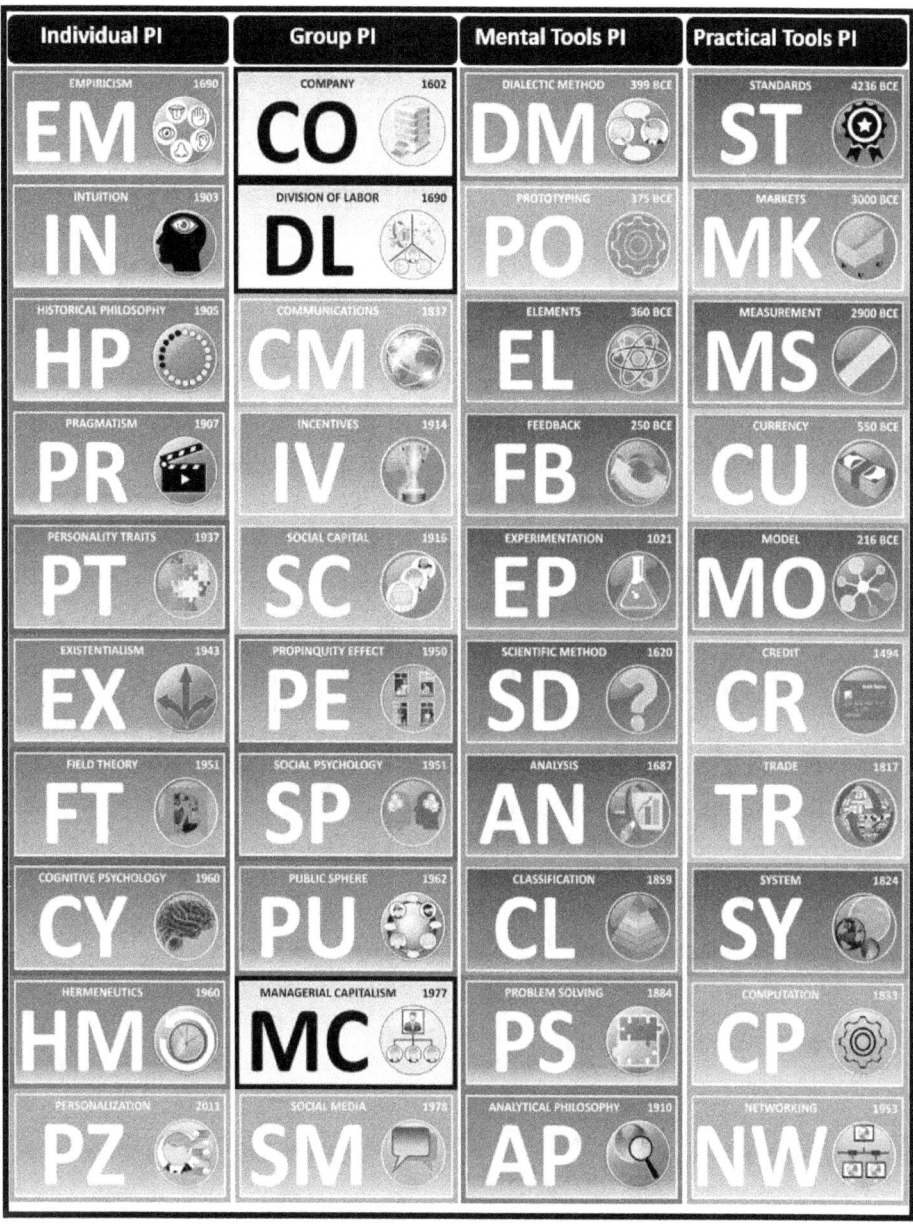

Figure 7 – Periodic Ideas Grouped by Function

The following table summarizes the alternate grouping of the periodic ideas reflected in the above diagram. Note: not all the periodic ideas neatly fit into one of these four categories and have been excluded from the above table.

FUNCTIONAL GROUPING	PERIODIC IDEAS
INDIVIDUAL PERIODIC IDEAS	Individual Periodic Ideas pertain to personal success and individual self-actualization. These include the periodic ideas of cognitive psychology, empiricism, existentialism, field theory, hermeneutics, historical philosophy, intuition, personality traits, personalization, and pragmatism.
GROUP PERIODIC IDEAS	Group Periodic Ideas relate to group interaction and group dynamics. These include the periodic ideas of communications, company, division of labor, incentives, managerial capitalism, propinquity effect, public sphere, social capital, social media, and social psychology.
MENTAL TOOLS PERIODIC IDEAS	Mental Tools Periodic Ideas are concepts that assist in critical thinking. These include the periodic ideas of analytical philosophy, analytics, classification, dialectic method, elements, experimentation, feedback, problem solving, prototyping, and scientific method.
PRACTICAL TOOLS PERIODIC IDEAS	Practical Tools Periodic Ideas provide practices and pragmatic ideas to make progress on projects. These include the periodic ideas of credit, computation, currency, markets, measurement, model, networking, standards, system, and trade. These applied concepts are useful throughout the life of a project.

Table 19 – Functional Grouping of Periodic Ideas

Individual Periodic Ideas pertain to personal success and individual self-actualization. While all the periodic ideas can be personally relevant, these ideas are, by their nature, focused on individuals. Most of the individual periodic ideas are philosophical and psychological because these disciplines explore the human psyche and human condition. Many philosophical inquiries relate to how an individual interacts with the world. Furthermore, there are entire areas of psychology devoted to the study of personality, and cognitive capabilities of your mind.

Group Periodic Ideas relate to group interaction and group dynamics. If you belong to a group, these ideas will benefit you. Groups are integral to communities, enterprises, families, and societies. The group periodic ideas span all the disciplines. In economics, *incentives* and *social capital* describe how groups can function efficiently. In philosophy, the *public sphere* is where a group discusses societal problems and inspire political action. In technology, *communications* and *social media* facilitate group interaction. In psychology, the *propinquity effect* is a means to form connections. *Social psychology* studies group interaction with group dynamics, interpersonal attraction, social cognition, and social influence. In business, the periodic ideas of the *company*, *division of labor* and *managerial capitalism* detail how groups in an enterprise can operate efficiently.

Mental Tools periodic ideas are concepts that relate to thinking. These periodic ideas will assist with critical thinking during a project. The *scientific method* is a systematic process of investigation. The scientific tools of *analysis* and *experimentation* allow you to gather and evaluate data. The scientific ideas of *classification*, *elements* and *feedback* are ways to think about the subject. *Analytical philosophy* encompasses the thinking methods of formal logic, conceptual analysis, deduction, and induction. The *dialectic method* is a dialogue-based process to encourage critical thinking. Practical *problem solving* provides a seven-step method to tackle a problem. In technology, *prototyping* is a means by which you can learn more about a concept.

Carlo Rovelli, a theoretical physicist, suggests that conceptual thinking complements practical activities. Philosophers have mental tools that engineers, and physicists need. These include accuracy of expression, attention to ambiguity, conceptual analysis, detecting flaws in arguments, devising new perspectives, seeking alternative theoretical explanations, and spotting conceptual weak points (Rovelli, 2018).

Practical Tools periodic ideas help you make progress on your projects. In economics, the periodic ideas of *credit* and *currency* provide a financial basis for your project. The economic ideas of *market* and *trade* suggest where and how your ideas will thrive. The scientific periodic ideas of *measurement*, *model*, and *standards* are practical concepts that unify your project. A *system* defines a group of interdependent elements that form a greater whole. The technology periodic idea of *computation* facilitates the analysis of your problems. *Networking* allows project elements to share and collaborate. These ideas are pragmatic and useful throughout the life of a project.

To practice using the periodic ideas, break down a big project into smaller tasks. Next, determine what resources, knowledge and time that tasks need. Then, try to apply the periodic ideas. When working alone, you can utilize the individual periodic ideas. When working in a group, you can apply the group periodic ideas. When you analyze or experiment, the mental tools periodic ideas can assist. The practical tools ideas provide the means to turn your ideas into reality.

Often, the combination of periodic ideas will open your mind to new avenues of thought. These combinations will consciously get you to pair two concepts that you would not have otherwise considered. Take any two periodic ideas at random. Then consider how they might cross-fertilize. You can consider how two periodic ideas working together is meaningful to you. For example, *creative destruction* (economic) and *prototyping* (technology) might suggest you try a rapid prototype approach. Periodic ideas can often get you to approach a problem from a different perspective. For instance, considering a problem from both a psychological and technological aspect broadens your thinking. Arthur Koestler said ideas arise from combining perspectives and frames of reference (Koestler, 1964). For example, combining the *public sphere* idea (philosophy) with the *virtual reality* (technology) idea would produce a virtual immersive environment where people could congregate and hold public debates.

People can get stuck in a rut when tackling a problem. The periodic ideas can get you to think about problems from a new perspective, or domain. For example, while working on a project you might infuse the psychology periodic ideas to add a social dimension to the project. Thinking about a project in a new way helps you make progress. Suppose you want to use the *division of labor* business idea in your project to divide tasks. You combine that with the *communication* periodic idea to allow teams to correspond about project tasks. Combining periodic ideas coaxes you to think outside the box.

Chapter 65 – CONCLUSION

The periodic ideas have been faithful companions in pivotal human affairs. These concepts have echoed down through history. They represent the pinnacle of human thought and achievement. These notions are among the most ingenious and enduring you will encounter. The periodic ideas span the domains of philosophy, science, technology, economics, business, and psychology. These concepts have affected the lives of billions of people across many generations. People wielding them have wrought prosperity and forged progress.

As you become familiar with the periodic ideas, they will broaden your perspective and empower you. They can serve as a muse, providing inspiration for creativity. You will find that these concepts recur in current affairs, in historical events, and in your daily life. Now that you are aware of them, you can observe how they continue to shape the lives of individuals everywhere. You will find many applications for these ideas in your endeavors.

The periodic ideas also synergize with my previous book, *The Four Elements of Thinking* (Cheung, The Four Elements of Thinking, 2019). The elements of earth, air, fire, and water correspond to reasoning, creativity, evaluation and synthesis. In air thinking (creativity), the periodic ideas can serve as inspiration during the ideation phase to generate ideas. The periodic ideas find use in earth thinking (reasoning) for *evidence, deduction,* and *induction.* For water thinking (synthesis thinking), the periodic ideas will help in *linking* and *perspective.* Furthermore, each of the periodic ideas are *pivots.* Fire thinking represents evaluation. The periodic ideas play a role in *judgment* and *contingency planning.*

The philosophy periodic ideas can guide you on your journey in life. You define what is meaningful to you. By doing so, you manifest your destiny. This is the philosophy periodic idea of *Existentialism.* The Latin phrase *carpe deum* means to "seize the day". Through existentialism, you seize life, *carpe vitae.* Empiricism would have you go forth into the world to explore it with your senses to make headway in your endeavors. Philosophers have developed critical thinking tools such as *analytical philosophy, the dialectic method,* and *pragmatism* to aid in your thinking. Use these ideas as a mental beacon to light your way. The philosophy periodic idea of practical *problem solving* gives you a seven-step method to work through challenges. *Intuition* provides insights without conscious reasoning through instinctive understanding. *Historical Philosophy* states that progress builds upon the accomplishments of the past. Remember the past to forge your future. *Hermeneutics* suggests we are a product of our time; and we, in turn, define the times. The *Public Sphere* gets you to engage in public debate to identify societal problems. You decide what groups to join and public debates engage in. Through public debate, you can inspire social improvement. The philosophy periodic ideas provide guidance, wisdom, and mental tools for your endeavors.

The science periodic ideas are useful assistants while working on any project. Use *Modeling* to help you visualize and learn about a problem or subject. The five steps of the *Scientific Method* are: question formulation, hypothesis development, prediction, testing, and analysis. This method develops scientific knowledge and can help you explore any subject. Employ *Experiments* to make a discovery, test a hypothesis or determine the efficacy of an idea. The *Elements* idea decomposes a project into atomic parts. Then, you use those elements in combinations and permutations to reveal new avenues of thinking. *Classification* provides you with insights on how to categorize and organize information. *Standards* provides you with rules or guidelines as criterion to measure against. The *Systems* periodic idea helps you define and frame a project in its environment. A system is a group of interdependent elements that form a complex whole. The systems idea coaxes you to think holistically about the structure and function of a project. The *Analysis* periodic idea gives you the tools to process your collected data or evidence. *Feedback* gives you a mechanism to maintain performance or to control a system or process. The *Measurements* science periodic idea creates a uniform system of weights and measures to align people that need to work together. The science periodic ideas allow you study a subject, tackle a problem, or progress on a project.

The technology periodic ideas provide methods and tools for you to wield. These tools are down-to-earth and invaluable for use in your projects. Use the technology periodic idea of *Prototyping* to gain practical knowledge in developing an emerging project. The *Communication* and *Social Media* periodic ideas facilitate connecting with people and engaging the public sphere. *Virtual Reality* allows you to explore and visualize through a simulated environment. Artificial Intelligence offers smart applications that can assist in your endeavors. *Robotics* introduces assistants that can support your pursuits. *Transportation Technologies* are a means by which you can deliver or obtain resources for your projects. The *Personalization* technology periodic idea customizes something making it unique and distinctive. The technology periodic ideas present practical tools to assist in your endeavors.

The <u>economic periodic ideas</u> allow you to make an impact on society. The world works through *Markets*. Markets constantly evolve and reinvent themselves through *Creative Destruction*. Fledgling enterprises use the economic periodic ideas of *Credit* and *Currency* to get off the ground. *Diminishing Returns* helps you intelligently assign resources to a project. The first person tasked to a job is the most effective. As more resources are allocated a project, the productivity of additional resources is less efficient. *Economic Cycles* cause industries to wax and wane. Capitalize on opportunities in times of prosperity and prepare for recessions before they happen. To reach peak performance, use *Incentives* to motivate groups and individuals. *Marginal Utility* is the change in benefit from an increased consumption of a good or service. To avoid waste, assess how many resources you need for a project and launch with that. *Social Capital* are the factors of social cohesion that allow groups to function efficiently. Finding a shared vision and shared values develops interpersonal relationships. The *Trade* economic periodic idea uses barter or exchange to get resources you need for a project. Economic ideas are crucial to give your ideas a firm footing.

The <u>business periodic ideas</u> are the cogs in the machinery of society. *Companies* start with a concept that cater to a need or desire of the people in society. The idea of *Intellectual Capital* urges you to identify the intangible assets that give your life meaning and bring value to society. The idea of *Division of Labor* suggests you assign people to specialized tasks to best utilize their talents. *Managerial Capitalism* suggests that you seek professional assistance to guide parts of your project to success. The business idea of *Multi-Divisional Forms* asserts that you should divide your project into separate focus areas or divisions.

The <u>psychology periodic ideas</u> are personal and intimate. *Personality Traits* are qualities that characterize an individual. The values and qualities you nurture make you unique. The *Propinquity Effect* asserts that people form relationships with those they repeatedly encounter. Physical and psychological proximity cultivate friendships. *Field Theory* states that we influence our environment and our environment shapes us. You decide where you go. You catalyze your destiny by choosing your environment. *Social Psychology* improves your social interaction skills. You can build rapport by mastering group dynamics.

Your social circles foster your personal growth. *Cognitive Psychology* is devoted to the study of mental processes and can improve your mental aptitude.

The periodic ideas have stood the test of time. Each of them has made a significant impact in their discipline. These concepts are relevant to the lives of common people. As you familiarize yourself with them, you will find practical applications for them in your everyday activities. A maestro gains proficiency in his craft over a lifetime. Similarly, to master the periodic ideas requires practice and perseverance. As they become familiar, you will observe them in action everywhere.

The philosophy periodic ideas guide you through your journey in life. The scientific concepts empower your thinking. The technology ideas provide tools to propel your projects to success. The economic ideas give your projects a social and financial footing. The business concepts show you how enterprises can transform lives. The psychology periodic ideas give you a deep insight into yourself and those around you.

The periodic ideas can play a crucial role in turning ideas into reality. Your life should be a constant work in progress. Devote your life to worthy causes and you will inspire others. The best ideas start with a single thought. One person who sets off with a desire to change the world and make it a better place. If you want to make a difference in the world, why not build from the ideas of some of the most brilliant minds in history? The periodic ideas are enduring and pivotal. Let these ideas guide and inspire you as you embark on new adventures during this wonderful journey, we call life.

Part IX – Appendices

Appendix-1 – THE PERIODIC TABLE OF IDEAS

The following diagram shows the full periodic table of ideas

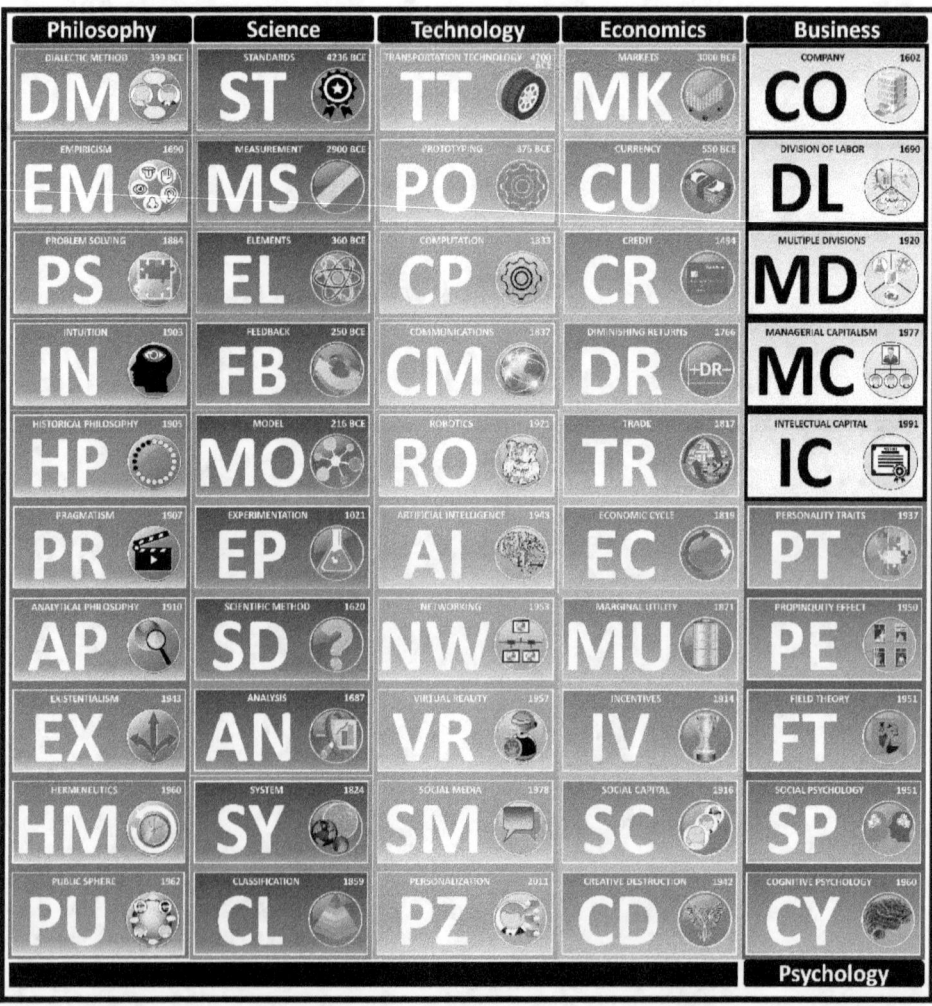

Figure 8 – The Periodic Table of Ideas (Appendix)

Appendix-2 – PHILOSOPHY PERIODIC IDEAS

The following table summarizes the periodic philosophy ideas.

PHILOSOPHY IDEA	ID	DESCRIPTION
DIALECTIC METHOD 399 BCE	DM	Socrates. The dialectic method is an exploratory process using dialogue to ask and answer questions, encourage critical thinking, coax out assumptions, and find contradictions to improve a hypothesis.
EMPIRICISM 1690	EM	John Locke. Empiricism states that knowledge primarily comes from our senses. Evidence discovered through experiments, sensory experience, observation, and experiment form the basis of our knowledge.
PROBLEM SOLVING 1884	PS	John Dewey. Problem solving is practical thinking with the aim of resolving a problem. The seven basic steps of problem solving are formulation, root causes, knowledge, ideation, selection, reasoning and evaluation.
INTUITION 1903	IN	Henri-Louis Bergson. Intuition is the ability to acquire knowledge without conscious reasoning. It includes the ability to access unconscious knowledge. Intuition includes insight, instinctive understanding, and unconscious cognition.
HISTORICAL PHILOSOPHY 1905	HP	George Santayana. Historical philosophy is a metaphysical naturalism stating that knowledge arises not just from pure reasoning but from the interaction of the mind and its environment. Progress builds upon the accomplishments of the past.

PHILOSOPHY IDEA	ID	DESCRIPTION
PRAGMATISM 1907	PR	William James. Pragmatism asserts that ideas have merit based on the practical consequences they have in everyday human experience. Knowledge is obtained through practical application of theory.
ANALYTICAL PHILOSOPHY 1910	AP	Bertrand Russell. Analytical philosophy encompasses formal logic, conceptual analysis, deduction and induction. The four steps of induction are pattern, hypothesis, experiment and theory. The four steps of deduction are theory, hypothesis, evidence and confirmation.
EXISTENTIALISM 1943	EX	Jean-Paul Sartre. Existentialism is the study of the human individual. Everyone can freely live life passionately and authentically by defining what will be significant and meaningful in their lives.
HERMENEUTICS 1960	HM	Hans-Georg Gadamer. Hermeneutics is the study of how humans interpret the world. We understand the world through interpretation. However, this interpretation is anchored to a historical era which creates biases and prejudices.
PUBLIC SPHERE 1962	PU	Jürgen Habermas. The public sphere is a place where people can congregate and freely discuss and identify societal problems. Through public debate in the public sphere, people inspire political action.

Table 20 – Periodic Philosophy Ideas (Appendix)

The following table summarizes the personal relevance of philosophy periodic ideas.

PHILOSOPHY IDEA	ID	PERSONAL RELEVANCE
DIALECTIC METHOD 399 BCE	DM	The dialectic method drives you to think critically, coax out assumptions, and find contradictions in a hypothesis. It inspires you to ask challenging open-ended questions as a basis to explore a subject.
EMPIRICISM 1690	EM	Empiricism encourages you to utilize your senses. It urges you to make first-hand observations and explore the world through sensory experiences. It gets you to hone your powers of observation.
PROBLEM SOLVING 1884	PS	Problem solving helps you methodically work through your problems in a seven-step approach. Practical problem solving allows you to intelligently conquer issues at work, home, community, and recreation.
INTUITION 1903	IN	Intuition allows you to acquire knowledge without conscious reasoning. Intuition causes you to make leaps of insight and arrive at an instinctive understanding that bypasses analytical reasoning. Intuition urges you to balance your hunches against rational thought.
HISTORICAL PHILOSOPHY 1905	HP	Historical philosophy spurs you to remember your mistakes and to avoid repeating them in the future. When you make mistakes and encounter failures, Historical philosophy encourages you to learn from them. Mistakes can be an effective teacher for you.
PRAGMATISM 1907	PR	Pragmatism advises you to consider how practical something is. It encourages you to live a practical life by using what works. Pragmatism urges you to take a hands-on approach to life's challenges.
ANALYTICAL PHILOSOPHY 1910	AP	Analytical philosophy helps you engage and develop your critical thinking. Its methods allow you to solve challenging problems.
EXISTENTIALISM 1943	EX	Existentialism inspires you to live life to its fullest by defining what is significant and meaningful to you.

PHILOSOPHY IDEA	ID	PERSONAL RELEVANCE
HERMENEUTICS 1960	HM	Hermeneutics gets you to consider how history, culture and historical context affect your reality filter. When you read historical texts, Hermeneutics helps you understand from the perspective of their traditions, prejudices and cultural norms. This helps you uncover your own biases, what Hans-Georg called a *"fusion of horizons"*.
PUBLIC SPHERE 1962	PU	The public sphere gets you to engage in public debate that aims to identify societal problems. Through public debate in the public sphere, you can inspire and influence social transformation. Social improvement begins with your ideas for social change.

Table 21 – Periodic Philosophy Ideas Personal Relevance (Appendix)

Appendix-3 – SCIENCE PERIODIC IDEAS

The following table summarizes the key Science Ideas.

SCIENCE IDEA	ID	DESCRIPTION
STANDARDS **4236 BCE**	ST	(Ancient Egyptians). Standards are a set of rules or guidelines established by an authority as a model, criterion, or measure. You can apply them as standards of assessment, conduct, criterion, instruction, or practices.
MEASUREMENT **2900 BCE**	MS	Khnum Khufu (Pharaoh). Measurement is the assignment of a number to a characteristic of an object or event. Researchers can then compare and analyze measurements. Metrology establishes a uniform system of weights and measures with fundamental units to link human activities.
ELEMENTS **360 BCE**	EL	Plato. Elements are the simplest chemical substances and are irreducible through chemical reactions. Elements can only be changed into other elements using nuclear methods. A *combination* merges two or more individual component elements. A *permutation* is a varied order or arrangement of a set of things.
FEEDBACK **250 BCE**	FB	Ktesibios of Alexandria. Feedback is defined as the return of a portion of the output of a process or system back to the input. Feedback is typically used to maintain performance or to control a system or process. Closed loop systems measure the output of a system and compare it to a desired target.

SCIENCE IDEA	ID	DESCRIPTION
MODEL **216 BCE**	MO	Aristarchus of Samos. Models in math and science make the world easier to understand through components based on existing knowledge. Models represent objects, phenomena, and processes in a simplified and objective way. Models simulate an observed phenomenon to facilitate understanding.
EXPERIMENT **1021**	EP	Ibn al-Haytham. Experiments are a scientific procedure undertaken to make a discovery, test a hypothesis, demonstrate a known fact, or determine the efficacy of an idea. It is a procedure under controlled conditions to verify, refute, or establish a hypothesis when trying to explain phenomenon.
SCIENTIFIC METHOD 1620	SD	Francis Bacon. The scientific method is a procedure consisting of systematic observation, measurement, and experiment. The five steps of the scientific method are question formulation, hypothesis development, prediction, testing, and analysis. These steps refine a hypothesis to explain natural phenomenon.
ANALYSIS **1687**	AN	Isaac Newton. Analysis is the processing of collected evidence and data to make sense of the information. Modern scientific evaluation is often accomplished through statistical analysis of data such as an Analysis of Variance (ANOVA) test.
SYSTEM **1824**	SY	Nicholas Carnot. A system is defined as a group of interacting, interrelated, or interdependent elements forming a complex whole. A system is also characterized by its structure, purpose, and function.
CLASSIFICATION **1859**	CL	Charles Darwin. In biology, classification is done with taxonomy which is the science of naming and classifying groups of organisms based on shared characteristics. Other systems of classification include phylogenetics, cladistics, systematics, economic taxonomy, and Bloom's taxonomy.

Table 22 – Periodic Science Ideas (Appendix)

The Periodic Table of Ideas

The following table summarizes the personal relevance of Science periodic Ideas.

SCIENCE IDEA	ID	PERSONAL RELEVANCE
STANDARDS **4236 BCE**	ST	Standards provides you with rules or guidelines as criterion to measure against. You can use them as standards of assessment, conduct, criterion, instruction, or practices. Standards of assessment allow you to test for outcomes.
MEASUREMENT **2900 BCE**	MS	Measurements allow you to synchronize with others to schedule meetings. It allows you to coordinate positionally to meet at a location. It establishes a uniform system of weights and measures aligning your tasks and activities with others.
ELEMENTS **360 BCE**	EL	Elements coaxes you to think about the atomic parts of your project. You can combine or permutate the elemental components of your project to unveil new avenues of thinking and exploration.
FEEDBACK **250 BCE**	FB	Feedback gives you a mechanism to maintain performance or to control a system or process. Through trial and error, feedback encourages you to learn from your mistakes. Social feedback allows group members to adjust behavior. Biological feedback gets you to listen to the signals that your body tries to tell you.
MODEL **216 BCE**	MO	Models assist in your ability to visualize and learn about a problem or project. You can use Models to represent phenomena and processes to aid in your understanding.
EXPERIMENT **1021**	EP	You can use experiments to make a discovery, test a hypothesis, demonstrate a known fact, or determine the efficacy of an idea. You can also use experimentation to test a claim or assertion.
SCIENTIFIC METHOD **1620**	SD	The five steps of the scientific method allow you to refine a hypothesis to explain phenomenon. This method is the basis of how scientific knowledge is developed and can help you think about any subject or problem.

SCIENCE IDEA	ID	PERSONAL RELEVANCE
ANALYSIS 1687	AN	Analysis gives you the tools to process your collected data from an experiment or project. Descriptive statistics characterizes data. Inferential statistics interprets data and draw conclusions. Analyses helps you make sense of gathered information by using statistical methods.
SYSTEM 1824	SY	A system is characterized by its environment, inputs, outputs, function, purpose and structure. Defining a system allows you to frame a problem in its environment. Delineating an interdependent complex whole allows you to analyze and work with the system.
CLASSIFICATION 1859	CL	Classification gives you insights on how to categorize and organize information. By identifying shared characteristics, you can organize information. Organized data can aid in comprehension or to plan a project.

Table 23 – Periodic Science Ideas Personal Relevance (Appendix)

Appendix-4 – TECHNOLOGY PERIODIC IDEAS

The following table summarizes the periodic technological ideas.

TECH IDEA	ID	DESCRIPTION
TRANSPORTATION TECHNOLOGY 4700 BCE	TT	Tepe Pardis. Transportation technologies use devices and systems to move people and cargo from an origin point to a destination. Its design factors include cargo, control, delivery, location, origin, positioning, speed, and steering. Transportation technologies include all types of vehicles from bicycles to spaceships.
PROTOTYPING 375 BCE	PO	Archytas. A prototype is an early model in advance of a release of a product created to test a concept. Prototyping allows designers to gain practical knowledge from an actual working system rather than a theoretical one.
COMPUTATION 1833	CP	Charles Babbage. A computer is a machine that can perform sequences of arithmetic, computational, or logical operations through a computer program. Computers control industrial and consumer devices assisting us in a wide variety of tasks.
COMMUNICATIONS 1837	CM	Sir William F. Cooke and Sir Charles Wheatstone. Communications technologies allow for a means of sending or receiving information at a distance. They are systems that can encode, store, retrieve, manipulate, transmit or receive information. The telegraph, telephone, cellular phone are examples of communication technologies.

TECH IDEA	ID	DESCRIPTION
ROBOTICS 1921	RO	Karel Capek. Robots are machines that can mimic human actions or substitute for humans in performing a task. Robots engage in walking, lifting, tasks, conversation, and cognition.
ARTIFICIAL INTELLIGENCE 1943	AI	Warren S. McCulloch and Walter H. Pitts, Jr. Artificial intelligence encompasses machines or computers that can perform cognitive functions often associated with the human mind, such as learning and problem solving.
NETWORKING 1953	NW	George Valley and Jay Forrester. Networking connects elements in a system together and brings them into contact with each other. It allows them to connect, share information, and operate together.
VIRTUAL REALITY 1957	VR	Morton Heilig. Virtual reality (VR) technologies create an immersive experience that can simulate the real world or an imaginary environment. Augmented reality (AR) is an interactive experience of a real-world environment where real world objects are enhanced by computer-generated information.
SOCIAL MEDIA 1978	SM	Ward Christensen and Randy Suess. Social Media technologies empower people to connect and share with others through the creation of virtual communities. Social media technologies are interactive applications that allow users to generate and share content through blogs, comments, posts, reviews, and videos.
PERSONALIZATION 2011	PZ	SRI International Artificial Intelligence Center. Personalization inventions customize or tailor something to an individual. A simple example are garments that are tailor-made to fit to an individual. Customized software applications allow us to unleash our creativity and express ourselves. Personal assistant software improves your productivity.

Table 24 – Periodic Technology Ideas (Appendix)

The Periodic Table of Ideas

The following table summarizes the personal relevance of technology periodic ideas.

TECHNOLOGY IDEA	ID	PERSONAL RELEVANCE
TRANSPORTATION TECHNOLOGY 4700 BCE	TT	Transportation technologies allow you to move people and cargo from an origin point to a destination. It is a means by which you can deliver or obtain resources for your projects.
PROTOTYPING 375 BCE	PO	Prototyping allows you to test a concept and gain practical knowledge. You can verify if an idea will work, find new avenues of exploration and gain experience with a problem.
COMPUTATION 1833	CP	Computer applications assist you in a wide variety of tasks. They increase your productivity and help in accomplishing goals. Computational applications can help you in statistical analysis or calculating tasks. Many productivity apps can increase your personal effectiveness.
COMMUNICATIONS 1837	CM	Communications technologies allow you to connect to others, engage in the public sphere, and link into social media. These technologies allow you to *connect*, *collaborate*, and *persuade*. You can connect to discuss, inform, and inspire. You collaborate to reach an objective. You persuade by a call to action, asking for help, or convincing someone.
ROBOTICS 1921	RO	Robots can assist or perform your daily tasks and chores. They can provide companionship when you are lonely. Robots can assist in your projects and endeavors.
ARTIFICIAL INTELLIGENCE 1943	AI	Intelligent smart applications can assist in your endeavors and improve your personal productivity. A variety of smart applications have been developed to tackle complex problems.

TECHNOLOGY IDEA	ID	PERSONAL RELEVANCE
NETWORKING 1953	NW	Networking allows your computer(s) to connect, share information, and operate together. Networked elements in your project are the foundation for collaboration. Networking allows elements to share information and perform operations together.
VIRTUAL REALITY 1957	VR	Virtual reality (VR) technologies empowers your ability to explore, prototype, and visualize. VR can create experiences that allow you to engage, explore, and learn in a VR environment.
SOCIAL MEDIA 1978	SM	Social Media technologies allow you to connect and share with others in an online community. They allow you to generate and share content through blogs, posts, reviews, and videos. Social Media empowers you to reach a large audience.
PERSONALIZATION 2011	PZ	Personalization allows you establish something unique to yourself. Customization creates something personally distinctive. Personalization caters to our craving for uniqueness. Personal assistant software improves your productivity.

Table 25 – Periodic Technology Ideas Personal Relevance (Appendix)

Appendix-5 – ECONOMIC PERIODIC IDEAS

The following table summarizes the ten periodic ideas in economics:

ECONOMIC IDEA	ID	DESCRIPTION
MARKETS **3000 BCE**	MK	Alfred Marshall. A market is a system where parties can exchange goods or services. Sellers offer wares or services in exchange for money. Markets serve as a mechanism to distribute resources and manufactured goods in society. The value of goods and services are established through transactions in the market.
CURRENCY **550 BCE**	CU	Jack Weatherford. Currency is a medium of exchange or a system of money which can serve as legal tender. Currency is traded for its economic value. Currency has four purposes: as a medium of exchange, a store of value, a measure of value and a standard of deferred payment.
CREDIT **1494**	CR	Luca Pacioli. Credit is the means which allows one party, the lender, to provide money or resources to another party, the debtor, for repayment later. Credit formalizes that reciprocity into a legally enforceable agreement which can extend to large groups of unrelated people.
DIMINISHING RETURNS **1766**	DR	Anne-Robert-Jacques Turgot. Diminishing returns is the decrease in the marginal output in production as the amount of a single factor of production is incrementally increased. The first person assigned to a job is the most effective. Subsequent people added are less and less effective.

ECONOMIC IDEA	ID	DESCRIPTION
TRADE 1817	TR	David Ricardo. Trade is the action of buying and selling of goods and services for money or something of value. Barter is trading things without money. Modern traders generally negotiate through a medium of exchange, such as money. A system that allows for trade is a market.
ECONOMIC CYCLE 1819	EC	Jean Charles Léonard de Sismondi. The economic cycle is the periodic boom and contraction in business cycles. It shifts between periods of economic growth and relative decline or stagnation. It is characterized by four repeating phases: expansion, boom, contraction, and depression.
MARGINAL UTILITY 1871	MU	William Jevons. Utility is the benefit from consuming a product. Marginal utility is the change in utility from an increase in the consumption of a good or service. *Cardinal utility* assigns a benefit value to subsequent units. *Ordinal utility* is concerned with the sequencing of additional units.
INCENTIVES 1914	IV	Jean-Jacques Laffont. Incentives are motivators that reward actions to produce a desired outcome. There are four types of incentives: financial, moral, personal, and coercive. Extrinsic motivators reward actions to yield a desired outcome. Intrinsic motivators are personal desires for self-improvement.
SOCIAL CAPITAL 1916	SC	Lyda Hanifan. Social Capital are factors of social cohesion that allows groups to function efficiently. These factors include personal relationships, shared identity, shared vision, shared norms, shared values, trust, cooperation, and reciprocity.
CREATIVE DESTRUCTION 1942	CD	Joseph Schumpeter. Creative destruction is a process through which something new brings about the demise of whatever existed before it. Capitalism and innovation create new products and markets even as they destroy the old ones.

Table 26 – Periodic Economic Ideas (Appendix)

The Periodic Table of Ideas

The following table summarizes the personal relevance of the economic periodic ideas:

ECONOMIC IDEA	ID	PERSONAL RELEVANCE
MARKETS **3000 BCE**	MK	Markets allow you to exchange goods or services with others. You can buy resources that you need. Through a market, you can adjust and balance resources for your projects. Markets can guide you to find customers for your idea and producers for your needs.
CURRENCY **550 BCE**	CU	Currency helps you attain necessities and facilitates your dreams. Money management is a basic life skill. Develop a financial strategy to balance your income against your expenses. You can save, plan and budget to realize your long-term goals. Break down large projects into manageable tasks. Money allows you to get the resources to complete those tasks.
CREDIT **1494**	CR	Credit can allow you to get the resources necessary to start a new project. Managing your credit is vital to your success in life. It is used as a gauge of financial standing by lenders.
DIMINISHING RETURNS **1766**	DR	You need to recognize the point of diminishing returns in order to maximize your time, effort and resources. As you continue to add resources to a project, those subsequent resources have decreased effectiveness in accomplishing the goal.
TRADE **1817**	TR	You can employ the concept of trade to buy and sell goods and services for money or something of value. You can barter to trade things without the use of money. If there is something you need, you may try to obtain it by trading away something you don't need.
ECONOMIC CYCLE **1819**	EC	The economic cycle suggests that you recognize that there are periods of boom and contraction which shift between growth and decline. You need to capitalize on opportunities in times of prosperity and yet prepare for recessions before they happen.

ECONOMIC IDEA	ID	PERSONAL RELEVANCE
MARGINAL UTILITY 1871	MU	Marginal utility suggests that there is only so much that you need. You should consider how many resources you need for a project and launch with that. You can add in a safety buffer for contingencies, but do not go overboard. Marginal utility asserts the excess resources will just sit idle.
INCENTIVES 1914	IV	Incentives motivate individuals and groups. Extrinsic motivations originate from external sources. Intrinsic motivations compel you based on your personal desires and values. Financial, moral, and personal incentives get you to excel. Financial and coercive incentives connect to your primal instincts of self-preservation and survival. Moral incentives appeal to your sense of social dedication and virtue. Personal incentives speak to your values and desire for self-actualization.
SOCIAL CAPITAL 1916	SC	You can use social capital to create social cohesion in a group. You can build trust and friendship to engender cooperation and reciprocity. Finding a shared identity, shared vision, shared norms and shared values develops interpersonal relationships.
CREATIVE DESTRUCTION 1942	CD	Creative destruction suggests that, if necessary, you let go of the old to make way for the new. Sometimes, to make way for new things to come into your life, you need to relinquish the old. New chapters in your life can flourish when old ones close. Creative destruction lets you navigate around market landmines and ride creative currents.

Table 27 – Periodic Economic Ideas Personal Relevance (Appendix)

Appendix-6 – BUSINESS PERIODIC IDEAS

The following table summarizes the periodic business ideas.

BUSINESS IDEA	ID	DESCRIPTION
COMPANY 1602	CO	Dutch East India Company. A company is a legal entity composed of an association of people for commercial or industrial purposes. Three ideas underpin the modern company: joint stock ownership, limited liability, and the company as a legal personality. Examples of companies include voluntary associations, business enterprises, and financial firms.
DIVISION OF LABOR 1690	DL	Sir William Petty. The division of labor is the separation of tasks in an organization or group. Assigning people to specialized tasks optimizes individual talent thereby improving group efficiency. Specialists in a group with unique capabilities complement other people with different skills.
MULTI-DIVISIONS 1920	MD	Alfred P. Sloan, Jr. The multi-divisional form (M-Form) is an organizational structure where a diversified company is separated into semi-autonomous units. The M-form frees top management from the minutia of daily operations and allows them to concentrate on corporate strategy, market positioning, and resource allocation among divisions.

BUSINESS IDEA	ID	DESCRIPTION
MANAGERIAL CAPITALISM 1977	MC	Alfred D. Chandler, Jr. Managerial capitalism relates to corporations that employ professional managers. Professional managers set objectives, organize activities, motivate teams, measure outcomes, and develop people in an organization. Managerial capitalism superseded patrimonial family-run capitalism.
INTELLECTUAL CAPITAL 1991	IC	Thomas Stewart. Intellectual capital are the intangible assets of a company. They are the nonphysical and nonfinancial assets that command value. They are typically classified into three categories: human capital, structural capital and relational capital.

Table 28 – Periodic Business Ideas (Appendix)

The following table summarizes the personal relevance of periodic business ideas.

BUSINESS IDEA	ID	PERSONAL RELEVANCE
COMPANY 1602	CO	You can use companies that can provide services and products for your project. You can reach out to associations, enterprises, or financial firms for their assistance or services. Companies can also provide opportunities for you to engage in and contribute to society at large.
DIVISION OF LABOR 1690	DL	You can use division of labor to assign people to specialized tasks to best utilize their knowledge and talents. Dividing a project into manageable parts facilitates people taking on its tasks. You can also look for specialists to help you.
MULTI-DIVISIONS 1920	MD	The multi-divisional form (M-Form) idea asserts that you should divide resources into specific focus areas. You can divide your project into separate divisions. Then, you can create autonomous teams or use specialists to manage those tasks.
MANAGERIAL CAPITALISM 1977	MC	Managerial capitalism suggests that you separate ownership from control of a project. For your project, see if there are experts that you can turn over project tasks to. When you delegate parts of a project where you do not have expertise, you can focus your time on where you do have competence.
INTELLECTUAL CAPITAL 1991	IC	Intellectual capital are the intangible assets that you have. Try to identify the intangible things that give your life meaning. You can then nurture and make the most of your human capital, structural capital and relational capital.

Table 29 – Periodic Business Ideas Personal Relevance (Appendix)

Appendix-7 – PSYCHOLOGY PERIODIC IDEAS

The following table summarizes the periodic psychology ideas.

PSYCHOLOGY IDEA	ID	DESCRIPTION
PERSONALITY TRAITS 1937	PT	Gordon Allport. Personality traits are characteristics or qualities that combine to form the distinct character of an individual. These traits motivate the essential drive and desires of a person. The big five personality traits are: agreeableness, conscientiousness, extraversion, neuroticism, and openness.
PROPINQUITY EFFECT 1950	PE	Leon Festinger, Stanley Schachter, and Kurt Back. The *propinquity effect* is the tendency of individuals to form close relationships with people they repeatedly encounter. The propinquity effect can arise from physical, psychological, or functional proximity. Similarly, the *mere-exposure effect* is a preference for something resulting from repeated exposure.
FIELD THEORY 1951	FT	Kurt Lewin. Field theory asserts that behavior is a product of the individual interacting with their environment. It describes behavior in terms of interrelationships between people and their psychological circumstances, social situation, and physical surroundings.

PSYCHOLOGY IDEA	ID	DESCRIPTION
SOCIAL PSYCHOLOGY 1951	SP	Kurt Lewin. Social psychology is the study of how the thoughts, feelings, and actions of individuals are affected by the actual, imagined, or implied presence of other people. It includes the study of attitudes, persuasion, social cognition, social influence, group dynamics and interpersonal attraction.
COGNITIVE PSYCHOLOGY 1960	CY	George Armitage Miller and Jerome Bruner. Cognitive psychology is devoted to the study of mental processes such as attention, language, memory, perception, problem solving, creativity, and thinking. You have two attention systems: exogenous is reflexive, and endogenous is deliberate. You have short-term, working, long-term, procedural, semantic, and episodic memory. Perception interprets stimuli from our senses.

Table 30 – Periodic Psychology Ideas (Appendix)

The following table summarizes the personal relevance of psychology periodic ideas.

PSYCHOLOGY IDEA	ID	PERSONAL RELEVANCE
PERSONALITY TRAITS **1937**	PT	Personality traits allows you to assess the motivations, drives, and desires of someone. People are driven by the habits, needs, and attitudes embodied in their personality traits. Thus, an understanding of personalities traits helps you collaborate, connect, and motivate people.
PROPINQUITY EFFECT **1950**	PE	The propinquity effect cultivates relationships through frequent contact. You can take advantage of this effect through social networking. You can nurture relations by physical, psychological, or functional proximity. The *mere-exposure effect* is a preference for something resulting from repeated exposure. Armed with that knowledge, you can navigate through life better.
FIELD THEORY **1951**	FT	Field theory suggests that we need to learn to adapt to changing environments and circumstances. Each new chapter you open in your life presents new actors, challenges, and plot twists. You can make changes through the Lewin three-stage process. First, *unfreeze* your mindset; next, *transform*; and then *freeze* into your new practice.
SOCIAL PSYCHOLOGY **1951**	SP	Social psychology improves your social interaction skills. Your mastery of attitudes, persuasion, social cognition, social influence, group dynamics and interpersonal attraction allows you to build rapport and create synergy with others.

PSYCHOLOGY IDEA	ID	PERSONAL RELEVANCE
COGNITIVE PSYCHOLOGY 1960	CY	With cognitive psychology, you can improve your attention span, creativity, critical thinking, language aptitude, memory recall, observation skills, and problem-solving competency. Awareness of the conclusions from cognitive psychology research can improve your mental aptitude. These include attentional blindness, dichotic listening tasks, the *McGurk effect*, *Miller's law*, and the serial position effect.

Table 31 – Periodic Psychology Ideas Personal Relevance (Appendix)

Appendix-8 – CANDIDATE PERIODIC IDEAS

CANDIDATE PHILOSOPHY IDEAS

AESTHETICS – Aesthetic Value, Affective Fallacy, Art Theory, Film Theory, Intentional Fallacy, Judgement of Sentiment, Literary Theory, Music Theory

ETHICS – Animal Welfare, Applied Ethics, Categorical Imperative, Consequentialism, Cynicism, Deontology, Ends vs Means, Environmentalism, Epicureanism, Hypothetical Imperative, Kantian Ethics, Meta-ethics, Moral Standards, Naturalism, Normative Ethics, Objectivism, Prescriptivism, Relativism, Sorites Paradox, Stoicism, Teleology, Universalism, Virtue Ethics

EPISTEMOLOGY – A Priori vs A posteriori, Analytic vs Synthetic, Cogito Ergo Sum, Deconstruction, Dialectic Method, Empiricism, Foundationalism, Hermeneutics, Historical Philosophy, Intuition, Masked Man Fallacy, Memory, Necessary vs Contingent, Perception, Phenomenology, Political Philosophy, Postmodernism, Pragmatism, Rationalism, Reason, Skepticism, Semiotics, Testimony, Tripartite theory, Truth, Turing Test, Vitalism

METAPHYSICS – Abstractions, Accident, Atomism, Cosmology, Determinism, Dualism, Essence, Existential Angst, Existentialism, Free Will, Humanism, Hume's Guillotine, Idealism, Materialism, Mind-body problem, Monism, Noumenon, Ontology, Particulars, Physicalism, Public Sphere, Pythagoreanism, Realism, Reductionism, Ship of Theseus & Identity, Subjectivism, Voluntarism

LOGIC – Analytical Philosophy, Aristotelian Logic, Computational Logic, Deductive Reasoning, Fallacy, Fuzzy Logic, Hypothesis, Inductive Reasoning, Inference, Logical Positivism, Mathematical Logic, Modal Logic, Modus Ponens, Monte Carlo Fallacy, Occam's Razor, Paradigm, Paradox, Philosophical Logic, Practical Problem Solving, Rules of Inference, Russell's paradox, Semantics

POLITICAL PHILOSOPHY – Classical Economics, Communism, Conservatism, Social Contract Theory, Social Theory, Utilitarianism

CANDIDATE SCIENCE IDEAS

NATURAL SCIENCES / BIOLOGY – Astrobiology, Biochemistry, Biogeography, Bioinformatics, Biological Engineering, Biomechanics, Biophysics, Biotechnology, Botany, Cell Theory, Chronobiology, Classification, Cognitive biology, Cryobiology, Ecology, Embryology, Epigenetics, Ethology, Evolution, Evolutionary Biology, Genetics, Homeostasis, Immunology, Inheritance, Marine Biology, Microbiology, Mycology, Nanobiology, Nomenclature, Paleontology, Pathobiology, Pharmacology, Phycology, Physiology, Physiology, Phytopathology, Quantum Biology, Sociobiology, Taxonomy, Theoretical biology, Virology, Zoology

NATURAL SCIENCES / CHEMISTRY – Agricultural Chemistry, Analytical Chemistry, Astrochemistry, Atmospheric Chemistry, Biochemistry, Chemical Engineering, Chemo-informatics, Environmental Chemistry, Geochemistry, Inorganic Chemistry, Materials Chemistry, Medicinal Chemistry, Neurochemistry, Nuclear Chemistry, Organic Chemistry, Pharmacology, Physical Chemistry, Phytochemistry, Radiochemistry, Solid-state Chemistry, Synthetic Chemistry, Theoretical Chemistry, Thermochemistry

NATURAL SCIENCES / PHYSICS – Acoustics, Aerodynamics, Agrophysics, Analysis, Applied Physics, Astrodynamics, Astrometry, Astronomy, Astro-particle Physics, Astrophysics, Atmospheric Physics, Bioacoustics, Biophysics, Celestial Mechanics, Chain Reaction, Classical Mechanics, Computational physics, Condensed Matter physics, Continuum Mechanics, Cosmology, Cryogenics, Deterministic, Discrete Energy Levels, Electroacoustics, Electromagnetics, Elements, Entropy, Experimentation, Exploration, Feedback, First Principles, Fluid Dynamics, Frames of reference, Galactic astronomy, Geophysics, Gravitational Physics, High Energy particle physics, Hybrid, Hydrodynamics, Hydrostatics, Induction, Inertia, Kinematics, Measurement, Metaphysics, Models, Molecular Physics, Natural Philosophy, Neuro-physics, Nuclear Physics, Optics, Particle Physics, Photonics, Planetary science, Plasma Physics, Pneumatics, Psychophysics, Relativity, Quantum mechanics, Relativistic Mechanics, Scientific Method, Scientific Paradigms, Solid-state physics, Standards, Static Equilibrium, Statistical Mechanics, Stellar astronomy, Stellar Astrophysics, Switching, Symmetry, System, Thermodynamics

FORMAL SCIENCES / LOGIC – Formal Logic, Informal Logic, Mathematical Logic, Modal Logic, Philosophical Logic, Predicate Logic, Propositional Logic, Syllogistic Logic

FORMAL SCIENCES / MATHEMATICS – Abstraction, Algebra, Algebraic Geometry, Analysis, Applied Mathematics, Number theory, Boolean algebra, Calculus, Categories, Chaos Theory, Cohomology, Combinatorics, Commutative property, Complex Analysis, Computational Mathematics, Constructive mathematics, Control Theory, Dedekind-Peano axioms, Differential Equations,

Differential Geometry, Differential structures, Differential Topology, Diophantine Geometry, Discrete Mathematics, Equivalence relations, Euclidean Geometry, Events, Field Theory, Fractal Geometry, Functions & Equations, Game theory, Geometry & Trigonometry, Graph Theory, Group Theory, Harmonic Analysis, Information Theory, Knot Theory, Logical equivalence, Manifolds, Mathematical Logic, Mathematical Operators, Mathematical Optimization, Mathematical Physics, Mathematical Proof, Metric Structure, Metric Topology, Model Theory, Modular arithmetic, Notation, Number Theory, Numerical Cognition, Operation , Operations Research, Optimization, Order Theory, Orders, Peano Postulates, Predicative mathematics, Probability Theory, Queueing theory, Radix economy, Riemann Geometry, Set Theory, Statistics, Tensor Theory, Theorem, Topology, Transforms, Variable & Constant, Vector Calculus, Vector Math, Zermelo-Fraenkel Set Theory

FORMAL SCIENCES / COMPUTER SCIENCES – Algorithms & Data structures, Artificial Intelligence, Computability Theory, Computational Complexity Theory, Computer vision, Cryptography, Data Compression, Data Mining, Dynamic Programming, Fast Fourier Transform Algorithms, Heuristic, Image Processing, Information Theory, Machine Learning, Object Oriented Programming, Optimization, Parallelism, Programming Languages, Recursion & Concurrency, Rendering, Semaphore, Simulated Annealing, Software development methodologies

CANDIDATE TECHNOLOGY IDEAS

MATERIALS TECHNOLOGY – Advanced Coatings, Bronze Working, Carborundum, Composites, Electroplating, Galvanizing, Glass working, Iron Working, Metallurgy, Nanotechnology, Photoelectric Materials, Piezoelectric Materials, Plastic, Shape Memory Alloy, Smart Materials, Steel Working, Stone Tools, Synthetic Fabrics, Synthetic Polymers, Teflon, Thermochromatics, Touchstone, Vulcanizing

ENERGY TECHNOLOGY – Anaerobic Digesters, Biomass Energy, Capacitor, Electric Battery, Electricity Transmission, Fire Working, Flywheel, Fusion Power, Generators, Heat Pumps, Hydroelectric systems, Nuclear Reactor, Oil, Solar Cells, Steam Engine, Steam ship, Water Wheel, Wind Turbine, Windmill

COMMUNICATIONS TECHNOLOGY – Audio Tape Recording (Cassette Tape), Cell Phone, Codes, Color Photography, Computer Networking, Encoding, Fax Machine, Fiber Optics, Internet, Internet of Things, Iterative, Motion Pictures, Paper, Printing Press, Protocols, Radio, Representation, Satellites, Smart Phone, Swarm, Switching, Teleconferencing, Telegraph, Telephone, Television, Typewriter, Videotape recorder, Wireless Communications, Writing

MEDICAL TECHNOLOGY – Anesthesia, Antibiotics, Artificial Organs, Aspirin Pain Reliever, Cloning, Computed Axial Tomography (CAT), Defibrillator, DNA

Sequencing, ECG, EEG, Genetic Engineering, Hospital, Magnetic Resonance Imaging (MRI), Microscope, Organ Transplants, Pacemaker, Penicillin, Polythene Colloids (Soap), PET Scanner, Stethoscope, Surgery, Ultrasound Imaging, Vaccine, X-Rays

CONSUMER & AGRICULTURCAL TECHNOLOGY – 3D Printing, Air Conditioning, Alarm Clock, Appliances, Artificial Dye, Artificial Fertilizer, Assembly Line, Ball Bearing, Barometer, Bottled / Canned Food, Calendar, Camera, Clock, Compact Disc (CD), Contacts, Contraceptives, Credit Card, Department Store, Dewar Flask (Vacuum Bottle), Digital Assistants, Digital Currency, Digital Photography, Electric Motors, Electrical Light Bulb, Electronic Gaming, Elevator, Eyeglasses Spectacles, GMO, Knife Plow, Language Translation, Loom, Mass Production, Match (Fire), Mechanical Clock, Mechanical Harvester, Microwave Oven, Personal Banking, Personalization Technologies, Phonograph (Gramophone), Photography, Refrigeration, Sewing Machine, Smart Cities, Smart Roads, Smart Utilities, Smart Wearables, Spinning Wheel, Spring Driven Clock, String Instruments, Sundial, Thermometer, Vacuum Cleaner, Velcro (Hook & Loop Fastener), Video Streaming, Videodisc, Watch, Wind Musical Instruments, Xerography, Zipper

COMPUTATIONAL TECHNOLOGY – Abacus, Artificial Intelligence, Augmented Reality, Barcode, Basic Tools, Calculator, Cryptography, Electromagnetic Seismograph, Electronic Computer, Facial Recognition, Gyroscope, Hardware, Industrial Research Lab, Information theory, Instrument Controllers, Integrated Circuit, Laser, Microprocessor, Mixed reality, Mobile Computing, Operating system, Optical Processor, Personal Computers (PC), Prototyping, Punch Card, Radio Astronomy, Radiometer, Robotics, Smart Security, Social Media, Software, Speech recognition, Star Catalog, Storage, Supercomputers, Superconductivity, Tablets, Tabulator, Telescope, Theodolite, Transistor, Vacuum Air Pump, Virtual Reality, Von Neumann Architecture, Wearables, Workstations

TRANSPORTATION TECHNOLOGY – Airplane, Astrolabe, Automobile, Balloon Flight, Caravel, Carburetor, Communication Satellites, Compass, Diesel Engine, Global Positioning Satellite, Helicopter, Horse Collar, Horse Shoe, Internal Combustion Engine, Interplanetary Spacecraft, Jet Propelled Aircraft, Lateen/Square Sail, Locomotives, Map Making, Navigation, Radar, Reusable Manned Spacecraft, Seaplane, Self-driving vehicles, Stirrup, Submarine, Wheel

WARFARE TECHNOLOGY – Artillery Predictors, Battleship, Bow & Arrow, Cannon, Drones, Gunpowder, Guns, Knight, Machine Gun, Nuclear Weapons, Repeating Firearms, Rocketry, Siege Warfare, Tank

CONSTRUCTION TECHNOLOGY – Carpenter's Square, Computer Aided Design, Concrete, Drafting Compass, Dynamite, Elevator Lift, Heating systems, Insulated Glazing, Interchangeability, Lathe, Line Gauge, Masonry, Plumbing,

Plumb-Line, Riveting Machine, Skyscraper, Smart Homes, Spirit Level, Suspension Bridge

CANDIDATE ECONOMIC IDEAS

MICROECONOMICS – Absolute Advantage, Allocative efficiency, Barter, Capital, Commodity, Competition & Cooperation, Competitive Market, Consumer, Consumption Good, Cost, Credit, Currency, Demand theory, Diminishing Marginal Utility, Duopoly, Engel's Law, Externality, Firms, Giffen Goods, Incentives, Independence Axiom (Allais Paradox), Investment Goods, Marginal Utility, Law of Demand, Market Economy, Market Equilibrium, Market failure, Market System, Monopoly, Monopsony, Oligopsony, Opportunity Cost (Weiser), Perfect Competition, Price Discrimination, Private Goods, Producer, Production, Production possibility frontier, Productive efficiency, Recession, Scarcity, Specialization, Supply and demand, Uncertainty and game theory, Veblen Goods (Luxury Item)

MACROECONOMICS – Aggregate Demand, Aggregate Supply (Marshall Cross), Anti-trust, Banking, Borrowing & Lending, Business cycle, Cartel Collusion, Circular Flow of Income, Comparative Advantage, Demand Deficiency (Negative demand), Diminishing Returns, Division of Labor, Economic Bubble, Economic Cycle, Economic Growth, Economy of Scale (Chandler), Equilibrium Theory, Exchange Rate, Export, Financing, Fiscal Policy, Free Trade, Genuine Progress Indicator, Gross Domestic Product, Growth, Happy Planet Index, Import, Inflation, Intangible goods, Intellectual Property, Investment, Invisible Hand, Joint Stock Company, Keynesian Multiplier, Liberalization of Trade, Malthusian Trap, Medium of Exchange, Monetary Policy, National Income Accounting, Non-Excludability, Non-Rivalry, Paradox of Value, Pareto Efficiency, Price System, Protectionism, Public Goods & Free-Riding, Public sector, Rational Choice Theory (Homo Economicus), Regulation, Ricardian Equivalence (Tax now/Tax later), Say's Law (Jean-Baptiste Say), Social Capital, Specialization of Labor, Sticky Wages, Subsidies, Tax Incidence / Burden, Taxation (Laffer Curve), Trade, Unemployment, Wages

OTHER – Adverse Selection, Arrow's Paradox, Asymmetric Information (Akerlof's Theory), Behavioral Economics, Collective Bargaining (Webb), Creative Destruction, Currency Crisis Model, Debt Relief, Development economics, Econometrics (Frisch), Economic Efficiency, Economic Liberalism, Economic Market Bubble, Ellsberg Paradox (Ambiguity Aversion), Entitlement

Theory, Exchange Rates, Factors of Production, Financial Instability, Game Theory (von Neumann & Morgenstern), Globalization, Human Capital, Information Economics, International economics, ISLM Model, Labor economics, Lucas Critique, Market Integration, Moral Hazard, Multiple Equilibriums, Nash Equilibrium (Cournot reaction curve), Phillips Curve, Pigouvian Tax (Externalities), Poverty, Productive Factors, Search Frictions, Signaling & Screening, Structural Change, Tariff, Theory of Value, Wage Labor, Welfare (Social transfer), Welfare economics, Winner's Curse (Auctions)

CANDIDATE BUSINESS IDEAS

BUSINESS ANALYTICS – Analytical Modeling, Behavioral Analytics, Business Intelligence, Business Planning, Cohort Analysis, Competitor Analysis, Customer Journey Analytics, Cyber Analytics, Decision Making, Enterprise Optimization, Financial Services Analytics, Fraud Analytics, Key Performance Indicators (KPI), Marketing Analytics, Market Basket Analysis, Modeling, Numerical Analysis, Predictive Pricing Analytics, Risk & Credit analytics, Supply chain analytics

BUSINESS MANAGEMENT – Anthony Triangle, Asset Management, Balanced Scorecard, Business Administration, Business Operations, Change Management, Commanding, Company, Conflict Resolution, Constraint Management, Controlling, Coordinating, Crisis Management, Critical Success Factor, Data Analysis, Decision Making, Design, Development, Division of Labor, Enterprise Modeling, IT Management, Leadership, Logistics, Management, Managerial Capitalism, Multi-Divisions, Operations Management, Organization, Planning, Poison Pill, Proport, QCD, Quality Assurance, Quality Management, Sales, Systems Development Life Cycle, Task Management, Time Management, Total Viable Systems Model, Wideband Delphi

ENTREPRENEURSHIP – Bootstrap-finance, Business Intelligence, Business Venture, Coaching, Cultural Entrepreneurship, Innovation, Project Entrepreneurs, Real Estate, Risk Taking, Social Entrepreneurship, Strategic Entrepreneurship

FINANCE – Accounting, Behavioral Finance, Capital Resource Allocation, Capital Structure, Circular Flow of Income, Computational Finance, Corporate Finance, Economics, Experimental Finance, Financial Econometrics, Financial Economics, Financial Market, Financial Mathematics, Financial Services, Fisher Separation Theorem, Modigliani-Miller Theorem, Personal Finance, Public Finance, Quantitative Behavioral Finance, Theory of Investment Value, Working Capital Management

HUMAN RESOURCE MANAGEMENT – Employee Mistreatment, Employee Training, Human Resource Consulting, Managing Transformation, Motivation, Occupational Stress, Onboarding, Organization Processes, Organizational Behavior, Organizational Culture, Organizational Development, Organizational Leadership, Organizational Psychology, Organizational Theory, Recruitment, Talent Management, Work Family Balance, Work-Life Balance

INTERNATIONAL BUSINESS – Accounting Standards, Corporate Culture, Cultural Literacy, Economic Policy, Economy of Scale, Export Regulations, Exports, Foreign-Exchange Market, Franchising, Free Trade, Globalization, Imports, International Finance, International Production, International Transactions, Labor Standards, Legal Systems, Multinational Companies, National Markets, Operational Risk, Political Systems, Supply Chain Management, Tariffs, Technological Advancement, Tourism, Trade Agreements, Trade Barriers

LOGISTICS – Configuration, Distribution Network, Handling, Information Flow, Inventory, Management Information Systems, Materials Handling, Outsourcing, Packaging, Production, Supply Chain Engineering, Supply Chain Management, Transportation, Warehousing

MANAGEMENT SCIENCE – Data mining, Decision analysis, Forecasting, Game Theory, Management Consulting, Mathematical Modeling, Operational Research, Optimization, Simulation, Social Network

MARKETING – Accounts, Advertising, Affinity Marketing, Brand, Brand Licensing, Consumer Behavior, Demand Chain, Destination Marketing, Distribution, Global Marketing, Industrial Marketing, Influencer Marketing, Loyalty Marketing, Media, Pricing, Product Management, Product Marketing, Promotion, Retail, Segmentation, Service, Social Marketing, Societal Marketing

PROJECT MANAGEMENT – Agile, Benefits Realization Management, Budget, Business Model, Case Study, Change Management, Communications Log, Critical Path, Critical Chain Project Management, Dependency, Earned Value Management, Event Chain, Fordism, Gantt Chart, GERT, Human Factors, International standards, Iterative and Incremental Project Management, Kanban, Lean Project Management, Phased Approach, Process-Based Management, Project Control Systems, Project Monitoring, Project Portfolio, Project Process, Project Production Management, Resource Allocation, Risk Management, Scheduling, Six Sigma, Stakeholder, Success Criteria, Task Analysis, Work Breakdown Structure

PUBLIC RELATIONS – Accounts, Audience Targeting, Brand Awareness, Communication Campaigns, Crisis Management, Event Management, Internal

Communications, Litigation Public Relations, Media Relations, Messaging, News Content, Opinion Leaders, Press Management, Press Releases, Social Media Marketing, Spokesperson Interviews, Trade Media
STRATEGIC MANAGEMENT – Benchmarking, Best Practices, Business Model, Business Strategy, Competitive Advantage, Concept-driven Strategy, Core Competence, Core Ideology, Corporate Strategy, Differential Value, Economical Strategy, Experience Curve, Horizonal Integration, Intellectual Capital, Portfolio Theory, Strategic Planning, Strategy Dynamics, Strategy Map, SWOT Analysis, Systems Thinking, Vertical Integration

CANDIDATE PSYCHOLOGY IDEAS

BEHAVIORAL GENETICS – Cognitive Ability, Diathesis Stress, Medical Illness, Nature vs Nurture (Galton), Personality, Psychiatric Illness
BIOLOGICAL PSYCHOLOGY – Behavioral Neuroscience, Behavior Brain Injury, Cognitive Neuroscience, Neuropsychology, Physiological Psychology
CLINICAL PSYCHOLOGY – Beck Depression Inventory (BDI), Cognitive Behavior Therapy (CBT), Cognitive Dissonance (Festinger), Collective Unconscious (Jung), Dysfunction, Existential Psychotherapy (Kierkegaard), Humanistic Psychology (Rogers), Medical Psychiatry, Miller's Law (7+/-2), Neuropsychology, Psychoanalysis (Freud), Psychodiagnosis, Psychodynamic, Psychological Assessment, Psychotherapy, Rational Emotive Behavior Therapy (Ellis), Systems Therapy
COGNITIVE PSYCHOLOGY – Attention (Broadbent), Behaviorism (Watson), Capacity for Decision (Frankl), Choice Theory (Glasser), Cocktail Party Effect (Cherry), Cognitivism, Cognition, Consciousness, Ego/Id/Superego (Freud), Emotion (Frijda), Experience, Experimental Psychology, False Memory Syndrome, Field Theory, Flashbulb Memories (Brown), Fluid-Crystallized (Cattell), Freedom of Attitude (Frankl), Functionalism, Gestalt Therapy (Perls), Language, Learning, Lewin's Change Model, Maslow's Hierarchy of Needs, Memory Retention (Ebbinghaus Experiments), Mental Processes, Mindfulness Meditation, Mood Congruent Processing (Bower), Motivation, Perception, Personal Construct Theory (Rowe), Positive Psychology, Problem Solving, Procedural-Semantic-Episodic Memory (Tulving), Reasoning, Reinforcement (Skinner), Seven Sins of Memory (Schacter), Suggestible Memory (Loftus), Zeigarnik Effect (Task Interruption)
COMPARATIVE PSYCHOLOGY – Animal Cognition, Behavioral Epigenetics, Conditioning (Pavlov), Conditioned Stimulus/Response, Ethology, Instinct,

Learning Environments (Thorndike), Law of Effect (Stimulus-Response), Operant Conditioning, Radical Behaviorism (Skinner), Theory of Contiguity (Guthrie)

DEVELOPMENTAL PSYCHOLOGY – Aging, Cognitive Development, Intellectual Development, Moral Development, Perception, Social development, Understanding

DIFFERENTIAL PSYCHOLOGY – Ability, Intelligence, Interest, IQ (Binet-Simon Test), Motivation, Self-Concept, Self-Efficacy, Self-Esteem, Temperament, Values, Wechsler Scale (WAIS)

EDUCATIONAL PSYCHOLOGY – Active Learning (Bruner), Attachment Theory (Bowlby), Cognitive Development, Constructivism, Eight Stages (Erikson), Empathizing-Systematizing (Baron-Cohen), Four Stages of Development (Piaget), Functionalism, Gestalt Psychology (Kohler), Humanistic Psychology, Hebb Association, Intelligence, Learning processes, Motivation, Operant conditioning, Piaget Cognitive Development, Race Studies, Self-Concept, Self-Regulation, Social Learning Theory, Structuralism

INDUSTRIAL PSYCHOLOGY – Human potential, Life Satisfaction, Management styles, Motivation, Occupational Health Psychology, Organizational Psychology, Productivity, Responsibility, Work environment

MORAL PSYCHOLOGY – Behavior, Judgment, Moral Behavior, Moral Conviction, Moral Development (Kohlberg), Moral Emotion, Moral Identity, Moral Intuition, Moralization, Moral Reasoning, Moral Values, Moral Virtues

PERSONALITY – Big Five Personality Traits (Tupes, Christal), Dissociative Identity Disorder (MPD), Eysenck's Scales, Five Family Roles (Satir), Lexical (Allport), Non-Productive Personality Types (Fromm), Personality Factors, Temperaments (Galen), Three Factor Model (Eysenck), Three Needs (McClellan)

SOCIAL PSYCHOLOGY – Aronson's First Law, Attitude Formation, Authority Figures (Milgram Experiment), Behavior, Belief Formation, Conformity (Asch), Festinger Cognitive Dissonance, Group Dynamics, Impression Management (Goffman), Interpersonal Attraction, Interpersonal Phenomena, Intrapersonal Phenomena, Mere Exposure Effect (Zajonc), Persuasion, Propinquity Effect, Schemas, Self-Concept, Social Cognition, Social Cognition Heuristics, Social Constructivism, Social Influence, Socio-political context (Martin-Baro), Stanford Prison Experiment (Zimbardo), Stereotypes

Part X – References

Appendix-9 – REFERENCES

Abbate, J. (2000). *Inventing the Internet (Inside Technology Series)* (58839th Edition ed.). Cambridge, MA, USA: The MIT Press.

Aczel, A. D., & Sounderpandian, J. (2005). *Complete Business Statistics.* New Delhi: MacGraw Hill Publishing Company, Limited.

Adler, M. J. (2010). *Dialectic.* Milton Park, Abington, Oxfordshire, England: Routledge.

Agichtein, E., Castillo, C., Donato, D., Gionis, A., & Mishne, G. (2008, February 11). Finding High-Quality Content in Social Media. *WSDM Proceedings of the 2008 International Conference on Web Search and Data Mining*, pp. 183-193.

Airbnb. (2020). *Airbnb Home Page.* Retrieved from Airbnb: https://www.airbnb.com/

Albusberger, N. (2017). *Determinants of Diffusion of Virtual Reality.* N/A: Independently Published.

Aldersey-Williams, H. (2011). *Periodic Tales: A Cultural History of the Elements, from Arsenic to Zinc.* New York City: Harper Collins.

al-Haytham, I. (1989). *The Optics of Ibn Al-Haytham: On Direct Vision Books 1-3.* London: Warburg Institute.

Allport, F. H., & Allport, G. W. (1921). Personality Traits: Their Classificaiton and Measurement. *Journal of Abnormal and Social Psychology*, 6-40.

Allport, G. W. (1937). *Personality: A Psychological Interpretation.* New York City: Henry Holt and Company.

Allport, G. W., & Odbert, H. S. (1936). *Trait Names: A Psycho-Lexical Study.* Albany, NY: Psychological Review Company.

Almereyda, M. (Director). (2017). *Marjorie Prime* [Motion Picture].

Amazon.com. (2020). *Amazon About Us Webpage.* Retrieved from Amazon.com: https://www.aboutamazon.com/

American Chemical Society. (2020). *Chemical Abstract Services Homepage.* Retrieved from Chemical Abstract Services : https://www.cas.org/

American Psychological Association. (2020). *APA Dictionary of Psychology.* Retrieved from American Psychological Association: https://dictionary.apa.org/

American Trucking Associations. (2020). *Reports, Trends, and Statistics.* Retrieved from American Trucking Associations: https://www.trucking.org/News_and_Information_Reports_Industry_Data.aspx

Amundson, R. (1985). The Hundredth Monkey Phenomenon. (K. Frazier, Ed.) *Skeptical Inquirer,* 348–356.

Anderson, D. J. (2005). *Kanban Successful Evolutionary Change for Your Technology Business.* Chicago: Blue Hole Press Inc.

Anderson, J. (2020). *Cognitive Psychology and Its Implications.* New York, NY: Worth Publishers.

Andreessen, M. (2000). *Mosaic -- The First Global Web Browser.* Living Internet. Retrieved from https://www.livinginternet.com/w/wi_mosaic.htm

Apple.com. (2020). *use Siri on all your Apple Devices.* Retrieved from Apple Support: https://support.apple.com/en-us/HT204389

Archibugi, D. (2001). Pavitt's Taxonomy Sixteen Years On: A Review Article. *Economics of Innovation and New Technology, 10*(5), 415-425.

Archimedes. (216 BC). *The Sand Reckoner (Archimedis Syracusani Arenarius & Dimensio Circuli)*. Seattle: Createspace.

Aristotle. (2012). *The Organon: The Works of Aristotle on Logic.* CreateSpace Independent Publishing Platform.

Aronson, E. (1972). *The Social Animal.* New York City: Viking Adult.

Asch, S. E. (1951). Effects of group pressure on the modification and distortion of judgments. In H. Guetzkow, *Groups, Leadership and Men: Research in Human Relations* (pp. 177-190). Pittsburgh, PA: Carnegie Press.

Asus. (2020). *Zenbo - your smart little companion.* Retrieved from Zenbo Asus homepage: https://zenbo.asus.com/

Bacon, F. (1620). *Novum Organum, the true directions concerning the interpretation of nature.* Oxford: Oxford University Press.

Bailenson, J. (2019). *Experience on Demand: What Virtual Reality Is, How It Works, and What It Can Do.* New York City: W. W. Norton & Company.

Bailer-Jones, D. M. (2013). *Scientific Models in Philosophy of Science.* Pittsburgh: University of Pittsburgh Press.

Bain, D. H. (1999). *Empire Express: Building the First Transcontinental Railroad.* New York City: Viking Adult.

Banting, F. G., & Best, C. H. (1922). The internal Secretion of the Pancreas. *The Journal of Laboratory and Clinical Medicine,* 251-266.

Barabasi, A.-L. (2014). *Linked: How Everything is Connected to Everything Else and What It Means for Business, Science and Everyday Life.* New York City, NY, USA: Basic Books.

Barr, S. M. (2014). *A Student's Guide to Natural Science.* Wilmington, Delaware: Intercollegiate Studies Institute.

Battelle, J. (2006). *The Search: How Google and Its Rivals Rewrote the Rules of Business and Transformed Our Culture.* London: Portfolio.

Baum, D. A., & Smith, S. D. (2012). *Tree Thinking: An Introduction to Phylogenetic Biology.* New York City: W. H. Freeman.

Beard, M. (2016). *SPQR: A History of Ancient Rome.* New York City: Liveright.

Bechara, A., Damasio, H., Tranel, D., & Damasio, A. (1997, Feb 28). Deciding advantageously before knowing the advantageous strategy. *PubMed*, 275. doi:10.1126/science.275.5304.1293

Bell, A. G. (1876). *United States Patent No. 174,465.*

Bellamy, E. (1889). *Looking Backward, 2000-1887.* Boston: Houghton Mifflin.

Bergson, H. (1903). *An Introduction to Metaphysics.* Indianapolis: Hackett Publishing Company.

Berners-Lee, T., & Cailliau, R. (1990, November 12). WorldWideWeb: Proposal for a HyperText Project.

Berners-Lee, T., & Fischetti, M. (1999). *Weaving the Web - The original design and ultimate destiny of the World Wide Web, by its inventor.* San Francisco: Harper.

Bernstein, W. J. (2009). *A Splendid Exchange: How Trade Shaped the World.* New York City: Grove Press Books.

Bertman, S. (2005). *Handbook to Life in Ancient Mesopotamia.* Oxford, UK: Oxford University Press.

Bertola, G., Grant, C., Disney, R., Bertaut, C. C., Bridges, S., Casolaro, L., . . . White, M. J. (2008). *The Economics of Consumer Credit.* Cambridge, Massachusetts: The MIT Press.

Bishop, C. M. (2006). *Pattern Recognition and Machine Learning.* New York City: Springer.

Blankenbaker, E. K. (2012). *Construction & Building Technology.* Tinley Park, Illinois: Goodheart-Willcox.

Bliss, M. (2007). *The Discovery of Insulin.* Chicago: University of Chicago Press.

Bloom, B. S., Krathwohl, D. R., & B., M. B. (1969). *Taxonomy of Educational Objectives; the Classification of Educational Goals.* Philadelphia, Pennsylvania: David McKay Company.

Bocca, G. (1959). *The Life and Death of Sir Harry Oakes.* New York City: Doubleday and Company.

Bontis, N. (1998). Intellectual capital: an exploratory study that develops measures and models. *Management Decision*, 63-76.

Boyer, C. B. (1959). *The History of the Calculus and Its Conceptual Development (Dover Books on Mathematics)* (First Edition ed.). Mineola, New York, USA: Dover Publications.

Boyle, R. (1661). *The Sceptical Chymist.* London: J. Cadwell.

Brandes, S. (1976). *American Welfare Capitalism, 1880-1940.* Chicago, Illinois USA: University of Chicago Press.

Brandt, S. (2015). *Introduction to Aeronautics.* Reston, Virginia: American Institute of Aeronautics & Astronautics.

Brin, S., & Page, L. (1998). The Anatomy of a Large-Scale HypertextualWeb Search Engine. *Computer Networks and ISDN Systems*, 107-117.

Broadbent, D. E. (1956). Successive Responses to Simultaneous Stimuli. *Quarterly Journal of Experimental Psychology*, 145-152. doi:doi:10.1080/17470215608416814

Brooks, F. (1975). *The Mythical Man-Month: Essays on Software Engineering.* Boston: Addison-Wesley.

Brown, R., & Kulik, J. (1977). Flashbulb Memories. *Cognition*, 73-99.

Bruner, J. S. (1956). *A Study of Thinking.* Hoboken, New Jersey: John Wiley & Sons Inc.

Campbell, G. (2019). *The Oxford Illustrated History of the Renaissance.* Oxford, England: Oxford University Press.

Carlson, D. (2012, December 21). *'Gangnam Style' Achieves Historic Feat: 1 Billion YouTube Hits.* Retrieved from Social News Daily: https://socialnewsdaily.com/6341/gangnam-style-achieves-historical-feat-1-billion-youtube-hits/

Carlson, E. (2013, March). *Know Thyself: How Mindfulness Can Improve Self-Knowledge.* Retrieved from Association for Psychological Science: https://www.psychologicalscience.org/news/releases/know-thyself-how-mindfulness-can-improve-self-knowledge.html

Carnegie, D. (1936). *How to Win Friends & Influence People.* New York City: Simon and Schuster.

Carnot, N. L. (1824). *The Reflections on the Motive Power of Fire.* Paris: Bachelier.

Cassidy, J. (2009). *Dot.Con: How America Lost Its Mind and Money in the Internet Era.* New York City: Harper Collins.

Casson, M., & Lee, J. S. (2011). The Origin and Development of Markets: A Business History Perspective. *Business History Review, 85*, 9-37. doi:10.1017/S0007680511000018

Cattell, R. B. (1946). *Description and Measurement of Personality.* New York City: World Book Company.

Cattell, R. B. (1957). *Personality and Motivation Structure and Measurement.* New York City: World Book Company.

Chandler, A. D. (1977). *The Visible Hand: The Managerial Revolution in American Business.* Cambridge: Harvard University Press.

Chaum, D. (1982). *Blind Signatures for Untraceable Payments.* Santa Barbara California: Department of Computer Science, University of California Santa Barbara.

Cherry, E. C. (1953). Some Experiments on the Recognition of Speech, with One and with Two Ears. *The Journal of the Acoustical Society of America*, 975-979. doi:doi:10.1121/1.1907229

Cheung, B. (2003). *32 Innovation Factors.* Bloomington, Indiana, USA: Xlibris Corporation.

Cheung, B. (2003). *3G Cellular Systems in 90 Minutes.* Philadelphia, PA, USA: Xlibris Corporation.

Cheung, B. (2005). *Renewable Systems in 90 Minutes.* Philadelphia, PA, USA: Xlibris Corporation.

Cheung, B. (2005). *Robotics in 90 minutes.* Philadelphia, PA, USA: Xlibris Corporation.

Cheung, B. (2019). *The Four Elements of Thinking.* Seattle: Independently Published.

Cheung, B., Gopal, K., DaSilva, V., Dwyer, T., Sudarsan, P., & Parasher, B. (2014). *USA Patent No. 8,755,805 B2.*

Cheung, B., Khawer, M. R., Sudarsan, P., & Gayde, R. S. (2018, March 13). *United States of America Patent No. 9,918,232.*

Cheung, B., Kumar, G., & Rao, S. A. (2005). Statistical algorithms in fault detection and prediction: Toward a healthier network. *Bell Labs Technical Journal, 9*(4), 171 - 185. doi:10.1002/bltj.20070

Cheung, B., N., K., N., K. G., & Putman, A. E. (2008). *USA Patent No. 7,443,804 B2.*

Cialdini, R. B. (2006). *Influence: The Psychology of Persuasion.* New York City: Harper Business.

Clausius, R. (1867). *The Mechanical Theory of Heat – with its Applications to the Steam Engine and to Physical Properties of Bodies.* London: John van Vorst.

Clement, J. (2019, November 19). *Number of monthly active Facebook users worldwide as of 3rd quarter 2019.* Retrieved from Statista: https://www.statista.com/statistics/264810/number-of-monthly-active-facebook-users-worldwide/

Clement, J. (2020, August 25). *Reach of most popular U.S. smartphone apps 2020 .* Retrieved from Statista: https://www.statista.com/statistics/281605/reach-of-leading-us-smartphone-apps/

Coleman, P. (2006). *Shopping Environments: Evolution, Planning and Design.* New York: Architectural Press.

Cooper, W. S. (1957). Sir Arthur Tansley and the Science of Ecology. *Ecology*, 658-659. doi:10.2307/1943136

Cooperman, T. (2019, March 27). *Recommended Daily Intakes and Upper Limits for Vitamin and Minerals.* Retrieved from Consumerlab Homepage: https://www.consumerlab.com/RDAs/

Coopersmith, J. (2015). *Faxes, The Rise and Fall of the Fax Machine.* Baltimore, Maryland, USA: Johns Hopkins University Press.

Copeland, B. J. (2010). *Colossus: The secrets of Bletchley Park's code-breaking computers.* New York City: Oxford University Press.

Copernicus, N. (1543). *On the Revolutions of the Celestial Spheres (De Revolutionibus Orbium Coelestium).* Nuremberg, Holy Roman Empire: Petreius, J. Retrieved from https://archive.org/details/on-the-revolutions-of-celestial-spheres

Copi, I. M., Cohen, C., & Flage, D. E. (2007). *Essentials of Logic* (Second ed.). Upper Saddle River, New Jersey, USA: Pearson Education.

Cotton, C., Cotton, C., Toney, T., Hilbert, G., & Jones, C. (2020). *Dude Perfect Youtube Channel*. Retrieved from YouTube: https://www.youtube.com/results?search_query=dude+perfect

Courtney, T. B. (2012). *The Law of Companies.* London, England: Bloomsbury Professional.

Cowan, H. J. (2012). *Time And Its Measurement: From The Stone Age To The Nuclear Age.* Whitefish, Montana: Literary Licensing.

Cowles, H. M. (2020). *The Scientific Method: An Evolution of Thinking from Darwin to Dewey.* Cambidge, Massachusetts: Harvard University Press.

Crossley-Holland, K., & Love, J. A. (2017). *Norse Myths: Tales of Odin, Thor and Loki.* Somerville, Massachusetts: Candlewick Studio.

D'Antonio, M. (2008). *A Ball, a Dog, and a Monkey: 1957 -- The Space Race Begins* (Reprint ed.). Simon & Schuster.

Darwin, C. (1859). *On the Origin of Species.* London: John Murray.

Das, R. (2014). *Biometric Technology Authentication, Biocryptography, and Cloud-Based Architecture.* Milton Park, Oxfordshire, England: Taylor & Francis.

Dasgupta, S. (2016). *Computer Science A Very Short Introduction.* New York City: Oxford University Press.

Daspit, T. (2020). *The Days They Changed the Gauge.* Retrieved from Southern Railfan Net: http://southern.railfan.net/ties/1966/66-8/gauge.html

Day, A. (1955). The Taxonomic Approach to the Study of Economic Policies. *The American Economic Review, 45*(1), 64-78.

Denning, S. (2018). *The Age of Agile: How Smart Companies Are Transforming the Way Work Gets Done.* New York City: Amacom.

Descartes, R. (1993). *Meditations on First Philosophy.* Indianapolis: Hackett Publishing Company.

Dewey, J. (1884). *Kant and the Philosophic Method.* Carbondale: Souther Illinois University Press.

Dewey, J. (1899). *the School and Society: Being Three Lectures.* Chicago: University of Chicago Press.

Dewey, J. (1938). *Logic - The Theory of Inquiry.* New York City: Saerchinger Press.

Dickinson, A. (1967). *Carl Linnaeus; Pioneer of Modern Botany.* London: Franklin Watts Inc.

Discovery Channel. (2020). *Mythbusters.* Retrieved from Discovery Channel: https://go.discovery.com/tv-shows/mythbusters/

Dodson, A. (2000). *Monarchs of the Nile.* Cairo, Egypt: The American University in Cairo Press.

Dodson, M. G. (2005). An Historical and Applied Aerodynamic Study of the Wright Brothers' Wind Tunnel Test Program and Application to Successful Manned Flight. *US Naval Academy Technical Report*, 1-168.

Dohrn-van Rossum, G. (1996). *History of the Hour: Clocks and Modern Temporal Orders.* Chicago, Illinois: University Of Chicago Press.

Dorf, R. C., & Byers, T. H. (2005). *Technology Ventures, from Idea to Enterprise.* New York, NY, USA: McGraw Hill.

Drucker, P. F. (2010). *The Practice of Management.* New York City: Harper Business.

Durant, W. (1926). *The Story of Philosophy: The Lives and Opinions of the Great Philosophers.* New York City: Simon & Schuster.

Durkheim, E. (1893). *The Division of Labour in Society.* London, England: Palgrave Macmillan.

eBay Press Room. (1995). *eBay: Our History.* Retrieved from eBay: https://www.ebayinc.com/our-company/our-history/

Ebbinghaus, H. (1913). *Memory: A Contribution to Experimental Psychology.* New York City: Teachers College Columbia University.

Ebeling, C. E. (2009). Evolution of a Box. *Invention and Technology*, pp. 8-9.

Edvinsson, L., & Malone, M. S. (1997). *Intellectual Capital: Realizing Your Company's True Value by Finding Its Hidden Brainpower.* New York City: Harper Business.

Einstein, A. (1948). A Message to Intellectuals.

Einstein, A. (2015). *Bite-Size Einstein: Quotations on Just About Everything from the Greatest Mind of the Twentieth Century.* New York City: St. Martin's Press.

Einstein, A. (March 2005). *Einstein's Miraculous Year: Five Papers That Changed the Face of Physics.* (J. Stachel, Ed.) Princeton, NJ, USA: Princeton University Press.

Etsy.com. (2020). *Etsy About Us Web Page.* Retrieved from Etsy Home Page: https://www.etsy.com/about

Fenna, D. (2002). *A Dictionary of Weights, Measures, and Units.* Oxford, England: Oxford University Press.

Ferguson, N. (2008). *The Ascent of Money.* London: The Penguin Press HC.

Festinger, L., Schachter, S., & Back, K. W. (1950). *Social Pressures in Informal Groups - A Study of Human Factors in Housing.* New York City: Harper & Brothers.

Field, J. (2005). *Social Capital and Lifelong Learning.* Bristol: The Policy Press.

Fisher, P. (1999). *Still the New World, American Literature in a Culture of Creative Destruction.* Cambridge, Massachusetts: Harvard University Press.

Fisher, R. A. (1921). On the "Probable Error" of a Coefficient of Correlation Deduced from a Small Sample. *Metron*, 3-32.

Fiske, A. P. (2000). Complementarity Theory: Why Human Social Capacities Evolved to Require Cultural Complements . *Personality and Social Psychology Review*, 76-94.

Fiske, S. T., & Taylor, S. E. (1991). *Social Cognition: From Brains to Culture.* New York City: McGraw-Hill, Inc.

Fiske, S. T., Gilbert, D. T., & Lindzey, G. (2010). *Handbook of Social Psychology.* Hoboken New Jersey: Wiley.

Five Elements Robotics. (2020). *Budgee Robot.* Retrieved from Five Elements Robotics homepage: https://5elementsrobotics.com/budgee-main/

Fleckner, A. M. (2020). Roman Business Associations. In G. Dari-Mattiacci, & D. P. Kehoe, *Roman Law and Economics Volume I: Institutions and Organizations.* Oxford, UK: Oxford University Press.

Fonsi, L. (2017, January 13). *Luis Fonsi - Despacito Ft. Daddy Yankee.* Retrieved from YouTube: https://www.youtube.com/watch?v=kJQP7kiw5Fk

Ford, H., & Crowther, S. (1922). *My Life and Work.* Garden City New York: Garden City.

Forsyth, D. R. (2013). *Group Dynamics.* Boston Massachusetts: Cengage Learning.

Freedman, W. L., Madore, B. F., Gibson, B. K., Ferrarese, L., Kelson, D. D., Sakai, S., . . . Kennicutt, R. C. (2001). Final Results from the Hubble Space Telescope Key Project to Measure the Hubble Constant. *The Astrophysical Journal, 553*, 47-72. doi:10.1086/320638

Frege, G. (1879). *Begriffsschrift (Concept Script).* New York City: Springer Spektrum.

Freud, S. (2012). *The Basic Writings of Sigmund Freud.* New York: Random House.

Fricker, J. D., & Whitford, R. K. (2004). *Fundamentals of Transportation Engineering: A Multimodal Systems Approach.* Upper Saddle River, New Jersey: Prentice Hall.

Gadamer, H.-G. (1960). *Truth and Method.* London: Sheed and Ward.

Garfinkel, S. L., & Grunspan, R. H. (2018). *The Computer Book: From the Abacus to Artificial Intelligence, 250 Milestones in the History of Computer Science.* New York City: Sterling.

Geeetech Blog. (2016, December 20). *Troubleshooting Guide to 19 Common 3D Printing Problems|Part One.* Retrieved from Geeetech Company Web Site: https://www.geeetech.com/blog/2016/12/troubleshooting-guide-to-19-common-3d-printing-problemspart-one/

Gelb, M. J. (2000). *How to Think Like Leonardo da Vinci: Seven Steps to Genius Every Day* (Reissue ed.). New York, NY, USA: Dell Publishing.

Gellius, A. (1927). *Attic Nights.* Cambridge, Massachusetts: Harvard University Press.

Gharajedgaghi, J. (2005). *Systems Thinking: Managing Chaos and Complexity : a Platform for Designing Business Architecture* (2nd ed.). Waltham, Massachusetts, USA: Butterworth-Heinemann.

Gibbs, R. W., & Gerrig, R. J. (1988). Beyond the Lexicon: Creativity in Language Production. *Metaphor and Symbolic Activity, 3*(3), 1-19.

Gladwell, M. (2002). *The Tipping Point: How Little Things Can Make a Big Difference.* New York City, NY, USA: Back Bay Books.

Glanz, J. (2010, April 6). Scientists Discover Heavy New Element. *New York Times*, p. Section A Page 18.

Goffman, E. (1959). *The Presentation of Self in Everyday Life.* New York City: Doubleday.

Goldsborough, R. (2013). *A Case for the World's Oldest Coin: Lydian Lion.* Retrieved from http://rg.ancients.info/lion/article.html

Goldstein, M., & Goldstein, I. (1981). *How We Know: An Exploration of the Scientific Process.* Boston, MA, USA: De Capo Press.

Goodfellow, I., Bengio, Y., & Courville, A. (2016). *Deep Learning.* Cambridge Massachusetts: The MIT Press.

Gower, B. (1996). *Scientific Method: A Historical and Philosophical Introduction.* Philadelphia: Routledge.

Grant, E. (2009). *Planets, Stars, & Orbs: The Medieval Cosmos, 1200-1687.* Cambridge, England: Cambridge University Press.

Grant, R. G. (2017). *Flight: The Complete History of Aviation.* New York: DK.

Grosvenor, E. S., & Wesson, M. (2016). *Alexander Graham Bell* (1 ed.). New Word City.

GSMA Intelligence. (2020). *The Mobile Economy.* GSMA.

Guilford, J. P., & Hoepfner, R. (1971). *The Analysis of Intelligence.* New York, NY, USA: McGraw-Hill.

Guinness World Records Ltd. (2019). *Guinness World Records 2019.* Oak Brook, IL: Portable Press.

Gummin, D. D., Mowry, J. B., Spyker, D. A., Brooks, D. E., Fraser, M. O., & Banner, W. (2017). 2016 Annual Report of the American Association of Poison Control Centers' national Poison Data System (NPDS): 34th Annual Report. *Clinical Toxicology*, 1072-1254.

Gupta, I., & Nagpal, G. (2020). *Artificial Intelligence and Expert Systems.* Herndon Virginia: Mercury Learning & Information.

Habermas, J. (1962). *The Structural Transformation of the Public Sphere.* Cambridge: MIT Press.

Halacy, D. S. (1970). *Charles Babbage, Father of the Computer.* Springfield: Crowell-Collier Press.

Hallgrimsson, B. (2012). *Prototyping and Modelmaking for Product Design.* London: Laurence King Publishing.

Halpern, D. (2004). *Social Capital.* Cambridge, England: Polity.

Hamilton, E. (2011). *Mythology: Timeless Tales of Gods and Heroes.* New York City: Grand Central Publishing.

Hancock, J. L. (Director). (2016). *The Founder* [Motion Picture].

Hanifan, L. J. (1916). The Rural Community School Center. *The Annals of the American Academy of Political and Social Science, 67*, 130-138.

Hanna, W., & Barbera, J. (Directors). (1962). *The Jetsons* [Motion Picture].

Harris, B. J. (2019). *The History of the Future: Oculus, Facebook, and the Revolution That Swept Virtual Reality.* New York City: Dey Street Books.

Harvard Business School. (2020). *Harvard Business School.* Retrieved from History of Harvard Business School: https://www.hbs.edu/about/history/Pages/default.aspx

Harvard University Department of Psychology. (2020). *Historic Faculty of Department of Psychology - George Miller.* Retrieved from Harvard University: https://psychology.fas.harvard.edu/people/george-miller

Hawkings, J., & Blakeslee, S. (2005). *On Intelligence: How a New Understanding of the Brain Will Lead to the Creation of Truly Intelligent Machines* (Reprint ed.). New York City, NY, USA: St. Martin's Griffin.

Hendler, J., & Golbeck, J. (2008). *Metcalfe's Law, Web 2.0, and the Semantic Web.*

Herbert, F. (1990). *Dune.* New York City, NY, USA: Ace Books.

Hertzsprung, E. (1913). On the spatial distribution of variable stars of the δ Cephei type. *Astronomical News*, 201-208.

Hetscheepvaart Museum. (2020). *Dutch Golden Age.* Retrieved from Hetscheepvaart National Maritime Museum: https://www.hetscheepvaartmuseum.com/goldenage

Hobsbawm, E. (1962). *The Age of Revolution: 1789 - 1848.* London: Vintage.

Holweg, M. (2007). The Genealogy of Lean Production. *Journal of Operations Management*, 420-437. doi:10.1016/j.jom.2006.04.001

Hook, S. V. (2009). *Johannes Gutenberg: Printing Press Innovator (Publishing Pioneers)*. Edina, Minnesota, USA: Essential Library.

Hubble, E. P. (1929). A relation between distance and radial velocity among extra-galactic nebulae. *Proceedings of the National Academy of Sciences of the United States of America, 15*(3), 168-173.

Hughes, R. (2014). *The Complete Detective: The Life and Strange and Exciting Cases of Raymond Schindler, Master Detective*. Seattle: M. Evans & Company.

Hughes, W. H. (1977). *Alexander Fleming and Penicillin*. New York City, NY, USA: Crane Russak & Company.

Hurlbut, C. S. (Ed.). (1976). *The Planet We Live On, An illustrated Encyclopedia of the Earth Sciences*. New York, NY, USA: Harry N. Abrams, Inc., publishers.

Huurdeman, A. A. (2008). *The Worldwide History of Telecommunications*. New York City: Wiley-IEEE Press.

Hyde, C. K. (2005). *The Dodge Brothers: The Men, the Motor Cars, and the Legacy*. Detroit Michigan: Wayne State University Press.

IBM. (2011). *Sabre - the First Online Reservation System*. Retrieved from IBM's 100 Icons of Progress: https://www.ibm.com/ibm/history/ibm100/us/en/icons/

Ingen Dynamics Inc. (2017). Retrieved from Aido Robot: http://aidorobot.com/

Instagram. (2020). *Instagram Home Page*. Retrieved from Instagram: https://www.instagram.com/

Interbrand. (2020). *Best Global Brands 2019 Rankings*. Retrieved from Interbrand: https://www.interbrand.com/best-brands/best-global-brands/2019/ranking/

International Union of Pure and Applied Chemistry. (2020). *International Union of Pure and Applied Chemistry Homepage*. Retrieved from International Union of Pure and Applied Chemistry: https://iupac.org/

Isakov, E. (2014). *International System of Units (SI): How the World Measures Almost Everything, and the People Who Made It Possible.* New York City: Industrial Press, Inc.

James, H. (2012). *Krupp: A History of the Legendary German Firm.* Princeton, New Jersey: Princeton University Press.

James, W. (1907). *Pragmatism A New Name for Some Old Ways of Thinking.* Mineola: Dover Publications.

Janesick, J. R. (2001). *Scientific Charge-coupled Devices.* Bellingham, Washington, USA: SPIE Press.

Jansky, K. G. (1933). Electrical Disturbances Apparently of Extraterrestrial Origin. *Proceedings of the Institute of Radio Engineers, 21*(10), 1387-1398.

Jech, T. (2006). *Set Theory* (3rd ed.). New York City, New York, USA: Springer.

Jevons, W. S. (1871). *The Theory of Political Economy.* New York City: MacMillan and Co.

Johnson, S. (2007). *The Ghost Map: The Story of London's Most Terrifying Epidemic--and How It Changed Science, Cities, and the Modern World* (Reprint edition ed.). New York City, New York, USA: Riverhead Books.

Jones, W. H. (2006). *Hippocrates Collected Works I*. Retrieved from Daedalus: Projects in Digital Humanities: https://daedalus.umkc.edu/hippocrates/HippocratesLoeb1/page.ix.php

Josephson, M. (1992). *Edison: A Biography* (1 ed.). Hoboken, NJ, USA: John Wiley & Sons, Inc.

Kalpakjian, S., & Schmid, S. (2013). *Manufacturing Engineering & Technology* (7th Ed. ed.). New York City: Pearson.

Kant, I. (2004). *Critique of Practical Reason.* (A. T. Kingsmill, Trans.) Mineola, NY, USA: Dover Publications.

Kant, I. (2008). *Critique of Pure Reason* (Revised ed.). (M. Weigelt, Ed., & M. Weigelt, Trans.) London, UK: Penguin Classics.

Kaplan, A. M., & Haenlein, M. (2011, November 24). Users of the world, unite! The challenges and opportunities of Social Media. *Business Horizons*, pp. 59-68.

Kennedy, J. F. (1962). *John F. Kennedy Moon Speech - Rice Stadium.* Retrieved from NASA: https://er.jsc.nasa.gov/seh/ricetalk.htm

Kickstarter.com. (2020). *Kickstarter About us webpage.* Retrieved from Kickstarter.com: https://www.kickstarter.com/about

Kierkegaard, S. (1992). *Either/Or: A Fragment of Life.* London: Penguin Classics.

Kim, D. H. (1994). *Systems Thinking Tools: A User's Reference Guide.* Arcadia, California USA: Pegasus Communications.

King, B. (2016). *Augmented: Life in The Smart Lane.* Singapore: Marshall Cavendish International.

King, M. L. (1968). *Strength To Love.* New York City: Pocket / Cardinal.

Kjellberg, F. (2020). *PewDiePie Youtube Channel.* Retrieved from Youtube: https://www.youtube.com/results?search_query=pewdiepie

Kleinbard, D. (2000). *The $1.7 trillion Dot.Com Lesson.* New York City: CNN Money.

Knoema. (2020, May 21). *Top Vehicle Manufacturers in the US Market, 1961-2016.* Retrieved from Knoema Enterprise Data Solutions Home Page: https://knoema.com/infographics/floslle/top-vehicle-manufacturers-in-the-us-market-1961-2016

Koestler, A. (1964). *The Act of Creation.* New York City, NY, USA: Dell publishing company.

Koetsier, J. (2013, March 1). *How Google searches 30 trillion web pages, 100 billion times a month*. Retrieved from Venture Beat: https://venturebeat.com/2013/03/01/how-google-searches-30-trillion-web-pages-100-billion-times-a-month/

Kozak-Holland, M. (2011). *The History of Project Management.* Ontario, Canada: Multi-Media Publications Inc.

Kramer, S. N. (1988). *History Begins at Sumer: Thirty Nine Firsts in Recorded History.* Philadelphia: University of Pennsylvania Press.

Krugman, P., & Wells, R. (2017). *Economics* (Fifth Edition ed.). New York City: Worth Publishers.

Laffont, J.-J., & Martimort, D. (2002). *The Theory of Incentives: The Principal-Agent Model.* Princeton: Princeton University Press.

Laing, G. (2004). *Digital Retro: The Evolution and Design of the Personal Computer.* Hoboken New Jersey: Sybex.

Lasn, K., & White, M. (2011, 2 2). *A Million Man March on Wall Street*. Retrieved from Adbusters: https://web.archive.org/web/20150402104218/https://www.adbusters.org/blogs/adbusters-blog/million-man-march-wall-street.html

Lavoisier, A. (1789). *Elements of Chemistry in a New Systematic Order containing All the Modern Discoveries (Traite elementaire de chimie).* Paris: Cuchet.

Lawrence, N., Jollant, F., O'Daly, O., Zelaya, F., & Phillips, M. (2009, May 19). Distinct roles of prefrontal cortical subregions in the Iowa Gambling Task. *Cerebral Cortex*, 1134-43. doi:10.1093/cercor/bhn154

Leavitt, H. S., & Pickering, W. (1912, March 3). Periods Of 25 Variable Stars In The Small Magellanic Cloud. *Harvard College Observatory Circular*, pp. 1-3.

Lehrer, J. (2010). *How We Decide* (Reprint ed.). New York City, New York, USA: Mariner Books.

Lerner, M. J., & Simmons, C. H. (1966). Observer's Reaction to the "Innocent Victim": Compassion or Rejection? *Journal of Personality and Social Psychology*, 203-210.

Leviathan, Y., & Matias, Y. (2018, May 8). *Google Duplex: An AI System for Accomplishing Real-World Tasks Over the Phone* . Retrieved from Google AI: https://ai.googleblog.com/2018/05/duplex-ai-system-for-natural-conversation.html

Levinson, M. (2016). *The Box: How the Shipping Container Made the World Smaller and the World Economy Bigger.* Princeton: Princeton University Press.

Lewandowski, K., Xu, Y., Pullan, S. T., Lumley, S. F., Foster, D., Sanderson, N., . . . Matthews, P. C. (2020, January). Metagenomic Nanopore Sequencing of Influenza Virus Directfrom Clinical Respiratory Samples. *Journal of Clinical Microbiology, 58*(1), 1-15.

Lewin, K. (1947). Frontiers in Group Dynamics: Concept, Method and Reality in Social Science; Social Equilibria and Social Change. *Human Relations*, 5-41. doi:10.1177/001872674700100103

Lewin, K. (1951). *Field Theory of Social Science: Selected Theoretical Papers.* New York: Harper & Brothers.

Lian, M. S., & Cess, R. D. (1977). Energy Balance Climate Models: A Reappraisal of Ice-Albedo Feedback. *Journal of the Atmospheric Sciences*, 1058-1062.

Lieberman, D. J. (2006). *How to Change Anybody, Proven Techniques to Reshape Anyone's Attitude, Behavior, Feelings, or Beliefs.* New York, NY, USA: St. Martin's Griffin.

Liebig, J. (1840). *Organic Chemistry in its Applications to Agriculture and Physiology.* Braunschweig, Germany: Friedrich Vieweg und Sohn Publishing Company.

Ling, S. J., Sanny, J., & Moebs, W. (2017). *University Physics Volume 1.* Surrey: Samurai Media Limited.

LinkedIn. (2020). *LinkedIn.* Retrieved from LinkedIn: https://www.linkedin.com/

Linnaeus, C. (1735). *Systema Naturae.* Leiden: Brill - Hes & de Graaf.

Locke, J. (1690). *Essay Concerning Human Understanding.* London: Thomas Basset.

Loftus, E. F., & Palmer, J. C. (1974). Reconstruction of Automobile Destruction : An Example of the Interaction Between Language and Memory. *Journal of Verbal Learning and Verbal Behavior*, 585-589.

Lowenstein, R. (2004). *Origins of the Crash: The Great Bubble and Its Undoing.* New York City: Penguin Books.

Lynch, K. M., & Park, F. C. (2017). *Modern Robotics: Mechanics, Planning, and Control.* Cambridge: Cambridge University Press.

Macdonald, K. (2007). *One Red Paperclip: How a Small Piece of Stationery Turned into a Great Big Adventure.* London: Ebury Press.

Maney, K. (2010). *Trade-Off: Why Some Things Catch On, and Others Don't* (1st ed.). New York City, NY, USA: Crown Business.

Mankiw, G. N. (2017). *Principles of Economics.* New York City: Cengage Learning.

Marie, P. (2018). *The Evolution of Agricultural Technology.* New York City: Rosen Education Service.

Marshall, A. (1890). *Principles of Economics.* London: MacMillan.

Martin, F. (2015). *Money: The Unauthorized Biography - From Coinage to Cryptocurrencies.* New York City: Vintage.

Martin, J. (2020, October 12). *11 Best Productivity Apps for 2020.* Retrieved from CloudApp: https://www.getcloudapp.com/blog/productivity-apps

Maytronics. (2020). *Dolphin Nautilus CC Robotic Pool Cleaner*. Retrieved from Maytronics homepage: https://maytronicsus.com/product/residential/nautilus-cc/

McCorduck, P. (1979). *Machines Who Think: A personal inquiry into the history and prospects of artificial intelligence.* New York City: W. H. Freeman.

McCulloch, W. S., & Pitts, W. (1943). A Logical Calculus of the Ideas Immanent in Nervous Activity. *Bulletin of Mathematical Biology*, 99-115.

McDonald's. (2020, March). *McDonald's - Our History*. Retrieved from McDonald's: https://www.mcdonalds.com/us/en-us/about-us/our-history.html

McGurk, H., & MacDonald, J. (1976, December 23). Hearing Lips and Seeing Voices. *Nature*, 746-748. doi: doi:10.1038/264746a0

McInerny, D. Q. (2005). *Being Logical: A Guide to Good Thinking* (Reprint ed.). New York City, NY, USA: Random House Trade Paperbacks.

Measurement Science Conference. (2020). *History of Metrology*. Retrieved from Measurement Science Conference: https://msc-conf.com/history-of-metrology/

Mehdipour, A., & Rashidi, H. (2013). Persian Bazaar and Its Impact on Evolution of Historic Urban Cores - the Case of Isfahan. *The Macrotheme Review*.

Mendeleev, D. I. (1901). *The Principles of Chemistry*. New York: P. F. Collier and Son.

Metcalfe, R. M., & Boggs, D. R. (1976, July). Ethernet: Distributed Packet Switching for Local Computer Networks. *Communications of the ACM, 19*(5), 395-404.

Michie, J. (2014). *Reader's Guide to the Social Sciences*. New York City: Taylor & Francis.

Micklethwait, F. (2005). *The Company, a Short History of a Revolutionary Idea* (Reprint ed.). New York City, NY, USA: Modern Library.

Milgram, S. (1963). Behavioral Study of Obedience. *Journal of Abnormal and Social Psychology*, 371-378.

Miller, G. A. (1956). The Magical Number Seven, Plus or Minus Two: Some Limits on our Capacity for Processing Information. *Psychology Review*, 81-97.

MIT Libraries. (2020). *MIT History*. Retrieved from MIT Sloan School of Management: https://libraries.mit.edu/mithistory/research/schools-and-departments/sloan-school-of-management/

Molles, M. (2012). *Ecology: Concepts and Applications* (7th International ed.). New York City, New York, USA: McGraw-Hill Education.

Montoya, R. M., & Horton, R. S. (2012). A meta-analytic investigation of the processes underlying the similarity-attraction effect. *Journal of Social and Personal Relationships*, 64-94. doi:10.1177/0265407512452989

Montoya, R. M., & Insko, C. A. (2008). Toward a More Complete Understanding of the Reciprocity of Liking Effect. *European Journal of Social Psychology*, 477-498.

Moran, T. P. (2010). *Introduction to the History of Communication: Evolutions and Revolutions.* New York City: International Academic Publishers.

Morison, S. E. (1991). *Admiral of the Ocean Sea: A Life of Christopher Columbus* (Reissue edition ed.). Boston, MA, USA: Little, Brown and Company.

Moscati, I. (2018). *Measuring Utility From the Marginal Revolution to Behavioral Economics.* Oxford England: Oxford University Press.

Moseley, H. G. (1913). The high-frequency spectra of the elements. *Philosophical Magazine*, 1024-1034.

Muller, J. (2010, December 2). *Ford Family's Stake Is Smaller, But They're Richer And Still Firmly In Control.* Retrieved from Forbes:

https://www.forbes.com/sites/joannmuller/2010/12/02/ford-familys-stake-is-smaller-but-theyre-richer-and-remain-firmly-in-control/#6950f8052174

Myers, R. (2003). *The Basics of Chemistry.* Westport, Connecticut: Greenwood Press.

NASA. (1976-2019). Spinoff Technology Transfer Program. *Spinoff.*

NASA. (2007, November 22). *Past Missions - Apollo: Mankind's first steps on the lunar surface.* Retrieved from National Air and Space Administration: https://www.nasa.gov/mission_pages/apollo/apollo11_audio.html

NBCLearn. (1962 (2015)). *Kennedy's Address at Rice University on space Exploration (Archival Film).* NBC Universal Media. Retrieved from https://highered.nbclearn.com/portal/site/HigherEd/browse/?cuecard=1249

Newton, I. (1687). *Philosophiae Naturalis Principia Mathematica (Mathematical Principles of Natural Philosophy).* London: Benjamin Motte.

Nietzsche, F. (1992). *Ecce Homo, How One Becomes What One Is, Friedrich Nietzsche* (Reprint Edition ed.). (T. R. Hollingdale, Trans.) London: Penguin Classics.

Nise, N. (2019). *Control Systems Engineering.* Hoboken, NJ: Wiley.

Nocera, J. (1994). *A Piece of the Action: How the Middle Class Joined the Money Class.* New York City: Simon & Schuster.

Nocks, L. (2007). *The Robot: The Life Story of a Technology.* Westport, Connecticut: Greenwood.

Norris, J. A. (2013). The Mineral Exhalation Theory of Metallogenesis in Pre-Modern Mineral Science. *Ambix,* 43-65. doi:10.1179/174582306X93183

Nye, D. E. (2015). *America's Assembly Line* (Reprint Edition ed.). Cambridge, Massachusetts, USA: MIT Press.

Oculus. (2020). *Oculus Quest 2 All-in-one VR*. Retrieved from Oculus Company Web Site: https://www.oculus.com/quest-2/

Offner, A. K., Kramer, T. J., & Winter, J. P. (1996). The Effects of Facilitation, Recording, and Pauses on Group Brainstorming. *Small Group Research, 27*(2), 283-298. doi:DOI: 10.1177/1046496496272005

Osborn, A. F. (1953). *Applied Imagination, Principles and Procedures of Creative Problem-Solving*. New York City, NY, USA: Scribner.

Osler, A. (1981). *Turbinia*. American Society of Mechanical Engineers. Tyne and Wear County Council Museums.

Pacioli, L. (1494). *Summa de Arithmetica, Geometria, Proportioni et Proportionalita*. Venice: Paganini.

Page, M. (2000). *The Creative Destruction of Manhattan, 1900-1940*. Chicago, Illinois: University of Chicago Press.

Page, S. E. (2018). *The Model Thinker: What You Need to Know to Make Data Work for You*. New York City: Basic Books.

Parissien, S. (2014). *The Life of the Automobile: The Complete History of the Motor Car* (First Printing ed.). New York City, NY, USA: Thomas Dunne Books.

Parthesius, R. (2010). *Dutch Ships in Tropical Waters: The Development of the Dutch East India Company (VOC) Shipping Network in Asia 1595-1660*. Amsterdam Netherlands: Amsterdam University Press.

Pasteur, L. (1854, December 7). Lecture at University of Lille.

Pedhazur, E. J., & Pedhazur Schmelkin, L. (1991). *Measurement, Design, and Analysis: An Integrated Approach*. New York City: Psychology Press.

Penzias, A. A., & Wilson, R. W. (1965). A Measurement of Excess Antenna Temperature at 4080 Mc/s. *Astrophysical Journal*, 419-421.

Petersen, P. B. (2004). *The Great Baltimore Fire*. Baltimore: Maryland Historical Society.

Peterson, L., & Peterson, M. J. (1959). Short-term retention of individual verbal items. *Journal of Experimental Psychology*, 193-198. doi:https://doi.org/10.1037/h0049234

Petty, W. (1690). *Political Arithmetick.* London: Robert Clavel.

Pickover, C. A. (2009). *The Math Book from Pythagoras to the 57th Dimension, 250 Milestones in the History of Mathematics.* Edison, New Jersey: Sterling.

Pierce, C. S. (1878, January). How to make our ideas clear. *Popular Science Monthly*, pp. 286-302.

Piggott, S. (1992). *Wagon, Chariot and Carriage: Symbol the Status in the History of Transport.* New York City: Thames and Hudson.

Pinterest. (2020). *Pinterest Home Page.* Retrieved from Pinterest: https://www.pinterest.com/

Plato. (1980). *Symposium.* Cambridge: Cambridge University Press.

Plato. (1992). *Republic.* Indianapolis, Indiana: Hackett Publishing Company.

Plato. (1998). *Phaedo.* (E. Brann, P. Kalkavage, & E. Salem, Trans.) Focus.

Plato. (2007). *Dialogues (Theaetetus).* DoDo Press.

Plato. (2012). *Crito.* Seattle: Amazon Digital Services LLC.

Plato. (2012). *Euthyphro.* Seattle: Amazon Digital Services LLC.

Plato. (2012). *The Apology of Socrates.* (B. Jowett, Trans.) Amazon Digital Services.

Plato. (360 BC). *Timeus.* Athens, Greece: MIT Classics. Retrieved from http://classics.mit.edu/Plato/timaeus.1b.txt

Poincare, H. (1929). *The Foundations of Science: Science and Hypothesis, The Value of Science, Science and Method* (Reissue edition (Dec 11, 2014) ed.). (G. B. Halsted, Trans.) Cambridge City, Cambridge, UK: Cambridge University Press.

Poker Listings. (2017, January 30). *Libratus Poker AI Beats Humans for $1.76m; Is End Near?* Retrieved from Poker Listings: https://www.pokerlistings.com/libratus-poker-ai-smokes-humans-for-1-76m-is-this-the-end-42839

Policastro, E. (1995). Creative Intuition: An Integrative Review. *Creativity Research Journal, 8*(2), 99-14.

Potts, D. T. (2012). *A Companion to the Archaeology of the Ancient Near East.* Hoboken, New Jersey: Wiley-Blackwell.

Proulx, N. (2017, December 8). Do You Have Any Unlikely Friendships? *New York Times*. Retrieved from https://www.nytimes.com/2017/12/08/learning/do-you-have-any-unlikely-friendships.html

Pugh, S. (1981, March). Concept Selection: a Method that Works. *Review of design methodology. Proceedings international conference on engineering design*, 497-506.

Purnell, C. (2017). *The Sensational Past: How the Enlightenment Changed the Way We Use Our Senses.* New York City: W. W. Norton & Company.

Quinn, T. J. (1991). *History of the Pavillon de Breteuil.* Retrieved from Bureau International des Poids et Mesures: https://www.bipm.org/en/about-us/

Rakov, V. A., & Uman, M. A. (2007). *Lightning Physics and Effects.* Cambridge, England: Cambridge University Press.

Ramotowski, R. (2012). *Lee and Gaensslen's Advances in Fingerprint Technology.* Boca Raton, Florida: CRC Press.

Ray, J. (2016). *Historia Plantarum (The History of Plants).* Sydney, Australia: Wentworth Press.

Reddit . (2020). *Reddit Homepage.* Retrieved from Reddit: https://www.reddit.com/

Redmond, K. C., & Smith, T. M. (2000). *From Whirlwind to MITRE: The R&D Story of The SAGE Air Defense Computer*. Cambridge, Massachusetts: The MIT Press.

Rees, M., Worden, P., Drake, F., Druyan, A., Werthimer, D., & Siemion, A. (2017, April 20). *Breakthrough Listen Initiative Publishes Initial Results*. Retrieved from Breakthrough Initiatives: https://breakthroughinitiatives.org/news/10

Reynolds, O. (1883). An experimental investigation of the circumstances which determine whether the motion of water shall be direct or sinuous, and of the law of resistance in parallel channels. *Philosophical Transactions of the Royal Society*, 84-99.

Ricardo, D. (1817). *On the Principles of Political Economy and Taxation.* Cambridge: Cambridge University Press.

Ride, W., Cogger, H. G., Dupuis, C., Kraus, O., Minelli, A., Thompson, F. C., & Tubbs, P. K. (2020, January 08). *International Commission on Zoological Nomenclature Code Online*. Retrieved from International Commission on Zoological Nomenclature Homepage: https://www.iczn.org/the-code/the-international-code-of-zoological-nomenclature/the-code-online/?article=5

Rieppel, O. (2019). *Phylogenetic Systematics: Haeckel to Hennig.* Boca Raton, Florida: CRC Press.

Riess, A. G., Casertano, S., Yuan, W., Macri, L., Bucciarelli, B., Lattanzi, M. G., . . . Anderson, R. I. (2018). Milky Way Cepheid Standards for Measuring Cosmic Distances and Application to Gaia DR2: Implications for the Hubble Constant. *The Astrophysical Journal, 861*(2), 1-13. doi:10.3847/1538-4357/aac82e

Roberts, A. (2006). *The History of Science Fiction.* New York: Palgrave MacMillan.

Robins, B. (1761). An account of the experiments, relating to the resistance of the air, exhibited at different times before the Royal Scoeity, in the year 1746.

In *Mathematical Tracts of the late Benjamin Robins, Esq* (pp. 200-217). London: J. Nourse.

Roskov, Y., Ower, G., Orrell, T., Nicolson, D., Bailly, N., Kirk, P. M., . . . Penev, L. (2019). *Species 2000 & ITIS Catalogue of Life, 2019 Annual Checklist.* Retrieved from Catalog of Life Org: www.catalogueoflife.org/annual-checklist/2019

Rothery, D. (2016). *Geology: A Complete Introduction.* Boston, Massachusetts: Teach Yourself.

Rovelli, C. (2018). Physics Needs Philosophy. Philosophy Needs Physics. *Foundations of Physics*(48), 481-491.

Ruegg, W. (1992). *A History of the University in Europe. Vol. 1: Universities in the Middle Ages.* Cambidge, England: Cambridge University Press.

Russell, B. (1910). *Principia Mathematica.* Cambridge: Cambridge University Press.

Russell, B. (1967). *A History of Western Philosophy.* New York City: Simon & Schuster.

Russell, S. J., & Norvig, P. (2009). *Artificial Intelligence: A Modern Approach.* Upper Saddle River: Prentice Hall.

S., L. (2015). *Who is Satoshi Nakamoto?* London: The Economist Magazine.

Sabre. (2020). *The Sabre Story.* Retrieved from sabre.com: https://www.sabre.com/files/Sabre-History.pdf

Sahakian, W. S., & Sahakian, M. L. (1993). *Ideas of the Great Philosophers.* New York City, New York, USA: Barnes & Noble Publishing.

Salo, U. (2006). *Ukko: The God of Thunder of the Ancient Finns And His Indo-european Family.* New York City: Institute for the Study of Man.

Santayana, G. (1905). *The Life of Reason: The Phases of Human Progress.* New York City: Scribner's.

Sartre, J.-P. (1943). *Being and Nothingness.* Paris: Editions Gallimard.

Sassoon, D. (2009). *Mona Lisa: The History of the World's Most Famous Painting.* New York City: Harper Collins.

Savage, A., & Hyneman, J. (Directors). (2010). *Mythbusters - Mini Myth Madness* [Motion Picture].

Scerri, E. (2013). *A Tale of Seven Elements.* Oxford, England: Oxford University Press.

Schaffel, K. (1991). *The Emerging Shield: The Air Force and the Evolution of Continental Air Defense, 1945-1960.* Washington, D.C.: Office of Air Force History, United states Air Force.

Schumpeter, J. (2008). *Capitalism, Socialism, and Democracy* (3rd ed.). New York City, NY, USA: Harper Perennial Modern Classics.

Schwab, K. (2017). *The Fourth Industrial Revolution.* New York City: Crown Business Publishing.

Science Forums. (2013, July 5). *How many possible chemical compounds are there?* Retrieved from Science Forums Homepage: http://www.sciforums.com/threads/how-many-possible-chemical-compounds-are-there.135244/

Scott, J. (Director). (2005). *BBS: The Documentary* [Motion Picture].

SETI Institute. (2020). *Early SETI: Project Ozma, arecibo Message.* Retrieved from SETI Institute: https://www.seti.org/seti-institute/project/details/early-seti-project-ozma-arecibo-message

Shannon, C. E. (1948). A Mathematical Theory of Communication. *Bell System Technical Journal,* 379-423.

Shannon, C. E., & Weaver, W. (1971). *The Mathematical Theory of Communication.* Champaign, Illinois: The University of Illinois Press.

Shields, C. (2013). *Aristotle (The Routledge Professors Series)* (2nd ed.). London, England, UK: Routledge.

Silver, D., Schrittwieser, J., Simonyan, K., Antonoglou, I., Huang, A., Guez, A., . . . Hassabis, D. (2017). Mastering the game of Go without human knowledge. *Nature*, 354-359.

Simmons, M. W. (2016). *Thomas Edison: American Inventor.* CreateSpace Independent Publishing Platform.

Simon, H. A. (1966). Scientific Discovery and the Psychology of Problem Solving. (R. Colodny, Ed.) *Mind and Cosmos*, 22-40. doi:DOI: 10.1007/978-94-010-9521-1_16

Simon, J. (2019, December 2). *AWS DeepComposer – Compose Music with Generative Machine Learning Models*. Retrieved from AWS News Blog: https://aws.amazon.com/blogs/aws/aws-deepcomposer-compose-music-with-generative-machine-learning-models/

Simons, D. J., & Chabris, C. F. (1999). Gorillas in our Midst: Sustained Inattentional Blindness for Dynamic Events. *Perception*, 1059-1074.

Simplicius. (2011). *On Aristotle Physics 1.3-4 (Ancient Commentators on Aristotle)*. (C. Taylor, & P. Huby, Trans.) London, England: Bristol Classical Press.

Singleton, R. A., & Straits, B. C. (2005). *Approaches to Social Research* (4th ed.). New York City, New York, USA: Oxford University Press.

Sismondi, J. L. (1819). *Nouveaux Principes d'économie politique (New Principles of Political Economy)*. Paris: Hachette Livre BNF.

Sloan, A. P. (1965). *My Years With General Motors.* New York City: McFadden.

Small Business & Entrepreneurship Council. (2016). *Facts & Data on Small Business and Entrepreneurship*. Retrieved from Small Business & Entrepreneurship Council: https://sbecouncil.org/about-us/facts-and-data/

Smith, A. (1776). *An Inquiry into the Nature and Causes of the Wealth of Nations.* London: W. Strahan and T. Cadell.

Smith, P. (2003). *An Introduction to Formal Logic.* London: Cambridge University Press.

SnapChat. (2020). *SnapChat Home Page.* Retrieved from SnapChat: https://www.snapchat.com/

Snedden, R. (2008). *Medical Technology.* London, England: Evans Brothers, Limited.

Sober, E. (2015). *Ockham's Razors: A User's Manual.* Cambridge, England, UK: Cambridge University Press.

Soby, L. M. (2016, November 30). *Elements 113, 115, 117, and 118 are now formally named nihonium (Nh), moscovium (Mc), tennessine (Ts), and oganesson (Og).* Retrieved from International Union of Pure and Applied Chemistry: https://iupac.org/iupac-announces-the-names-of-the-elements-113-115-117-and-118/

Sombart, W. (1913). *Krieg und Kapitalismus (War and Capitalism).* Berlin, Germany: Duncker & Humblot.

Soni, J., & Goodman, R. (2017). *A Mind at Play: How Claude Shannon Invented the Information Age.* New York City: Simon & Schuster.

Stackowiak, R., & Kelly, T. (2020). *Design Thinking in Software and AI Projects: Proving Ideas Through Rapid Prototyping.* New York City: Apress.

Standage, T. (2014). *The Victorian Internet: The Remarkable Story of the Telegraph and the Nineteenth Century's On-line Pioneers.* New York: Bloomsbury.

Stearns, P. N. (2012). *The Industrial Revolution in World History* (4th Edition ed.). London, England, UK: Routledge.

Stevin, S. (1585). *Decimal arithmetic: Teaching How to Perform All Computations Whatsoever by Whole Numbers Without Fractions, by the Four Principles* of Common Arithmetic: Namely, Addition, Subtraction, Multiplication, and Division. (R. Norton, Trans.) London: Imprinted by S.S. for Hugh Astley.

Stewart, J. V. (2001). *Intermediate Electromagnetic Theory.* New Jersey: World Scientific Publishing Company Inc.

Stewart, T. A. (1991, June 3). Intellectual Capital: Brainpower. *Fortune*, p. 44.

Stewart, T. A. (2010). *Intellectual Capital: the New Wealth of Organization.* New York City: Random House.

Stross, R. E. (2007). *The Wizard of Menlo Park: How Thomas Alva Edison Invented the Modern World.* New York City, NY, USA: Broadway Book.

Styron, W. (1979). *Sophie's Choice.* New York City: Random House.

Sullivan, E. (2001). *Academic Costume Code and Ceremony Guide.* New York: Walter de Gruyter.

Sutton, C. (2004, October 29). *Internet Began 35 Years Ago at UCLA with first message ever sent between two computers.* Retrieved from Computer Science University of California Los Angeles: http://internetanniversary.cs.ucla.edu/

Sveiby, K. E. (1997). *The New Organizational Wealth: Managing & Measuring Knowledge-based Assets.* Oakland, California: Berrett-Koehler Publishers.

Swart, K. W. (1969). *The Miracle of the Dutch Republic as seen in the Seventeenth Century (University College London Inaugural Lecture).* London, England: H.K. Lewis & Co. Ltd. Retrieved from Diana Muir Appelbaum.

Tansley, A. G. (1935). The use and abuse of vegetational terms and concepts. *Ecology*, 284-307.

Terrell, D. B. (1967). *Logic, a Modern Introduction to Deductive Reasoning.* New York City, New York, USA: Holt, Rinehart and Winston.

The Blind Cafe. (2015). *The Blind Cafe.* Retrieved from https://www.theblindcafe.com/

Thieman, W. J., & Palladino, M. A. (2018). *Introduction to Biotechnology* (Fourth Edition ed.). New York City: Pearson.

Thompson, F. (2005). *Fordism and Post-Fordism and the Flexible System of Production.* Salem: Willamette University. Retrieved from http://www.willamette.edu/~fthompso/MgmtCon/Fordism_&_Postfordism.html

Thompson, L. (2003). Improving the Creativity of Organizational Work Groups. *Academy of Management Executive, 17*(1), 96-109. doi:DOI: 10.5465/AME.2003.9474814

Tobias, R. B. (2012). *20 Master Plots: And How to Build Them.* Cincinnati, Ohio: Writer's Digest Books.

Tro, N. J. (2016). *Chemistry: A Molecular Approach* (4th ed.). New York City, New York, USA: Pearson.

Trochim, W. M. (2001). *The Research Methods Knowledge Base* (Second ed.). Cincinnati, OH, USA: Atomic Dog Publishing. Retrieved from http://www.atomicdogpublishing.com

Tupes, E. C., & Christal, R. E. (1961). Recurrent personality factors based on trait ratings. *United States Air Force Aeronautical Systems Division Technical Report*, 61-97. doi:10.1111/j.1467-6494.1992.tb00973.x

Turgot, A.-R.-J. (1766). *Reflections on the Formation and Distribution of Wealth.* Library of Econmics and Liberty.

Turing, A. (1936). *On Computable Numbers, with an application to the Entscheidungsproblem.* London: London Mathematical Society.

Twitch.tv. (2020). *Twitch.tv Home Page*. Retrieved from Twitch.tv: https://www.twitch.tv/

Twitter. (2020). *Twitter Home Page*. Retrieved from Twitter: https://twitter.com/

Uber. (2020). *Uber About Us Web Page*. Retrieved from Uber: https://www.uber.com/us/en/about/

Ubtech. (2020). *Lynx with Amazon Alexa*. Retrieved from Ubtech Hompage: https://www.ubtrobot.com/products/lynx-with-amazon-alexa?ls=en

Underwriters Laboratories. (n.d.). *Underwriters Laboratories News Room Press Release*. Retrieved from Underwriters Laboratories: https://www.ul.com/newsroom/pressreleases/underwriters-laboratories-publishes-first-safety-standard-for-portable-generators/

United States Patent and Trademark Office. (2017, December 21). *Patent Full Text Database*. Retrieved from United States Patent and Trademark Office: http://patft.uspto.gov/netahtml/PTO/index.html

Urry, L. A., Cain, M. L., Wasserman, S. A., Minorsky, P. V., Reece, J. B., & Campbell, N. A. (2016). *Campbell Biology (Campbell Biology Series)*. New York City: Pearson.

Van Dijck, J. (2013). *The Culture of Connectivity: A Critical History Of Social Media*. New York City: Oxford University Press.

Vera, D., & Crossan, M. (2005). Improvisation and Innovative Performance in Teams. *Organization Science, 16*(3), 203-224.

Verschuur, G. (2015). *The Invisible Universe: The Story of Radio Astronomy* (3rd ed.). New York City: Springer.

Von Neumann, J. (1945). *First Draft of a Report on the EDVAC*. Philadelphia: University of Pennsylvania.

Wagner, I. (2020, February 12). *Automotive manufacturers - Estimated U.S. market share held by selected automotive manufacturers in 2019*. Retrieved from Statista Home Page: https://www.statista.com/statistics/249375/us-market-share-of-selected-automobile-manufacturers/

Wallas, G. (1926). *The Art of Thought*. London, UK: Jonathan Cape.

Warfel, T. Z. (2009). *Prototyping: A Practitioner's Guide.* New York City: Rosenfled Media.

Wark, K. (1983). *Thermodynamics.* New York City, NY, USA: McGraw Hill Book Company.

Watson, J. B. (1913). Psychology as the Behaviorist Views It. *Psychological Review,* 158-177.

Watson, J. D., & Crick, F. H. (1953). Molecular Structure of Nucleic Acids: A Structure for Deoxyribose Nucleic Acid. *Nature, 171*(4356), 737-738.

Watson, L. (1979). *Lifetide. published.* London, UK: Hodder & Stoughton .

Weatherford, J. (1998). *The History of Money.* New York City: Crown Business.

Webber, M. E. (2019). *Power Trip: The Story of Energy.* New York City: Basic Books.

Webster's New World Dictionary (College ed.). (1984). Simon and Schuster.

WeChat. (2020). *WeChat Home Page.* Retrieved from WeChat: https://www.wechat.com/

Wharton School. (2020). *The Wharton School.* Retrieved from History of Wharton: https://www.wharton.upenn.edu/history/

White, M. M. (2011). *Occupy Wall Street: We are the 99 percent - About.* New York City: The Occupy Solidarity Network, Inc. Retrieved from http://occupywallst.org/about/

Williams, D. M. (2020). *Cladistics: A Guide to Biological Classification.* Cambridge: Cambridge University Press.

Willis, A. J. (1997). The Ecosystem: An Evolving Concept Viewed Historically. *Functional Ecology,* 268-271.

Wilson, R., & Watkins, J. J. (2013). *Combinatorics: Ancient & Modern.* Oxford: Oxford University Press.

Winchester, S. (2019). *The Perfectionists: How Precision Engineers Created the Modern World.* New York City: Harper Perennial.

Winston, W. (1994). *Operations Research: Applications and Algorithms* (3rd ed.). Belmont, California, USA: Duxbury Press.

Wittgenstein, L. (1922). *Tractatus Logico-Philosophicus.* (F. P. Ramsey, & C. K. Ogden, Trans.) Austria: Annalen der Naturphilosophie.

Wong, K. D. (2012). *Fundamentals of Wireless Communication Engineering Technologies* (1st ed.). Hoboken, New Jersey, USA: John Wiley & Sons Publishing.

Wonning, P. R. (2018). *A History of Time - A Chronicle of Calendars, Clocks and Time Zones.* Evansville, Indiana: Mossy Feet Books.

Wood, M. (2019, December 2). *Announcing AWS DeepComposer with Dr. Matt Wood, feat. Jonathan Coulton.* Retrieved from YouTube: https://www.youtube.com/watch?v=XH2EbK9dQlg

World Intellectual Property Organization. (2019). *World Intellectual Property Indicators 2019.* Geneva, Switzerland: World Intellectual Property Organization.

World Trade Organization. (2018). *World Trade Statistical Review .* Geneva: World Trade Organization.

Worx. (2020). *Worx Landroid Robotic Mower.* Retrieved from Worx homepage: https://www.worx.com/landroid/en/

Wozniak, S., & Smith, G. (2007). *iWoz: Computer Geek to Cult Icon: How I Invented the Personal Computer, Co-Founded Apple, and Had Fun Doing It* (Reprint ed.). New York City, NY, USA: W. W. Norton & Company.

Yates, F. A. (1966). *The Art of Memory.* Milton Park, Oxfordshire, England: Routledge and Kegan Paul.

Yeates, L. B. (2004). Thought Experimentation: A Cognitive Approach. Kensington, New South Wales, Australia: University of New South Wales.

Yenne, B. (1993). *100 Inventions that shaped world history.* San Mateo, CA, USA: Bluewood books.

Youngdahl, K., Hammond, B., Sipics, M., Hicks, R., & Cicchini, D. (2013). *The History of Vaccines.* Philadelphia, PA, USA: The College of Physicians of Philadelphia.

YouTube. (2019). *YouTube for Press*. Retrieved from YouTube: https://www.youtube.com/about/press/

YouTube. (2020). *YouTube Home Page*. Retrieved from YouTube: https://www.youtube.com/

Zajonc, R. B. (1968). Attitudinal effects of mere exposure. *Journal of Personality and Social Psychology*, 1-27. doi:https://doi.org/10.1037/h0025848

Zeigler, B. P., & Praehofer, H. (2000). *Theory of Modeling and Simulation: Integrating Discrete Event and Continuous Complex Dynamic Systems.* Cambridge Massachusetts: Academic Press.

Zeilik, M. (2002). *Astronomy - The Evolving Universe.* Cambridge, England: Cambridge University Press.

Zimbardo, P., Haney, C., Banks, W. C., & Jaffe, D. (1972). *The Stanford Prison Experiment: A Simulation Study of the Psychology of Imprisonment conducted August 1971 at Stanford University.* Philip G. Zimbardo, Inc.

Zuse, K. (1993). *The Computer - My Life.* New York City: Springer.

www.ingramcontent.com/pod-product-compliance
Lightning Source LLC
Chambersburg PA
CBHW072027230526
45466CB00020B/960